A MUSICIAN'S NARRATIVE

MY GRANDMOTHER, Mrs. CAMPBELL
Painted by Sir John Watson Gordon in 1819

A
MUSICIAN'S NARRATIVE

BY
SIR ALEXANDER CAMPBELL MACKENZIE
K.C.V.O.

WITH FOUR PLATES

CASSELL AND COMPANY, LTD
London, Toronto, Melbourne and Sydney

First Published 1927

Printed in Great Britain.

FOREWORD

ALTHOUGH the peaceful persuasion of indulgent colleagues has often encouraged a lame pen, it is to spontaneous generation that this my story—written at leisure in the evening of a fairly long day—owes its existence.

Whatever else Nature withheld, she certainly endowed me with that mental faculty which, at will, reproduces with photographic accuracy scenes and events as if they were of yesterday; and as I have been surrounded by music since childhood, retrospection gains an added charm.

The pleasures of memory are, however, too often clouded by sad recollections. *Jean qui Rit*—to me always a pleasant fellow—has another and a much less cheerful visage to turn when recalling the many things he would rather not have said or done. Just my case! But if sincerely-felt regrets atone for frequent lapses, then I have suffered my full share of penitential moments.

Should, therefore, these—still incomplete—jottings need justification, it lies in the opportunity provided to express my gratitude for the happiness brought by many treasured friendships into an unusually prolonged and busy professional life, during the course of which there can have been but few phases unknown, or personal participation therein denied me.

While most thankfully acknowledging the valuable assistance of my friend William Wallace during the progress of these pages, and the care bestowed upon the preparation of this "Narrative" by the publishers, I trust that the use of the preceding word on its title page may not be thought presumptuous.

A. C. M.

London, August, 1927.

CONTENTS

CONTENTS

LIST OF PLATES

PART I

EDINBURGH—SONDERSHAUSEN—LONDON

A MUSICIAN'S NARRATIVE

CHAPTER I

EARLY YEARS AND RECOLLECTIONS

" We are all going to the play, or coming home from it."
—" Old Curiosity Shop "

THIS rapid glance at my native city—beautiful for situation and always conscious of its dignity—may scare off a few, otherwise patiently disposed, readers at the outset; but the fact that I was born in Nelson Street, Edinburgh (August 22, 1847), has, before now, inclined me to ignore well-meant signals and take the consequences. The well-remembered street-pictures were then somewhat more gaily coloured. Dress-coated, tall-hatted "Posty" was resplendent in royal scarlet and gold braid, while the slower-footed " Peeler " wore blue swallow-tails and the shiniest and hardest of toppers; an inconvenient and unpractical garb made still more conspicuous by white " ducks " in summer. On long benches at street-corners sat groups of discharged veterans (generically called " Highland porters "), some of whom may have served with Wellington, and now did—one may hardly say " ran "—errands for the families to whom they had individually attached themselves. The trusted retainer who had adopted us was no Highlander, but an Irish ancient answering to the name of Patrick in the squeakiest voice and richest brogue.

As the " scent of the rose still clings to the vase," the smell of honest Pat's pipe of strongest " twist " lingers yet in my nostrils.

The Great Pandolfo's ancestors sold their Italian *Immagini* in the streets, and impatient nurses reprimanded troublesome

3

children by suggesting the impending arrival of a " Dummy Doctor." The execrated memories of Burke, Hare[1] and the Resurrectionists being still very much alive.

My earliest recollection is that of the wizened, be-cowled figure of my great-grandfather crouched in an arm-chair, surrounded by his daughter and her husband, while their son— my father—held me by the hand. Four generations!

My next one is that of a very old and picturesque family mansion, at the foot of Stockbridge, where, in one of the immensely large rooms then let to some ancient female pensioners, dwelt my old nurse. On my visits Nannie would sit by the fireside reciting long passages from Burns by heart—and with a keen appreciation of their humour—to me. Oddly enough I remember being struck with the effect of the short line: " To sport that night; " " Fu' blythe that night," etc., ending each verse of *Halloween*.

At the University the ageing Sir William Hamilton drew innumerable students to his class-room, and the noble figure of Professor Wilson (" Christopher North ") might be seen swinging along, his hair streaming in the wind. His glorious *Noctes Ambrosianæ* were over, but he still contributed to *Maga*.

Sir Walter Scott's friend, Willie Allan, occupied the presidential chair of the Scottish Academy of Arts, and another of his favourites, William Henry Murray, who produced the " Waverley " dramas, was manager of the Theatre Royal in dear, dirty old Shakespeare Square, where the General Post Office now stands.

That fine actor, the " Great Murray," deserved all the esteem he enjoyed as a cultured gentleman, prominent citizen and manager. But the fact that he was the grandson of Bonnie Prince Charlie's detested secretary (" Traitor Murray,"

---

[1] Fifteen years later an old blind man in a white smock-frock, selling bootlaces and matches in Trafalgar Square, was pointed out to me as the same Hare who cheated the gallows by turning King's Evidence, and on comparing dates I have no reason to doubt the accuracy of the statement. Having found employment, his identity was discovered by his mates, who threw him into a lime-pit.

as I often heard him called) preyed on his mind in later years and caused him to become morose and hypochondriacal.

These morbid feelings were in some measure justifiable, because in 1847 many staunch Jacobites could still express themselves strongly; and when on tour with his company the sensitive man was occasionally compelled to realize it. " We'll hae nae Murrays here," was an irate landlady's answer to a request for rooms. " Fause loons! Curses on the name! " were not agreeable greetings.

The brothers John Sobieski and Charles Edward Stuart had not long left Edinburgh. After flaunting banners in Elginshire for about twelve years they went to Austria in 1845 or '46. Their pretensions to the honour of being sons of the Prince were fairly disproved in the *Quarterly Review* of June 1847.[1]

Poets and composers (such as Lady Nairne) had kept a fascinating tradition alive and the glamour of Scott was over it all.

Incidentally be it said that the purely Jacobite melodies of that period have an unmistakable essence of their own and differ considerably from the rest of our national tunes. How this came to pass has always been an interesting puzzle to me.

My youngest brother was the popular manager's godson, and possessed a silver mug which bore the odd inscription:

To William Murray Mackenzie from William H. Murray, Esquire, of—what?

The last word and query alluded to the confiscated estate of Broughton belonging to the faithless secretary. Unfortunately this interesting relic was stolen, and found its way to the melting-pot a few years ago.

The actor, whom I have seen on the stage, was often in our house, and died in 1852.

The Edinburgh stage had for long held an exceptional reputation and continued to attract the best English actors, who were supported by excellent resident companies, the

[1] If for nothing else they were remarkable for longevity, John dying in London in 1872 and Charles in France in 1880.

members of which were familiar and highly-respected person-
alities. I have always felt grateful to my father for introducing
me so early to the wonders of Theatre-land, for, so to speak,
I was born into two professions.

My introduction to the region known as " Behind " took
place on an occasion when, in a fright at the sudden appearance of a strange animal cautiously creeping down a very steep
and narrow staircase with a huge tail tucked under its arm, I
timidly squeezed against the wall to let it pass.

" Don't be afraid; I'm only the cat! " a kindly voice
assured me.

He who has forgotten his first pantomime gets no sympathy from me.

The names of some of the " stars " I saw show the liberality of the education which henceforth was to be mine.[1]

In a grim piece, *Presumption*, the huge, weird figure of
Frankenstein's monster in glittering greenish bronze, en-
deavouring to catch sounds of music with its hands, and
dashing off with the screaming child of its artist-creator, is
before me now.

T. P. Cooke was a splendid pantomimist as well as actor,
and his " Monster " was surely the first Robot seen on the
stage. Besides Mackay (the famous "Baillie" returned to
work after financial mishaps), Miss Nicol (admirable comic
actress), and other worthies of local celebrity, there were
Henry Webb (Dromio), Miss Glyn, Rebecca Isaacs (fine
singer and actress), Priscilla Horton, young Marie Wilton (in
pantomime), the Bateman children (*ætat*, respectively 8 and
6), of whom the elder, Mrs. Crowe, became a valued teacher
under me at the R. A. M., and Alfred Wigan.

During the recent revival of *The Beggar's Opera* I was
asked whether I had seen it before. I had!—on February
14, 1853, when a certain John Sims Reeves played the amorous
captain. I make no pretence of having been sufficiently

---

[1] That trustworthy book, " The Annals of the Edinburgh Stage," by J. C.
Dibdin (Edinburgh, 1880), not only enables me to verify dates and statements,
but contains many references to my father's connexion with the theatre.

precocious to understand the plot, but the scenes, Macheath, Peachum, and Lockit, and the rest of the disreputable crew are distinctly remembered.

It is on record that the distinguished tenor was to have been heard during the previous season, but had disappointed an expectant house. On that occasion, although the bill had suddenly to be changed, a crowded audience, in sympathy with the manager, generously accepted the situation and kept their seats.[1]

Ira Aldridge (coloured tragedian), Ben Webster in *Janet Pride* and a one-act piece with a marvellous change to a striking likeness to Napoleon; Charles Mathews in *The Great Gun Trick* (a skit upon Professor Anderson, the so-called " Wizard of the North "), conjuring cleverly in immaculate shirt-sleeves; Mr. Sands (the "Man-Fly") walking head-downwards across the ceiling, stand out, among others, in my memory.

And the first orchestral music I can clearly recollect to have heard was Locke's (or Purcell's?) music to *Macbeth*.

The introduction of comic songs between the acts may not have been an artistic innovation, but in the persons of their perpetrators, Sam Cowell and young J. L. Toole, proved a successful one. Who can say that the tunes were not good ones, or that the melancholy histories of *Vilikins and his Dinah* and the *Ratcatcher's Daughter* were not morally instructive?

This brings me to the subject of Opera, which, even in the questionable shape in which it had been presented just before my time, had always been popular, our playgoers being keen lovers of music. The odd adaptations of master works for which Sir Henry Bishop was chiefly responsible were then beginning to pass from the boards. Is it not told that Mozart's *Figaro*, " translated, altered and arranged by Henry R. Bishop," was given with ten songs and six dances by the ruthless adapter? What would now be said of performances

[1] Dibdin : " The Annals of the Edinburgh Stage," p. 450.

of *Il Barbière* in which the part of Figaro was spoken? Yet Murray played it when the Count Almaviva (Edmund Edmunds) was the only male vocalist in the cast, and there were other instances of a similar treatment of *Don Giovanni* and *Masaniello*.[1]

Mr. Edmunds, who left the stage at an early period of his life to become a popular teacher of singing, told me that, as a lad, he had played in Drury Lane with Edmund Kean, and had also taken part in the production of *Der Freischütz* in 1824. Of a marvellous vitality and attaining to a great age, he and I were colleagues and friends when I left Edinburgh in the late 'seventies.

My initiation into the ever-fascinating realm of Opera had an exciting result, as the handsome young timpanist, George Loveday (afterwards Toole's business-manager), beside whom I sat, realized during a performance of *Norma*.

The Arch-Druid (Herr Zelger) was an exceptionally imposing man with a great voice and an appropriately large stomach. His appearance in flowing white robes, when slowly stalking forwards to the footlights, proved too awe-inspiring for a child's nerves, and I slid down between the kettledrums for safety. In that ignominious position I remained until a convenient moment arrived when I could be restored to my seat and senses by the drummer, to a gentle accompaniment of titters from the members of the orchestra.

Of somewhat later date is the recollection of a black-maned head swaying over a violin. August Manns' eccentric movements while playing or conducting were not "arrived at," as was occasionally suggested, but natural to the man. In 1855—a year previous to his appointment at the Crystal Palace—he travelled as leader with an opera company (Reeves and Mr. and Mrs. Weiss among its members), and his

---

[1] There was something of a craze for dramatic versions of French opera libretti in those days. Thus I witnessed a costly production of *La Juive* with a long procession (partly equestrian) round the auditorium ; and of an acting edition of *Le Prophète* a vivid impression remains.

8

subsequent friendship with my father, with whom he alternated as leader when in Edinburgh, was so generously extended to myself that his name must appear frequently in these pages.

Despite the many time-honoured gibes at our affection for the pipes, the Scot's favourite instrument is the violin. In almost every farmhouse a fiddle hung within easy reach, and the fame of the best local performers was jealously guarded. Nor was its manufacture confined to a number of skilled craftsmen—such as Duke, the Hardies, etc.—but had a peculiar fascination for amateur makers of all classes. Indeed the fiddle is to be held responsible not only for our earliest national music, but also for a considerable amount of genial conviviality.

The name of the younger Hardie was a familiar one in our house, and I firmly believed that any mishap, to crockery or anything else, could be remedied by sending for Tom, who was as well-known for his ingenuity as a highly-skilled workman as for his unreliable habits. My father once kept him under lock and key in a room in our house until his task of repairing was done, freedom plus money being a dangerous combination.

Sire of two generations of musicians, the famous Neil Gow and his contemporaries McIntosh, McGlashan, Marshall (all Highlanders), and others, contributed largely to the spirited dance music with which their vigorous violin-playing was identified. But, however striking their natural gifts may have been, their musical education was of a primitive kind.

Good reel players still existed in numbers, and I can recall the exciting effect a large, picked band of violinists —led by my father, who had gathered them together from all parts of Scotland—produced on an enthusiastic audience by the long strings of alternating strathspeys and reels which succeeded each other without break. The changes were effected by the simple plan of passing the name of the next tune round.

I doubt whether any of the performers could read music. The necessary " snap," strong up-bow jerk of the wrist and exaggerated accentuation, are features not easily captured even by the most accomplished violinists.

It may be that in the person of Neil Gow's son, Nathaniel (composer of *Bonnie Prince Charlie*, *Flora Macdonald*, and the ever-popular *Caller Herrin'*, 1766-1831), the first trained Scottish musician made his appearance. Although his knowledge may not have amounted to much, his songs show an admirable natural talent, and we Scots owe a good deal to his gifts.

But there is one—though his work is forgotten, if it was ever sufficiently appreciated—whose memory merits the highest respect. Judged alone by the orchestral and pianoforte arrangements of our national melodies which were so prominent a feature in the Theatre Royal, James Dewar (leader in SirWalter's day) must have been a first-rate musician. MSS. in my possession prove high attainments, then very rare in Scotland. His affectionate pupil, my father, joined the orchestra (a year after Scott's death) at the age of thirteen, and succeeded his master in 1845. It was his humorous boast that, when sitting in the orchestra at rehearsal without a part on his desk, Paganini had spoken to him. The great virtuoso asked: " Who is this boy? " and told him, no doubt in choice Italian, to go away. The incident happened in 1832 and confirms the story that the artist would not suffer the presence of unwanted listeners. In this instance, however, the precaution proved fruitless, as the boy certainly did hear him from a dark corner of the theatre.

Another of Dewar's contemporaries, in some respects a more generally cultivated man, the learned, unassuming and able musician Finlay Dun, was probably the first of us all who sought improvement in his art in other countries. He studied under Baillot and Crescentini in Paris, an example which was followed by my father, who contrived on his own earnings at an early age to secure tuition from the famous Lipinski (Dresden) and, later, from my own master Sainton

(London). These preparatory struggles may serve some spoon-fed scholarship-holders as object lessons in self-help, as well as inspire gratitude for the numerous educational benefits enjoyed in present days.

My parent, an admirable violinist and talented musician, besides collecting and arranging " The National Dance Music of Scotland," [1] contributed several additions to genuine Scottish song; among others, *Bonny Bonally*, *The Grey Hill Plaid*, and *The Nameless Lassie*, all written by his poet-friend James Ballantyne.[2] Internal evidence causes me to conclude that he knew more about the musical setting of *Ilka Blade o' Grass* (popularized by the tenor, John Wilson) than is supposed.

Ballantyne, Wilson and the young composer were cronies and enthusiastic workers in the field of national song, of which some of the best specimens, finding their way into collections, become traditional while their authors' names fade out of ken. In the case of *The Nameless Lassie*, its composer is now as nameless as his lassie. I have often heard it played and sung in the streets, and once, when leaving a concert on a snowy winter's night in Glasgow, I stood listening, tearfully, to the touching melody played on a clarinet in a side-street.

No instrumentalist can be so harrowingly depressing as a street clarinet! Recently I heard this melody well performed by the band of a Highland regiment. The conductor knew nothing more about it than its title, until he was informed that it was written by my father considerably over seventy years ago. But there is a melancholy satisfaction even in this kind of post-appreciation.

Under somewhat similar conditions that experience has already been mine. A tune of my own, evidently so racy of the soil as to have been accepted as a genuine antique of long forgotten parentage, was innocently reproduced as such, and

---

[1] Since re-published by Novello & Co.

[2] Ballantyne (a friend of Charles Dickens), beginning as a house-painter, became an authority on the art of glass-painting and was commissioned to execute the stained-glass windows in the House of Lords.

for some years I have enjoyed the pleasure of hearing myself played and whistled " incog."

As early as 1846 my father conducted Mendelssohn's music to *Antigone,* when Helen Faucit recited; and that his theatre orchestra must have been a superior one is proved by a playbill of 1848, in my possession, when it played the overtures to *William Tell, Midsummer Night's Dream, Oberon* and *Fidelio* on the same evening. A letter " To — Mackensie (*sic*) Esq." from Bochsa (the harpist) referring to his visit with Madame Anna Bishop, is dated:

> Edinburgh,
> March 26, 1847.

MY DEAR SIR,—

Mde. Bishop begs me to express to you her sincere thanks for your kindly attention and kindness during her theatrical engagement here. Allow me also, my dear Sir, to say that *I* feel much obliged to you for the great pains and the care you have taken to render the performances as effective as possible. Indeed, I may declare, that you *have done* your duty!

Believe me, my dr. Sir, with kind regards from Mad. B.

> Yours very truly
> CH. BOCHSA.

As I am sure the gentlemen of your orchestra have done their best, please to offer them from our parts, our thanks and good wishes.

In those days our " nobility and gentry " had not yet acquired the " London habit," and spent their winters in the Scottish capital. They " patronized " my father's Annual Benefits at the theatre, when a concert was invariably included. Here is one of these programmes (1848) of which the heading reads oddly now. The harpist, E. H. Dibdin, was the grandson of Charles of sea-song fame, and Carl Drechsler (of Dresden), a 'cellist of reputation and the master of the best German players of their day—Grützmacher, Cossman, Lindner, etc.

Playbills then promised good value and were of inordinate length.

Last Night but Six of the Company's Performing here this Season.

MR A. MACKENZIE'S BENEFIT,

UNDER THE IMMEDIATE PATRONAGE OF

THE LADY PATRONESSES OF THE ASSEMBLIES:

Right Honourable Countess of Leven and Melville—Right Honourable Lady Mary Browne Constable.
Right Honourable Lady Isabella Gordon—Right Honourable Lady Charlotte Fletcher.
The Right Honourable Lady Harriet Suttie—The Right Honourable Lady Elizabeth Douglas.
Honourable Mrs Bouverie Primrose—Honourable Mrs Ramsay of Barnton.
Honourable Lady Menzies—Lady Mackenzie of Coull—Lady Honyman of Armadale—Mrs Wedderburn
Mrs Buchanan of Auchentorlie—Mrs Thomson Bonar—Mrs Fullerton—Mrs Mackenzie of Applecross.
Mrs Cockburn—Mrs Maitland of Dundrennan—Mrs Mackay of Bighouse—Mrs Mercer of Gorthy.

Major Dyson and Officers of the Third Dragoon Guards,

And Lieut.-Colonel Sir Hew Dalrymple, Bart., and Officers, 71st Regiment.

This Evening, THURSDAY, May 11, 1848, will be performed the celebrated Comedy, in Three Acts, entitled

The CLIMBING BOY.

John Strawberry, Esq., Member for the Borough of ——, by Mr MURRAY.
Sir Gilbert Thornoliffe, M.P., by Mr R. YOUNGE—Merriment, a Rewell Catholic Clergyman, by Mr WEEKLEY
Jack Bunzard, in the Service of Mr Strawberry, by Mr RAY
Coattail, Steward to Sir Gilbert, by Mr HENRY—Chiffonier, an Upholsterer, by Mr S. LAKE
The Climbing Boy by Mrs W. H. EBURNE, her First Appearance here this Season.
Jack Rag, a Nondescript, by Mr LLOYD—Bates, a Police Inspector, by Mr NICHOLSON—Servant by Mr CARROLL
Miss Prudence Strawberry, Sister to John Strawberry, Esq., by Miss NICOL.
Rebecca, Wife to Bunzard, by Miss VIVASH—Lucy Smartruff, Waiting-maid to Rosalie, by Miss DAVIS
Jenny, Servant to Miss Prudence Strawberry, by Miss HARRIET COVENEY.
Rosalie de Monneville, Daughter of Sir Gilbert, by Miss COVENEY

After which, MR LLOYD WILL SING THE NEWHAVEN FISHWIFE.

In the course of the Evening

HERR DRECHSLER

WILL PERFORM A

FANTASIA ON SCOTCH AIRS ON THE VIOLONCELLO

COMPOSED BY KUMMER;

MR HENRY E. DIBDIN

WILL PERFORM A GRAND SOLO ON THE HARP;

AND

MR A. MACKENZIE

WILL PERFORM A FANTASIA ON THE VIOLIN.

After which, for the First Time in this City, a New Farce entitled

THE BED-ROOM WINDOW.

Baron de Rosebach by Mr RAY—Casimir Wengel, his Nephew, by Mr VAUDREY
Joseph Halt, a Soldier, by Mr WILLIAM HOWARD—Trapp, a Peasant, by Mr LLOYD.
Bertha by Mrs C. A. TELLET—Clara by Miss VIVASH.

The whole to conclude with, for the First Time these Five Years, the admired Melo-Dramatic Romance, from the celebrated Poem by
Sir WALTER SCOTT, and adapted to the Stage by THOMAS DIBDIN, Esq., entitled The

Lady of the Lake.

Sir Roderick Vich Alpine Dhu, a powerful Outlaw, by Mr EDMUND GLOVER,
Douglas, Father to Ellen, by Mr R. YOUNGE—Malcolm Graeme, Suitor to Ellen, by Mr WEEKLEY,
Fitzjames, Knight of Snowdon, by Mr WYNDHAM,
Brian, a Fiend-like Hermit, attached to Roderick, by Mr RAY—Allan Bane, a Minstrel, attached to Douglas, by Mr JOSEPHS,
Norman by Mr FREEMAN—Sandy by Mr HENRY—Murdoch by Mr C. LLOYDS—Malise by Mr CARROLL—Herbert by Mr S. LAKE
Lady Margaret, Mother to Roderick, by Miss CLEAVER—Blanche of Devan, a Maniac, by Miss COVENEY,
Ellen, the Lady of the Lake, by Mrs C. A. TELLET.

To-morrow, RURAL FELICITY—And other Entertainments.
On Saturday, a popular Comedy—And a Variety of other Entertainments.
On Monday, PAST & PRESENT—THE SWISS COTTAGE—THE BRITISH LEGION—And THE GENTLE SHEPHERD,
BEING FOR THE BENEFIT OF MRS C. A. TELLET.
On Tuesday, THE COUNTRY SQUIRE—THE BOLD DRAGOONS—And THE FALLS OF CLYDE
BEING FOR THE BENEFIT OF Miss ROSE DEWAR.
On Wednesday, SWEETHEARTS AND WIVES—THE IRISH LION—And BEN THE BOATSWAIN.
BEING FOR THE BENEFIT OF THE Misses COVENEY,
AND THE LAST NIGHT BUT ONE OF THE COMPANY'S PERFORMING THIS SEASON.

Edinburgh, an educational centre, attracted a number of German musicians who came, saw, and—remained. Ever since the much-travelled and somewhat overrated Chevalier Neukomm was invited to undertake a greatly needed improvement in our choirs and Church music—long before the obnoxious "kist o' whustles" gradually began to be tolerated —our characteristic predilection for the foreign teacher steadily increased. In my youth there was a real need of their presence, and to the beneficial influence of the men of that day we are so greatly indebted that no excuse need be offered for exhuming some of their names.

Among our family's best friends were several admirable men: the burly, jolly Bavarian, Johann Dürrner, a part-song writer of deserved popularity in his own country, who became my guardian, but only survived my father by less than a couple of years.

The lanky, grotesque-looking Hanoverian 'cellist, Georg Hausmann (uncle of the better-known Robert of the Joachim Quartet). Unlucky in love, our good friend made a voluntary exit from this world.

The amiable Küchler, and others, who, *via* opera companies, found their way to where better luck awaited them.

The genial old Frenchman Théophile Bucher (once a flautist of renown before becoming a teacher of singing), who repaid our hospitality by leaving his money to the " Reid Chair of Music " for a scholarship bearing his name.

Tom M. Mudie—in the first batch of R.A.M. students— the Hargitts, etc., all worked companionably together.

Keen musicians and busy men, the surreptitious pleasures of ensemble playing could only be indulged in on Sunday mornings during church hours in some friendly back drawing-room. Such desecrations of the Sabbath being liable to be visited by the rigour of the law, the ire of landladies and neighbours, the fearful joy of quartet playing had frequently to be snatched in our house. On one occasion a sharp-eared policeman interrupted the harmony. " But this is sacred music," said my father, showing him a quartet by Haydn.

14

Whether this undeniable fact, or the half-crown and a dram convinced the departing constable, remained purely a matter of conjecture. Often have I seen my father writing his pantomime and other theatre music on Sunday mornings with a violin on the table in case a gentle pizzicato had to be resorted to when the pianoforte had to remain closed.

These were dreary days, with their long climbs—to an accompaniment of the clangour of the combined bells of every kirk—from Heriot Row to St. Giles, where Jenny Geddes launched her cutty-stool at the Dean's head in 1637. Interminable discourses often aroused feelings of admiration within me for the excellent dame.[1]   Then the slow sauntering back, after the weirdly-sung Doxology, for vehicles were taboo.

Although discipline, compared with that of other Scottish homes, was decidedly imperfect in our house on the Seventh Day, the ever-remaining impression is that of a stupefying boredom which had the reverse of a beneficial influence on the youthful mind.

My mother, a sweetly pretty, gentle and retiring young woman, had an exaggerated horror of publicity—much at variance with her keen aspirations for her husband's success —and never ceased to preach the undesirability of putting oneself en evidence.

To counterbalance this constitutional reticence she possessed a remarkable fund of quaint humour, which she retained in old age, even when stricken with a long and painful malady.

Her mildly-expressed dislikes were poetry and French-women, and more than once I was warned never to marry one of the latter. In regard to that wish, at least, she has been obeyed.

The custodian of the Select Subscription Library, whose

---

[1] One sermon, heard at another church, certainly left a lasting impression. A reverend and eloquent McBoanerges chose the subjects of *La Traviata* and *Crinoline*. Of that wicked opera he could hardly have spoken from personal experience, but the female section of his congregation clearly resented his denunciation of the prevailing fashion.

patience and trust must have been wonderful, probably regarded me as a freak, for I was allowed to climb ladders, haul out and sprawl over books, before carrying off much miscellaneous literature for home consumption. Ours being a family of avid readers, I made acquaintance with Scott, Smollett, Dumas, and many other authors more or less fitted for my years. By frequent visits to the theatre and a " Kenny Meadows " edition, an early introduction to Shakespeare was added, which certainly surprised the German school-masters I was destined to meet.

This habit of reading once had a disastrous result. I had developed an aptitude for dancing and became a favourite show-boy at the popular Mr. Robert Low's [1] annual public exhibitions. The " fling," " hornpipe," and a memorable *Pas de Deux* with the little daughter of the great editor of *The Scotsman*, Alexander Russel, were among my early terpsichorean efforts. A brand-new Highland costume had been made for my first appearance on any stage, and, after having been carefully dressed, I was told to wait in the dining-room until my mother had completed her own attire. Kneeling with my back to a blazing fire, and a book propped on a chair before me, I became absorbed in its contents, but oblivious of the fact that my beautiful kilt was smouldering and smoking until the smell of burning wool pervaded the house and brought my mother in haste into the room. Alas, for the " garb of old Gaul! " What remedies and repairs were effected I know not, but I performed my solo that afternoon in spite of the conflagration.

In 1856, when musical affairs called my father to London, I (aged eight) followed him by sea. All the wonders as well as trivial happenings during that visit are stamped on my memory. The Crystal Palace (Manns only at the beginning of his great work), the Thames Tunnel (a world's wonder then), the Earthquake of Lisbon at Wylde's " Great Globe," which stood in the middle of Leicester Square.

---

[1] Teacher of dancing to the Royal Family at Balmoral, and composer of some well-known reels and strathspeys.

MY MOTHER
(*Circa* 1846)

When in 1911 our R.A.M. orchestra had to meet in the Portman Rooms until The Duke's Hall was ready for occupation, imagination carried me back to my first visit to Madame Tussaud's. There was the spot where I addressed an old gentleman—seated with snuff-box in hand—who slowly turned his head the better to view the figures.

"Please, sir," piped the small boy, "can you tell me when the music commences?" The question was repeated before I caught my father's merry eye and realized that Mr. William Cobbett was not in the least interested in music, but continued to gaze at his waxen confrères. The enthusiastic Mr. Walter W. Cobbett of our own day does, happily, not share that indifference.

With little old Madame herself, the Sleeping Beauty, the stalwart Policeman and the Giant, the rooms were peopled again.

Shift the scene to the Princess's Theatre, with Charles Kean and his wife in *The Winter's Tale;* "Time" (the prologue) rolling forward on a great ball; the Sheepshearing Scene; Autolycus (Horatio Saker); the statue at the end of the play, and a little girl—whose better acquaintance I am proud to have made in after years—Ellen Terry as Mamillius . . . The excellent music was by John L. Hatton, whom I knew when his mind was failing, and he had no recollection of this beautiful production.

At Covent Garden I witnessed a performance of *Der Freischütz* (in English), during which several awkward and mirth-provoking mishaps occurred. Kaspar's luxuriant black wig refused to accompany him to the nether regions, stuck fast in the trap and remained in full view of the audience.

Yet another theatre, The Queen's, familiarly known as "The Dusthole," in which for obvious reasons we remained but a very short time. On the shabby stage a melodrama, *The Poison Island of Java;* in the audience not a few in equally dingy shirt sleeves, the so-called dress-circle ornamented by pewter-pots, and vendors of beer with their cans circulating freely among the audience.

Standing in a conspicuous place, we were evidently attracting unwelcome attention when my father whispered, "Time to go, my boy," our curiosity being quickly satisfied.[1]

From boyhood to the end of a short life, constant work, late hours, heavy family responsibilities and a determination to excel in his profession, had undermined my father's constitution. The earliest admission of this carefully-guarded knowledge, and of his views regarding my education, were indicated in a letter (July 1, 1857) from Burntisland—where we were enjoying the sea-bathing—in which he wrote that he " fully intended to take Alick to Germany, but did not feel well enough for such a journey." The postponement only lasted for one month.

I was present when an eager crowd awaited the arrival of the steamer from Edinburgh which was expected to bring the result of the trial of Madeleine Smith. Whether the attractive personality of the accused or the romantic nature of the case was responsible for the evident sympathy with the prisoner, I know not; but when my father stepped on shore, saying, " She has got off! " the news was received with something resembling a cheer.[2]

[1] On this site " The Prince of Wales " and, subsequently, " La Scala " Theatres were built.

[2] In after-life I occasionally met the advocate who defended her, in the person of the Right Hon John Inglis, Lord Justice-General, in whose house I taught music.

CHAPTER II

THE selection of Sondershausen (Schwarzburg-Thuringia) instead of a better-known musical centre, such as Leipzig, is maybe worth an explanation.

Johann Gung'l (nephew of the famous Josef, himself a talented dance composer) visited our city with his band, with the usual result that several of its members remained. *Ubi bene, ibi Patria.* At the time, Hungarian, Austrian and Bavarian bands were very popular. One Kalozdy travelled with his men arrayed in gorgeous scarlet national costumes; and I remember seeing the violinist Reményi at the time, but his roaming disposition prevented him from settling anywhere for long.

A young German 'cellist, Günther Bartel, found his way into the theatre orchestra, and this admirably-trained musician was consulted regarding the most advantageous place for educational purposes. That my friend-to-be was thoroughly justified in suggesting his native town is undeniable. Sondershausen, long known for its exceptionally fine orchestra, had become a centre of attraction for the most advanced musical thinkers in Germany on account of the novelties produced and the amount of so-called *Zukunfts Musik* to be heard there, and, with Weimar, the little *Residenz-Stadt* shared this enviable reputation.

Leipzig, although the birth- and meeting-place of the *Davidsbündler* and the home of their champion, Dr. Franz Brendel (himself a Thuringian), notoriously lagged a long way behind.

As the weather had been exceptionally bad it was decided to postpone our departure for a week. The glorious panorama of the Firth of Forth (as far as the Bass Rock) which our windows commanded showed a very boisterous sea. Nevertheless, a silly boy tearfully protested against delay.

" Maybe, my boy, you'll wish yourself back again sooner than you think! " Prophetic words, for little more than a couple of months later the boy had bitter reason to reflect and repent.

I have no means of verifying it now, but have always understood that the ship in which we were to have sailed came to grief. Be that as it may, the passage to Hamburg was a sufficiently trying one to make me feel uncommonly sorry for myself.

The first music I heard in Germany was the overture to *Fingal's Cave* (in the restaurant on the Alster Basin) while guided by my father's explanatory comments.

The railway carried us as far as Hildesheim, whence began long and tedious stretches in the *Schnellpost*. There were at least thirty-six separate states, mostly with their own coinage, regulations, and manners. This peculiar state of matters in Northern Germany is illustrated by the fact that we were assisted, at midnight, by an enlightened medical man who was good-natured enough to exchange some English sovereigns (for thalers and groschen) which had been flatly refused by governmental *Postamt* officials. We were then permitted to resume our journey. Presumably, such an incident is not likely to happen now.

The *Schnellpost*, with its postillions in huge jack-boots, stiff, pointed hats, and bugles slung across their cut-away jackets (just like their colleague of Longjumeau—minus his pigtail), was a picturesque institution. These riders, always addressed as *Schwager* (brother-in-law) were a cheery set of men who blew lusty and long fanfares when approaching the numerous turnpikes or clattering through a village.

At night-time the frequent awakenings, by lanterns thrust through the window by an official demanding passports, were perhaps the worst discomforts. But on the wide and splendidly-kept *Chaussées*, bordered all the way by carefully-watched fruit-trees, the service was good as we sped through Erfurt and Nordhausen (where the famous Schnapps is made, and pigs have as brief a life as in Chicago) to Schwarz-burg-Sondershausen.

The British were popular enough in Saxony, Hanover and Thuringia—Heinrich Heine's persistently bitter denunciations of former days in the *Augsburger Zeitung* notwithstanding. Unbounded admiration for our inventions, steel-products, etc., was constantly expressed and all *Englische Waare* considered incomparable. But the ignorance of the North German about us was astonishing. The national malady *Spleen* and *Die Englische Krankheit* (rickets) accounted for all our eccentric habits.

About Scotland, thought to be a more or less uncivilized country, many strange questions were put to the *Kleine Schotte* as I came to be called.

" Do they use pocket-handkerchiefs in Scotland, too? " said a Schwarzburger woman to me. After a deep breath, I managed to gasp out an affirmative reply.

My father, under the worst possible medical advice, spent some weeks undergoing unsuitable treatment at Alexis Bad, but kept up his bright spirits until concealment was no longer possible. My mother, ignorant of immediate danger, wrote to me in her quaint way from the dismal place: " You would be surprised to see the invalids feed. It is more like a menagerie of voracious animals than a hospital. Whether dinner is the only meal they take I don't know, but it looks like it."

The already doomed man reported to a brother as to Sondershausen:

It is a charming place, and Alick, I think, will be happy with them the Bartel family). The music is first-rate, supported entirely by the Grand Duke. The people pay nothing to hear the Concerts, and the charge for the Theatre when open—which is only for four months— is *Erster Rang*, ninepence,[1] Pit, sixpence and fourpence, and Gallery, two-

Ninepence for the dress-circle is, I fancy, an understatement; it was slightly more than that.

pence. We took a drive the other day to the "Possen," a hunting lodge, when we came upon a respectable-looking man who turned out to be the Grand Duke of Schwarzburg-Sondershausen. He entered into conversation and showed us about the place and lifted Alick to see the deer. We think of coming home by the Rhine. That passage from Leith will never get me again.

Thoroughly unfit for the journey, his last words as he stood at the door of the *Postwagen* were: "My boy, I shall never see you again."

The ominous prediction was fulfilled in a few weeks. Increasing weakness caused him to fall when stepping into a vehicle and the accident hastened the end, which came within a fortnight of his arrival at home.

From among the many tributes to his popularity and appreciations of his talents I quote these verses which appeared in *The Scotsman* two days after his death.

IN MEMORY OF THE LATE ALEXANDER MACKENZIE

Alas! dear friend, and art thou gone?—
  Younger than he, by many years,
Who sings thy dirge with heartfelt moan,
  And views thy grave with heart-wrung tears
Who feels a brother's loss in thee—
Brother in love and minstrelsy.

A grateful glorious task was thine—
  To conjure up with wondrous art
The melodies of Auld Lang Syne,
  And make them thrill through every heart
In plaintive lays, in lilts of glee—
All owned thy magic mastery.

From the deep fountains of the soul
  Thou madest the glistening tear-drops flow,
When under thy subdued control
  We heard the low sad tones of woe,
Wafting the soul to doleful days
Of "Flodden Field" and "Yarrow Braes."

Through peasant's cot, through baron's hall,
  Thy mellow lilts spread joyous glee:
At rural dance, at regal ball,
  Even beauty borrowed grace from thee:

MY FATHER
(*Circa* 1846)

And hearts were linked in love's strong chains
When bounding to thy matchless strains.

While Scotland mourns her minstrel gone,
    And all our breasts with sorrow thrill,
Let's pray that his young orphan son [1]
    In time his father's place may fill:
And thus our country still shall be
The home of simple melody.

October 12, 1857.   JAMES BALLANTYNE.

[1] Mr. Mackenzie's eldest son, a boy of ten years of age, inherits his father's musical talent, and is being educated in Germany.

The unexpected blow had a peculiar effect upon a boy rendered all the more lonely by strange surroundings and an unfamiliar language.   I took it into my small head that thirty-three years was to be the utmost limit of my span of life, and one day, when strolling in our garden, bounded by the ancient town wall, I heard my father's voice calling " Alick " so distinctly that I ran into the street in expectation of meeting him at the front door.

Hallucination or not, the astounding impression remains to this hour.   Certainly for several months I experienced a prolonged spell of that unexplainable and undesirable possession, the " Celtic gloom," until that morning on which I awoke to understand and speak German—suddenly, as it seemed, for the interval between is almost a blank.

A good old Frenchwoman, Mdlle. Lagaude, of unprepossessing and witch-like appearance, had prepared me sufficiently well to enter school.   Shortly after that event I was duly presented to *Seine Durchlaucht der Fürst*, when he visited it, as a curiosity.   But we knew each other already, for I had met him again at the *Possen* when I had inspected his gorgeous watch with its richly-jewelled coat of arms—made in London, as the simple old gentleman delighted to tell me.

When ten years before ('47-48) the good citizens, infected by the prevailing fever of discontent, thought it necessary to relieve their feelings by a demonstration under the palace windows, they were thus dismissed by the then reigning *Fürst* in broad Thuringian dialect:

C   23

"*Jetzt aber, Kinder, thut mir den Gefallen und macht dass Ihr Alle nach Haus kommt.*" (But now, children, do me the favour to get away home.) The request was obeyed and the great revolution ended.

My affectionate *Haus-Mutter*, Frau Bartel, had, when a child, seen Napoleon at Erfurt, but the dignified and reticent old dame was not communicative on the subject of her youthful days.

The district had been, I believe, under the Emperor's rule until 1813, and the number of ludicrously-corrupted French words still in common use was fearful and wonderful. While the lingering memories of the invaders seemed not to be of an unpopular kind, a general dislike of *Die Preussen* was unmistakably apparent. Many elderly people still respectfully addressed their parents as "*Sie*" instead of the familiar "*Du*," and some customs and rights were of past centuries.

On market-days the prices of all articles of food were fixed to a *pfennig* by the *Bürgermeister*—the cost of living was almost unbelievably low. The regulations of the many Trade-Guilds, with their apprentices, journeymen and masters, were as actively real as in the days of Hans Sachs.

The *armer Reisende* (poor journeyman) begging his way from town to town, identification book in hand, was never refused the small alms at any door, and many times have I handed them over. At night he had to report himself at the *Herberge* (shelter). An odd sight on spring mornings was the arrival of the town swineherd, who drove the pigs to the meadows and returned them to their owners at the close of day. Time after time have I watched the porkers detach themselves from the main body and briskly run up their own doorsteps: thus Teufelsdröckh saw them behave at Entepfuhl in his boyhood.

Whether unaided instinct or the effect of a long-thonged whip determined the unerring selection of the right house was a problem I tried, unsuccessfully, to solve. In any case, it remains an object-lesson in Teutonic thoroughness.

My good mentor, old August Bartel, *Kammermusiker* and *Stadtmusiker*, besides being an able musician was known as a *Lebemann* (viveur), and also as a mighty hunter for whom the wild boar and other game in the Thüringer Wald provided ample sport. I accompanied him on one of his expeditions to the Kahlenberg, a completely barren mountain plateau famous as the site of a fierce battle with the Huns. We entered a hut, built into a dug-out, of which the roof only was visible. From the interior a wooden pipe ran as far as a high and bare tree to which an owl was tied by a rope which could be pulled in the hut. During this process the frightened bird danced and flapped its wings, its shrill screams attracting the curiosity of birds (chiefly birds of prey, such as hawks, etc.), which would perch upon the surrounding trees—easy shots from the interior of the hut. But neither my persistent tugging at the rope, nor the owl's *vocalises*, had any effect, and game and luncheon bags returned empty. The whole proceeding struck me as so screamingly funny that I might have changed places with the owl had I not thought it better to repress my mirth.

Bartel, while holding a principal post in the Ducal Orchestra, happened to be one of the very last representatives of the *Stadtmusiker* (town musician: *vulgo, Stadtpfeifer*), whose prescriptive rights were to provide music at funerals, weddings, balls, *Kermessen* and other entertainments within his district; he therefore had to teach and maintain a given number of apprentices who lived in his house. In no sense one of them, I arrived just in time to witness the rapidly approaching end of these old-world conditions. The duties of this ancient guild were gradually being handed over to the Military Band (of a standing army of *circa* 300 men) already well-known for its excellence, with a corresponding compensation for lost privileges.[1]

[1] The " Thuringians " played in London with great success at a time when our best bands had not attained that superiority over those of any country which they now may claim. That popular and powerful agent for good is, in recent years, indebted to the unwearied efforts of the now retired—after fifty years' service—Lt.-Colonel J. Mackenzie Rogan, C.V.O.—for its vastly improved conditions and status in our musical life.

During my first year, our house, like Caliban's Isle, was "full of strange noises." In one room a couple of violinists—good ones—practised. A clarinettist blew his loudest in the wood-cellar; a double-bass grunted in the wash-house; a trombone was heard from a corner in the garden, while other wind-instruments added to the din from various parts of the house. I attended the rehearsals of the small orchestra with my violin (trying my 'prentice hand on second oboe parts), and met with much kindness and friendly service from the young men. All was conducted with military discipline, and I have held the master's violin while he slapped a misbehaving young stalwart's face previous to running him from the room. This unpleasant incident occurred shortly before the expiration of his official authority, when temptation to rebel seemed irresistible. While an excessive outward politeness prevailed, the classes were very sharply divided and the trail of militarism was over it all.

The punishments meted out to awkward recruits by inhuman *Feldwebel* were brutal, and I often shuddered to see and hear these bullies delivering resounding blows on the ears of their peasant victims at drill. The military bandsmen still bore the old name *Hoboisten*. Note also the subtle distinction between *Musiker* and *Musikus*; the latter term implied an inferior grade, and on a *Reiseschein* (journey pass) I am so described.

Although the before-mentioned old Frenchwoman was the only person who spoke English, there was one who vainly imagined that he did. Some wiseacre considered that my attendance at the English class taught by this oddity would help my progress in German. Logically the idea seemed correct, but as no English ever heard on land or sea was spoken in it the class remains a treasured joke.

A quaint being was our Oberlehrer Haesler, with his pursed lips and general air of being crushed by the weight of superior knowledge. A pupil of Spohr, and a good, though dry, violinist, he divided his occupations between schoolmastering and the Court Orchestra. After the performance of one of his late master's concertos he proudly informed me that it had taken him eleven years to learn. I was not impressed by the fact.

His knowledge of our language had been gained solely from Shakespeare—*via* Schlegel's translations—and his Elizabethan turns of speech in conversation were as funny as his pronunciation. When in 1862 he visited London and its Exhibition, I was glad to be of service to the good, but helpless, man, whose ' Whither go we now?" "Prythee, let us hence!" etc,. astonished many a cabby as much as they amused his quondam pupil.

Now and then, in the class, I was sorely tempted to intervene. But on one occasion when my class-mates (all very much my seniors) were gravely informed that I had been sent to Germany because of the very inferior education to be had in Edinburgh, my youthful ire was roused beyond repression. Then arose the boy, and boldly answered him in his own tongue.

"*Sie vergessen, Herr Oberlehrer, dass Edinburg eine grosse, berühmte Universitäts-Stadt ist!*" (You forget, sir, that Edinburgh is a great and famous University town). This to the surprise of my fellow-scholars and consternation of their master. The study of *Julius Cæsar* was resumed with difficulty.

I was not sorry when it was thought convenient to remove me at an early date, as it entailed leaving home before 8 o'clock on dark winter mornings—no light being provided in the class-room, with an obligatory candle in my pocket—only to waste time and temper. It was not until nearly two years after my arrival that the worthy burghers enjoyed the benefit of the gaslight.

Then came my confirmation. The Lutheran Church service, with its sermons of moderate length and powerful chorales with ingenious interludes by the organist—whose varied impromptu "figuration" accompanying each verse constituted a test of his ability—was both new and grateful.

At school my progress in German was rapid, the cause

of the only severe reprimand being that I ignored boys of my own age and favoured intimacy with my elders. Wonderful paternal interest! Once when summoned from home to appear before a master, the expected wigging proved to be a compliment on an essay, which I had to convince him —not without difficulty—was my own unaided work. He actually honoured me by reading it to his class, with comments on the many grammatical errors, but high praise for its descriptive and imaginative passages, which were compared favourably with other laboured efforts before him.

While the compulsory *Turnerei* and *Ausflüge* (school trips) did not appeal to me in the least, I took my lusty share in shouting the *Freiheits Lieder* of Arndt, Körner, Fallersleben and other forerunners of *Die Wacht am Rhein* and *Deutschland über Alles*. Brought up in this atmosphere of love for the Fatherland, it has ever been a source of wonder to me that we have not thought it necessary to foster a like spirit of patriotism in our children in a similar manner. Have we no worthy equivalents for these songs in British literature and music?

The conditions under which I began my musical education could not have been bettered. To the simple, submissively contented mode of life, the active cult of the most advanced musical tendencies displayed by the fine Court Orchestra—conducted by a man whose devotion to progress had won an exceptional reputation for it—provided a strange contrast. Not so many miles away Liszt was fighting for the Music of the Future at Weimar.

Our orchestra had among its members a number of celebrities. Conzertmeister Uhlrich (my master) had shared the first desk with Ferdinand David during the later years of Mendelssohn's reign at Leipzig. For him Max Bruch wrote his first and most popular violin concerto; Himmelstoss, an excellent 'cellist; the famous contrabassist Simon— looking like Samson and nicknamed " the bass tamer " (*Bassbändiger*); Heindl, the Viennese flautist, who made his name when travelling with young Anton Rubinstein; Kellermann, a sweet-toned clarinettist; the horn virtuoso, Meyer (as yet I have not heard his match)—like Vivier, a wit. Although he had visited London professionally, his knowledge of English was confined to this single sentence: " Waaiterr, a pint porrterre and four ecks! " Mayhap the genial man's excessive corpulence was attributable to a too frequent repetition of this order!

These and others—artists all—were modestly satisfied with a pleasant life, moderate pay, and a pension to look forward to.

Kapellmeister Eduard Stein, known far beyond the limits of the little town as a cultured leader among modern musicians, had the affectionate regard of all. The pale, intellectual face, with long straggling wisps of black hair carefully trained over a bare skull, presented a perfect picture of a German *Gelehrter*. A dreamer and student of theology in his youth, he had discarded the sacred science for that of music, married an actress, and devoted himself to the pioneer's discouraging task which made his orchestra famous.[1]

Soon I became his pupil, falling under the spell of his refined and gentle nature. For all his ultra-modernism, a liberal-minded eclectic, he bestowed as much care upon Auber, Verdi or Gounod as upon Berlioz, Liszt or Wagner. In this respect, to my mind, an ideal conductor.

Stein's occasional fits of absent-mindedness were only exhibited in the theatre during a drama or play, when he had to be roused from meditation and warned of a coming cue; but even with this precaution there were awkward contretemps and subsequent official snubs (*Nasen*) for himself and orchestra.

With three schoolfellows a quartet of violins was formed, for which the music had to be arranged by ourselves from operas and other sources; our practising being done in a small room behind the shop of the Hof-Konditor Krause,

---

[1] Stein's predecessor had been the talented and cheerful Gottfried Hermann, whose vacated post Schumann proposed to fill when matters became uncomfortable at Düsseldorf. I met Hermann when he visited us from Lübeck.

at whose son's instigation the wondrous combination came into existence. Although the noises produced may have been fearsome at times, the experience was of service. We also saved our pocket-money to buy music, the arrival of which was eagerly awaited from Holle of Wolfenbüttel. My own predilection was for Mozart's sonatas, the order of choice depending upon the available amount of groschen— the larger works having sometimes to wait until an affluent week came round. My bookcase testifies that Mozart's and Beethoven's sonatas (in Liszt's cheap edition) were all gradually acquired in this way.

I have good reason to remember a narrow escape from death—one of three—and the agonizing struggle it occasioned. During an exceptionally hot summer a series of tickets was taken to allow me to bathe in a covered shed erected in an old mill on the River Wipper. The greasy, moss-grown, wooden floor had been made too short, and on entering the bath I stepped beyond its unseen limits and slipped into the river. By sheer luck I managed to grasp the narrow edge of the slippery boards before being swept under the revolving mill-wheel a few yards below. To maintain that insecure grip against the force of the rushing stream was extremely difficult, but fear lent strength; inch by inch I succeeded in gaining a stronger purchase upon my slender hold and gradually pulled myself back to safety. Seconds seemed hours during that fight for life, for had I been swept into the wheel there would have been a speedy end of me. I kept strict silence about it at home, but paid no further visits to the mill.

In the summer of '59, entrusted with the responsibility of taking care of myself, I made a leisurely journey to Hamburg on my way to spend a month at home. It was always my luck to hear the basso Karl Formes in Opera whenever I passed through Hamburg, and the North Sea invariably behaved badly to me. On arriving at Leith on a Sunday at an unexpectedly early hour, I felt strangely helpless when discovering that much of my native tongue had been left behind in Germany; nor were the mild family jokes at my expense greatly to my liking.

The return journey was made through Holland—I lingered some days in Rotterdam—where there had been an inundation and a large tract of the country was still under water. The sails of windmills, roofs of houses, tree-tops with boats and barges sailing round them provided many odd and sad sights from the train. A stop had to be made at Hanover, where I was charged with the delivery at the house of Georg Hausmann's father of some lithographic portraits of his unfortunate son. And before stepping into the now familiar *Postwagen* I could not resist spending some time at Cassel. These independent trips, made *solus,* at so early an age taught me much, as I never missed an opportunity of finding my way to picture galleries or theatres.

In the following summer I set forth to meet an aunt and her friend at Brussels, where these adventurous ladies awaited my pilotage through Saxony after an instructive visit to the picturesque Flemish and Belgian towns. At Antwerp we saw the famous armless copyist painting with his toes.

We explored the sights and art-treasures of Bruges under the self-appointed guidance of a burly, well-spoken gentleman who occupied rooms (evidently permanently) in our hotel. One night, after the ladies had retired, he invited me to his apartments on the top floor. The walls were adorned with rapiers, pistols, guns, Indian clubs, and other athletic and sporting paraphernalia which he exhibited with evident satisfaction. But an excited manner and flushed appearance were not much to my taste, and when he started to give practical illustrations of their uses, while gradually divesting himself of his garments, the situation became uncomfortable, as I had to keep dodging him round the room. Finally, when a pair of heavy clubs were swung closer and closer to my head, I thought it wise to get as near to the door as would enable me to make as rapid an exit as possible. Thoroughly frightened when I appeared below, the angry proprietor declared that, had he known, he would not have allowed me to pay that visit to the gentleman upstairs. Before leaving, I was informed that my eccentric friend belonged to a distinguished Irish family.

Making the beautiful capital of Saxony our head-quarters, we revelled in its wonderful picture gallery, the gems in the Green Vault, and—the Opera closed—in the attractions of one of the best theatres in Germany.

It is something to have seen Emil Devrient (famous actor, brother-in-law of the great Leonora in the successful revival of Beethoven's *Fidelio* in 1822, and a link with Goethe's time) [1] if only in the comic part of a German Uriah Heep. Though advanced in years he seemed in full possession of his gifts.

The wild scenery of Saxon Switzerland fascinated me. Did not an ancient guide sing Kaspar's *Drinking Song* on the self-same spot where the seven bullets were cast, in the identical *Wolfschlucht*, and cry—in a rasping bier-bass—" Hilf, Zamiel! " And did I not believe in the absolute truth of it all?

In the month of August one does not expect to hear much music in Leipzig or Berlin, but in the latter city I witnessed the most ludicrously bad operatic performance within my recollection, and that rendering of *Die Braut von Lammermoor* in the Royal Opera House deserves to be recorded. The name of the Edgardo—Herr somebody, *als Gast* (as " star ") has happily escaped me, but the extraordinary costumes worn by all concerned were a source of delight which amply recompensed the Scottish eye for the torture of the ear. The peculiar cut and brevity of these wonderful kilts were doubtless designed and specially adapted to an exceptionally hot summer. Nor did the renowned orchestra shine on that occasion.

On the whole—with notable exceptions—the singing on the German operatic stage was not then of a superior order (often such as would not have been tolerated in unmusical

[1] See " Goethe's Letters to Zelter," by A. D. Coleridge, p. 447.

Britain), and I was frequently amazed to note that so few of the natives seemed to be aware of the fact.

Immediately after returning to Sondershausen, full of delightful impressions, I was laid low by a severe attack of gastric fever. Dangerously ill for some weeks, I was nursed back to health by the anxious care of my dear friends. No doubt the illness was caused by the indifference to the elementary principles of sanitation then prevailing all over Germany.

CHAPTER III

MUSICAL RECOLLECTIONS OF GERMANY

FEW lads can have had such exceptional chances of hearing the amount and variety of music as were mine. Considering the number of works with which I became acquainted—some of them, more's the pity, hardly to be revived again—in Opera alone my schooling was extensive. The singing may not have been of the highest excellence (while it compared favourably with that to be heard on many of the more celebrated operatic stages), but ensemble and orchestra playing were as perfect as the artistic conscience could achieve. Our Fürst had a carriage running on rails which conveyed him each evening directly from the dining-room to his box in the theatre.

Fidelio, Don Juan, Zauberflöte, Seraglio, Figaro, Frei-schütz, Preciosa, Méhul's *Joseph* (little Benjamin's simple and touching song always made me cry), *Dame Blanche, Jean de Paris, Zampa, Masaniello, Le Maçon, Lestocq, Fra Diavolo,* and the fine *Gustave, ou Le Bal Masqué. La Juive, Robert le Diable, Les Huguenots* (I must be one of the few left who have heard its Fifth Act!) and *Dinorah, William Tell* and the immortal *Barbière.* All in German, and none of the finicking nonsense about operas in their own language. Verdi was not popular at the time. Then there were Lortzing's *Czar und Zimmermann,* and his amusingly childlike *Wildschütz.* This composer (his own librettist and a genius who still holds his own in Germany) had, during his latter and unprosperous years, travelled much in our district, singing in and conducting his own operas under depressing circumstances in villages.[1] Friends told me

---

[1] I wonder whether his *Hans Sachs* did not put another composer on the track of *Die Meistersinger.*

that they had seen him act Kaspar and play the double-bass when not on the stage. As he had died as recently as 1856, affectionate recollections were still quite fresh.

A performance of *Fidelio* is unforgettable because the Florestan happened to be sung by a very obese tenor (with a fearful squint) carrying what is impolitely called a *Bier-Bauch*. When in the Dungeon Scene he rose from the straw in a starving condition imagination flatly refused to support the illusion.

Heinrich Dorn's precursor to a greater work *Die Nibelungen* came from Berlin, but none had a kind word for the dull opera.

Tannhäuser, the scene of which is laid at the not far distant Wartburg, had an added local interest for us. Spohr's difficulties over its production at Cassel in '53 were not yet forgotten, and Wagner's works were only gaining a foothold slowly. The old violinist-composer's personality was still keenly remembered in Sondershausen, and his daughter Rosa (harpist) when on a visit to her father's friends was pointed out to me.

In the winter of '61 I was present at an admirable performance of *Tannhäuser* (an opera which reached Covent Garden in an Italian version fifteen years later) and of *Faust*. As the latter had seen the footlights only three years previously, this was quick work for a small *Fürstenthum*, and emphasizes the interest and activity in these musical regions. As an R.A.M. gallery-boy I witnessed one of the first London performances at Her Majesty's Theatre with this memorable cast: Tietjens, Trebelli, Guiglini, Santley and Gassier.

A harmony lesson was interrupted by the arrival of this score. The parcel eagerly opened, Stein at once proceeded to play and explain the opening scenes to me. Many years later, at my request, Gounod honoured me by a sight of the original MS. score, making characteristic remarks as he turned the pages over.

During the last month of my stay (1862) I saw Offenbach's *Orphée* seeking his wife in Hell, and *Lohengrin* leaving his in Brabant. The outrageously funny French work was then wildly careering through Germany, while the romantic masterpiece had to knock at every stage door for admittance. Wagner (who had heard his opera for the first time in '61 in Vienna, although Liszt had produced it eleven years before in Weimar) was, to my knowledge, keenly anxious concerning its reception in Sondershausen, as many influential critics had been present on this occasion. Another thirteen years passed before the arrival of the Knight of the Swan in the Thames (again Italianated); the schoolboy's experiences were therefore considerably in advance. None of us in Sondershausen noticed any extravagances either in *Tannhäuser* or *Lohengrin* to justify the carping criticisms and objections raised. The fuss made in London anent their unintelligibility, want of melody, etc., amazed me. Was it good or ill humour which caused Costa, when repeating part of the finale to Act 1, to call out " Bring back the Goose " ?

Just then, too, the book of *Tristan* was issued and eagerly read; much fun was poked at its involved literary style. Criticism was mild in comparison with the ridicule—a witty Berlin journalist, Paul Lindau, did his best—evoked by the uncouth alliterative language of *The Ring*. It all helped, however, to keep the combative composer's name on every tongue.

Confessing patience to be exhausted, the poet declared —in 1862—that hopes of ever witnessing a performance of his work had ceased along with the expectation of looking forward to the leisure and pleasure necessary to the completion of its musical composition. Yet, in spite of unconscionable lengths, scenic difficulties almost impossible to overcome, giants, dragons, birds, beasts, exorbitant orchestral demands, and all the other obstacles he heaped up to impede acceptance, Wagner's towering genius and superhuman energy gradually silenced opposition. The ever-growing admiration of that monumental achievement is unparalleled.

Is there any other work which the most ardent *fanatici per la musica* would permit to interfere with their dinner hours?

Our open-air Sunday concerts in the Loh (the site of a disused tannery) had a wide reputation for fine performances of the most advanced music of the day, the programmes ranging from Mozart to Schumann, thence to Liszt, Wagner and Berlioz. Brahms, as an orchestral composer, was not yet known.

On field-days when such works as the *Symphonie Fantastique, Harold in Italy, Mazeppa* or *Tasso* were given, a goodly number of critics from Leipzig, Berlin, etc., were among the audience. In a very wide space, surrounded by woods, the covered orchestra was placed. On the stroke of three o'clock our gorgeously-attired Hof-Marschal von Wurmb (typical Court autocrat of the period) raised his long, gold-knobbed staff of office to announce the coming of the Fürst and his party, which was then solemnly conducted by him to an elevated pavilion. The illustrious family could never have heard the opening bars of the first pieces, as the music started promptly at the signal, when they were still some distance away.

I frequently wondered whether the simple townsfolk, for whom these ear-feasts were provided gratis, really understood all or much of the music they were privileged to listen to. Certainly, in their homely dialect, they criticized the novelties as keenly as a Scottish congregation would discuss the soundness of its minister's theology.

Strict etiquette, caste observance, and perpetual *Deckeln* (lifting of headgear) prevailed. With many exaggerated obeisances and much clicking of heels, the aristocratic "Vons"—the tiny army required a vast number of officers —kept rigorously within their own circle, never conversing with the Bürger class.

On a red-letter day, Liszt, with a party of disciples, arrived from Weimar to hear his *Mazeppa* and another of his recently written works. His then still slim, upright

37

figure made him appear somewhat taller than he was. The thin lips, ascetic, colourless face, and thick mane (already quite grey) covered by a hat which seemed too small for his head, fascinated me. Watching him eagerly all the afternoon, even trifling matters left an impression, and I noted that his grey kid gloves did not nearly cover the hands which had captivated multitudes. Although still residing at Weimar, his official position as conductor had already been vacated in weary disgust at the intrigues and persistent opposition which culminated in the maltreatment of his friend Cornelius's *Barbier von Bagdad*. Quite unlike the genial, kind-hearted old man I was privileged to know so well in after-time, he looked grim, stern and melancholy. Not long afterwards he left for Rome, only to be disappointed in his marriage project, and thus it was in the most troubled period of a phenomenally brilliant life that I saw him first in '61. Liszt aged rapidly.

My friend Bartel, to whose advice I owed all these advantages, returned to his native town and was joined by an elder brother from Russia, where he had been in the service of the music-loving but eccentric Prince Galitzin as 'cellist in a quartet party led by young Berthold Tours. The Prince, who afterwards travelled in Europe as conductor of his own Russian choir, was, I take it, the son of Beethoven's admirer, and so intensely fond of music that he would rouse his quartet out of their beds in the middle of the night for a performance.

These enthusiastic brothers introduced me to the glories of chamber music. Occasionally being permitted to try my skill on a second violin part, I became and remained an ardent *Schumannianer*.

Oddly enough, although the most modern orchestral music had ceased to surprise or startle, the earliest published work of a certain César Franck, viz: *Three Pianoforte Trios*, seemed to be the strangest, most incomprehensible composition of the day. (I have never seen or heard them since.) Yet had not a point already been reached that we pencilled

"Yes, play, it is quite right," into the parts of Bülow's *Julius Cæsar* overture? Fairly fitted to occupy a humble seat as *Voluntär* in the orchestra, I was permitted to take one among the second violins.

As Hans von Bülow remarked to me, referring to his small hand which could barely stretch an octave, "*Die Natur hat mich wahrlich nicht zum Pianisten gemacht;*" (Nature certainly did not make a pianist of me) so I might say that the same mother had not been kind to me as a violinist. She endowed me with an incurable defect—a hot, perspiring hand. These concerts took place in summer when the sun's rays and heated atmosphere of the closed-in shell in which we played became sometimes intolerable. The ingenious idea of filling my left trouser pocket with bran with which to keep my hand dry was not exactly a success. After the first dip a paste covered my fingers and spread over strings and finger-board until a pudding-like mass distinctly hampered my executive powers. That secretly-tried remedy was not repeated.

Another uncomfortable experience was mine when Liszt's pupil Ratzenberger played his master's *Concerto in E flat* at an evening concert at Court. Published only five years before, that now popular work had been as yet very rarely performed and was considered to be the last word in pianism.[1] The composer only played it twice in public. Etiquette ordained the provision of a white waistcoat, and *Frack*, as well as my first white necktie. The Concerto calls for energetic vigour on the part of all concerned, and—no chairs being permitted except for 'cellists—we stood on a highly-polished floor. Its surface being exceedingly slippery, I was much more concerned for my feet than my fingers, but I managed to keep my balance and skated through the piece without the tumble I expected every minute in full view of the Court.

But the time drew near for leaving those from whom I

[1] Played in London for the first time by Frits Hartvigsen at a Philharmonic Concert in 1872.

had enjoyed an affection only given to a son. Stein's and Ulrich's tuition had been of the best, experience in the orchestra invaluable, and I had soaked in as much music and German literature as any lad of my age could reasonably be expected to carry. There were some feeble attempts at composition to show. A Polka (modestly entitled *Faust !*) was followed by a comic duet which I brought to Stein one morning when by chance the Theatre Director and principal tenor Sowade arrived during the lesson. Greatly amused, the two men started to sing it, to the gratification of the composer. A *Festmarsch* found a place in an evening programme, as a kindly adieu to the *Schotte*. Stein's rapid scoring of the piece in my presence was the only lesson in instrumentation I ever had in my life. Finally, some pieces for violin and piano, which probably assisted me to a scholarship in London.

The last and newest orchestral works I heard were the Prelude to *Tristan*, and, hot out of the publisher's oven, Liszt's *Faust Symphony*.[1] The slow movement *Gretchen* left a vivid impression.

Then *Schwager* blew his horn, whisked me off Londonwards, and ended these delightful schooldays.

The excitement of these last days affected me in a strange way. Arriving at the station at Cassel, the name of my destination could not be recalled. I got no farther than the request for a ticket to . . . ? The train was due to start, and my intended route was only discovered by the considerate help of the officials. Happily, history has never repeated itself, and this remains the only occasion when I suffered the ugly experience of a complete loss of memory.

At Rotterdam the amiable old father of Berthold Tours—and chief musician of the town—welcomed me kindly into his family circle. Our conversation must have been odd, for my hosts knew no English, I, no Dutch; nor was German of much help to us.

---

[1] Liszt's own copy of Goethe's works, in which the verses used in the Finale are marked by the composer, is a valued possession of mine.

CHAPTER IV

LONDON in 1862, aged fifteen. I was to await the coming of a relative in rooms situate in a street running riverwards from the Strand. The sitting-room contained a fine portrait of Wellington, by Sir Thomas Lawrence. I had seen enough of the artist's work to recognize that fact. But a surprise was in store for me when the stately proprietress entered, and, standing before the picture, presented the living image of the Iron Duke to my astonished eyes.

Meanwhile, acting upon orders, a visit to Manns was immediately made. Very long hair curling down over the checked shawl upon my shoulders, and a turban hat (*vulgo :* pork-pie) on my head, made me so much an object of annoying attention that I resolved to appeal to the nearest barber on my return from the Crystal Palace. The artist was found near Blackfriars Station and his scissors did their office. But my aunt's exclamation on the following morning proved that the shearing had not been done with sufficient thoroughness.

" Boy, what a head of hair! "

Said the parlourmaid complacently, " Oh mum, you should 'a seen 'im yesterday! "

Another sacrifice had to be made before my relative would consent to walk abroad with me. Be the incident noted solemnly: once more history refused to repeat itself !

The intentions of my well-meaning family regarding myself were of the vaguest, and resulted in several premature quests. Mr. Arthur Chappell passed me on to the popular conductor, Alfred Mellon, who received me on Covent Garden stage one morning when I interrupted his conversation with a handsome young man—Charles Santley. Wallace's *Love's Triumph* and Balfe's *Puritian's Daughter* were, I think, running at the time. But a very boyish appearance did not encourage confidence and no suggestion of an immediate engagement followed.

To Prosper Sainton I went with a request for advice and a hope of lessons from my late father's master. The cheery Frenchman solved the problem in his own good-natured way, and to my lasting gratitude. Too much occupied to accept me as a private pupil, he suggested my entering the R.A.M., in which he would be *obliged* to teach me (at a much smaller fee); and after examining my compositions, he foresaw a chance of success for me in the competition for the "King's Scholarship," provided I became a student at once. On his recommendation to the Principal I was immediately enrolled and placed in his own class.

The school, of which period of a precarious existence the most recently published intimate history[1] only tells us that it "muddled along for the next few years," was then emerging from one of its many transition stages and ruled by a Board of Professors.

Fortunate in having the Principal and Sainton as masters, it was by no means any fault of theirs that I did not shine during my studentship. The former, Charles Lucas, a kindly-disposed if somewhat gruff personage with a roughish humour of a dry kind, was Costa's principal 'cellist, organist of Hanover Chapel, partner in a publishing firm, and an excellent musician of the old school. Liking him well— even to the extent of cordial agreement with his repeated statement that I was the worst contrapuntist he had ever met—I learned much.

Later on, when the ambiguous term "academic" came prominently into fashion and used in no complimentary sense, the remembrance of Lucas's censures encouraged me to think that, being no galled jade, I need hardly wince. Although much good and earnest work was undoubtedly

[1] "A History of the Royal Academy of Music," by F. Corder, 1922.

being done, I felt as if I were suddenly dumped into a totally different atmosphere. While the first two concertos and the earlier sonatas were taught and performed, Beethoven's later works were perhaps considered beyond our comprehension.

Dussek, Hummel, Moscheles—all of indisputable merit—Mendelssohn and Bennett provided the staple fare in the pianoforte department. Chopin was rarely played, Schumann almost unknown; the prevailing disregard, or mayhap ignorance, of the music I had heard so frequently was a source of wonder to me. Such mild liberties as may have been taken with the established canons of Harmony and Composition not infrequently called forth sarcasms referring to "Young Germany and Young Scotland." But these occasional "scraps" did not disturb the pleasant relationship between master and pupil, and a stricter discipline was of rare benefit to me.

One or two of the young men (there were not many, all told) still wore the blue coat adorned with shining buttons and the cap with R.A.M. in gilt letters: a naval uniform which soon disappeared. With Lucas conducting at the piano, to the accompaniment of much snuff, our little orchestra practised in what had been the drawing-room of the Carnarvon family mansion in Tenterden Street, Hanover Square; but these rehearsals provided me with more amusement than interest.

During the second week of studentship an ex-student (John Ratcliffe, flautist) asked me to deputize for a violinist on that same evening at the St. James's Theatre (Miss Herbert in *Lady Audley's Secret*), and, anxious for work, I never henceforth lacked an engagement. Thus I gained an early and varied experience of the rougher side of an orchestral musician's life. However useful it may have been to me, it was not then to be recommended to every boy as a safe preparation for a more ambitious career.

Sainton's prediction was fulfilled: within one term as a paying student the institution received no more of my mother's money. I was then engaged at Dion Boucicault's

43

newly-erected Westminster Theatre (on the site of "Astley's"). Playgoers showed no great inclination to cross the river to see the finely-acted drama *Jeannie Deans*; nor did a panto-mime, *Lord Dundreary* (without dialogue) meet with any success. Thereby hangs a tale. I had to inform the musical conductor of my inability to attend its final rehearsal as the competition for the King's Scholarship had been fixed for that morning, and was warned by him of the inevitable result of my absence. After waiting all day in nervous expectation, the last candidate—myself—was called at a very late hour in the afternoon. Hungry and tired I reached the theatre just in time for the overture. On the following night I received the expected dismissal from M. Rivière, to whose reprimand I was able to reply, " Well, sir, so be it; but I've got the Scholarship." This letter was in my pocket:

December 23, 1862.

Sir,—

As Chairman of the Royal Academy of Music I congratulate you on your election to one of the King's Scholarships for which you have been a candidate and which you are entitled to hold for two years, subject always to your strict attention to the Rules and Regulations, copy of which are herewith forwarded to you and which you are re-quired to sign and which I beg you will return to the Secretary imme-diately.

The following are the conditions on which the King's Scholars will hold their Scholarship. "If an elected King's Scholar shall not make satisfactory progress in the opinion of the Board of Professors at the end of his or her first year's instruction he or she will be deprived or suspended from the privileges of the scholarship as the Committee may direct." I am, Your obedient Servant,

G. CLERK,[1] *Chairman.*

Thus a coveted prize and a discharge were mine; but the composer of *Spring, gentle Spring*, thinking better of it, returned to reinstate me on the same evening.[2]

[1] Sir George Clerk of Pennycuick, Bart.

[2] At that time the obnoxious practice of " farming " theatre orchestras prevailed, and a large section of the profession was dependent upon one or two conductors, who provided bands to the managements. The rates of payment will not bear comparison with those of to-day. My modest stipend —at the first desk—was a weekly guinea to begin with.

On the same day the brilliant pianist, the late Agnes Zimmermann, was re-elected for another year to the only scholarship of the kind then in England. Only two recipients, Mr. William Shakespeare and Francis Ralph, followed me before an exhausted capital compelled its lapse.

Tended by old friends of my family in rather distant Walworth, my nightly walk homewards [1]—fiddle-case tucked under the arm—was rendered none the more cheerful by the scare provided for a terrified London by garroters. Keeping well in the middle of the road, we all carried knuckle-dusters or other defensive weapons—mine a cheap sword-stick which would have puzzled me to put to any use.

After an absurdly long period of seemingly uncheckable ruffianism, the necessary—but happily not harmless—cat was applied, and lo! the brutal assaults ceased within little more than a week. A lesson yet to be learned by the more tender-hearted sentimentalists of to-day.

Soon I had to remove to a more convenient neighbour-hood nearer to the R.A.M., but not before joining—from a coign of vantage at the "Elephant and Castle"—in the hearty cheers and welcome on the occasion of the entry into London of the beautiful "Sea King's daughter" with her affianced, the young Prince of Wales, in February, 1863.

One morning, when on my way to the Academy, a stout gentleman of unmistakably German origin asked to be directed on his way. Answered in his own tongue, he questioned me as to the particular part of Germany which had the honour of giving me birth. Further conversation revealed him to be none other than my old friend the Arch-Druid who had inspired me with so much awe in Edinburgh. Strange meeting with Orovisto in Kennington Park after more than ten years!

[1] There were no buses at late hours and the first attempt—by an American —to run a horse-tramway service succumbed to a public outcry.

CHAPTER V

MUSIC AND THE THEATRES OF THE 'SIXTIES

THE Academy was miserably equipped for its lofty purpose; there being no adequate waiting-room for the boys, much of their spare time was spent, notwithstanding "Old Ben's" frequent sarcastic addresses to "Gentlemen and Gentlemen's sons," in the front hall or in Tenterden Street. The queer old fellow's surname—Badman—was "hushed up." Many of us took our midday meal at cheap eating-houses or at public bars. But where to find a dinner on Sundays was the weekly puzzle, for only a few hospices were open, and even then only for a short time. I often trudged to a chop-house in Hungerford Market and so witnessed the gradual demolition of this picturesque old square. Of music or entertainment there was none; therefore, forced to take long solitary walks, my knowledge of the town soon became almost as extensive as Sam Weller's. London could be as lonely as Glencoe.

To George Honey, the original Soupnour in Macfarren's *Robin Hood*, I owed many a pleasant evening which otherwise would have been spent in solitude. The popular comedian possessed a sonorous, though untrained, bass voice of which he was justly proud, and his ambition was to sing in Oratorio. The fact that he was not permitted to appear as an exponent of sacred music became a standing grievance. But even my close friendship with the creator of the part of Eccles could not bring me to adopt his view.

On week days at Pamphillon's dining-rooms (demolished to make way for the Oxford Circus Tube Station) I frequently met Charles Keene, a quaint, Quixote-like figure in rough tweeds, with an ancient Sir Walter Raleigh clay pipe rarely removed from its lips except to discuss bagpipes, of which instrument the famous *Punch* artist seemed to be inordinately fond. The harmonious subject was perhaps the chief cause of his conversing so much with a youngster from the North.

Nearly at the same time as myself certain young musicians (my seniors), all of whom were to play leading parts in the musical progress of their country, returned from Germany —Arthur Sullivan, Franklin Taylor and Walter Bache. The last proceeded to Rome to study with Liszt before settling in London. Sullivan, ex-student of the R.A.M. and first holder of the Mendelssohn Scholarship, reaped an immediate success with his evergreen *Tempest* music (written in Leipzig) at the Crystal Palace on April 5, 1862.

Shortly after that more important event in our history than is now conceded, a little black-haired, rather nervous young fellow appeared at one of our rehearsals in Tenterden Street. Introduced by the Principal, we cheered him lustily. He listened to our efforts for some time and before leaving was invited to return soon to place some of his compositions on our desks. But Sullivan, having heard us, knew better and came no more. Nor did I see him again until many years had passed, and then under different conditions. From subsequent conversations with him I gathered that he had no particularly pleasant recollections of his early days in the old school: indeed, had transferred his allegiance to a newer institution. But during the latter years of his life I had the great satisfaction of welcoming his warm good-will towards our Alma Mater.

Constant occupation in the evenings could not be favourable to adequate private study, and I once found myself totally unprepared for an examination in piano-playing. The enemy had to be faced. I boldly began to improvise, starting off in A minor and taking care to end in the same key. George Macfarren—the only examiner who spoke—startled me by asking the name of the piece. May Heaven forgive the answer!—"An Impromptu by Schubert." I was not surprised when G. A. M. informed me that he was unacquainted with "that one," but realized what the consequences would be if a repetition were demanded! But to my intense relief, nothing more was said, and a cheeky boy made a rapid exit from the room. The fact that a good deal of Schubert's piano music was not yet well-known in England, and that I might perhaps have learned the piece in Germany, may possibly have prevented the lynx-eared Macfarren from pursuing further inquiry. Nevertheless, I have never ceased to wonder at my escape, and would certainly not advise any student to run a similar risk to-day.

Rubinstein and other renowned artists had been repeatedly heard in London, but they seemed to have made little or no impression upon what appeared to me to be a pretty, limpid, but colourless style of piano-playing then in vogue —and so taught for another twenty years.

Spohr's pupil, Henry Blagrove, a silver-toned and extremely neat executant, but cold interpreter, acted as Sainton's substitute during his rare absences; and the genial organist of St. Paul's took over Lucas's classes on a few occasions. Kindly old John Goss generously offered me a share of his luncheon at lessons, but as it consisted of dry biscuits the tempting invitation was gratefully declined. His modest, lovable manner is still remembered. At the Monday "Pops" there were chances of hearing Vieuxtemps (then at the height of his fame), Arabella Goddard and Alfred Jaëll, whose rotundity of figure barely allowed his deft fingers to reach the keyboard. Of another great artist, the already dying Ernst, I had one fleeting glance when I saw him walking with evident difficulty in Oxford Street. The bent figure and probably the yellowest face ever seen on man made a lastingly painful impression upon me.

At the Promenade Concerts in Covent Garden (bearing that excellent conductor, Alfred Mellon's name) there were, beside the more popular excerpts from the Classics, much Mendelssohn and some Gounod—then slowly becoming known—to be heard.

Adelina Patti's sister, Carlotta, the young pianist Marie

Krebs, and the monocled, moustachioed Levy, famous cornet player, were the attractions. Mellon, who had learnt his business in theatre orchestras, was the most efficient British conductor of his day, and fully deserved the affectionate popularity he enjoyed during an all too short life.

The "Proms" continued after his death with more or less success for some years under conductors of varying ability, but, though serving their ostensible purpose as an educational factor to some extent, could hardly be taken into serious account. Refreshment bars, a mixed assortment of female music-lovers, and the air of general "larkiness" during the performances of those typical British waltzes which were *de rigueur*, afford a vividly enlightening contrast with Sir Henry Wood's wonderful programmes and the enthusiastic demeanour of a present-day Promenade audience.

The prevailing taste then catered for may have been at its lowest when a much-advertised Turkish (or Arab) artist was imported to perform solos—clad in gorgeous attire—on a weird-looking instrument. But we knew that the illustrious Oriental was none other than a member of a well-known British family of wind-instrumentalists and a familiar figure in our orchestras. Whether his instrument was an early specimen of that fearful wildfowl, the saxophone, or a disguised bass clarinet, matters little. The present popularity of the former is undeniable, albeit inexplicable.

True, the Philharmonic Society was steadily doing its duty, as it had always done for 115 years. The latest comer among the great composers, Schumann, was granted an occasional hearing. But the larger public was already enjoying the beginnings of that liberal education at the Crystal Palace upon which so much of our musical progress then depended.

Then, as now, English Opera kept sending up S O S signals. In 1863 pathetic appeals for assistance were as frequent as fruitless, and the courageous Pyne and Harrison combination at Covent Garden had to succumb to adverse circumstance. The following quotation from *The Theatrical*

Observer of 1864 (and unfortunately still applicable) reveals the state of affairs.

Up to the very last there has been no diminution in the energetic struggles made by these enterprising managers to secure for National music a name in their own country. The success which attended their efforts in America was not imitated in England. . . . With such material at their disposal—with an amount of talent and energy rarely exhibited —it appears to us most surprising—incomprehensible indeed—that at the end of eight seasons we have not what every Englishman ought to be proud to assist in obtaining—a National Opera.

Yet more incomprehensible in this present year of Grace!

The prominent operatic composers of that day, whose names still live, could not be charged with indifference to the cause, for new works were provided with a greater facility than would now be deemed possible or expedient. I was present at one of the last performances of Balfe's *Blanche de Nevers* (founded on "The Duke's Motto") and regretfully noted the depressing effect of undue haste upon a scanty audience. The most fruitful period of their activity appears to have ended with *Lurline* and *Robin Hood* in 1860. The deserved successes of *The Bohemian Girl, Satanella, Maritana* and *Lurline* were not to be easily repeated. With all these melodious and attractive young women I made acquaintance when an Academy vacation permitted the acceptance of a short engagement as leader with George Cooper's Opera Company at Birmingham. The manager, Spohr's pupil and an excellent violinist, only entered the orchestra on one evening for a few minutes to play an obbligato in *Lurline*. His amiable wife—Madame Tonnelier on the bills—was an accomplished singer and actress.

The experience gained in playing a pair of operas nightly practically at sight (after short rehearsals), was varied and valuable, as I knew little about English opera then.

In another and less ambitious direction, attempts were made to popularize native operas. "Mr. German Reed invites communications with anyone who can assist him in his plans for establishing 'Opera di Camera' as in institution."

The industrious Macfarren (whose seriously conceived *Helvellyn* deserved better success at Covent Garden) had already contributed two charming little works—*Jessie Lea* and *The Soldier's Legacy*—and Balfe added his *Sleeping Beauty* to the well-intentioned scheme. Opera in English kept fighting gallantly for existence, although in '65 it became acquainted with strange bedfellows: *Faust* and a pantomime *The Lion and the Unicorn*; *Satanella*, alternating with Gounod's *Mock Doctor*, preceded *Cinderella* at Her Majesty's. But then at Drury Lane—shades of Phelps and Irving!—we find *Henry VIII* and *Hop o' my Thumb* on the same bill.

Beginning with Boucicault's *Colleen Bawn* and *Jessie Brown*—in the latter drama the relief of Lucknow became a personal matter, to be continued in good earnest under the stage by the excited combatants—I remained at Drury Lane during several memorable seasons. It was at the Olympic Theatre, during the run of *The Ticket of Leave Man*, that I made my first appearance as a soloist in London. The members of the band were in the habit of filling in the long waits before bringing down the act-drop to slow music of the kind technically known as "keyhole," by card-playing. I was in my place in the empty orchestra one night when an act was nearly at its end. No one appeared. It was too late to give warning, and a hurried scramble to seats would have been disastrous. The end came, the bell tinkled, and a single violin played the touching melody as the curtain descended. The doors were gently opened, but the delinquents were wise enough to remain outside.

"Thank you, my boy, you've saved me from a wigging," said the conductor.

Something similar happened at Drury Lane in an "afterpiece" which ended with a dance. Neither the conductor nor his subaltern appeared, and I boldly mounted the throne, led the fairly large band, and thus made my debut as a conductor. On this occasion, however, my chief had evidently not escaped.   Nervously pulling his moustache, he said to me on the following day, "My boy, I wish you would grow a beard."   A brief remark, but full of meaning.

The peculiarities of several prominent foreigners, such as the beautiful Stella Colas and Mde. Beatrice, had to endure much good-natured banter from sundry graceless journalists. In *Bel Demonio* I enjoyed the spacious style and pronounced accent of the romantic Fechter.   "Thus bad *beg*ins and worrrse *rrre*mains *be*'ind."

About this time I was drafted into the stage band at Covent Garden, employed to play behind the scenes in the *Ballo in Maschera* and on the stage (in dominos) in *Don Giovanni*.   In order to hear as much of the fine singing (of Graziani and others) I took care to be in my place as long as possible before our services were required.

Sometimes after these performances Sainton (Costa's leader) would greet me at the morning lesson with, "You all play damn bad last night!"

In extenuation be it said that Verdi chose the worst possible key for the strings (D flat) in that piece of dance music.

At the close of one of the rehearsals Mario swaggered ostentatiously across the stage, grinning at Costa, while puffing vigorously at two large cigars, one in each hand.   It was his genial way of protesting against a notice prohibiting smoking which had been put up by the management.   I heard that exceptionally fine artist and graceful actor on several occasions.

At Drury Lane I saw much which invariably conjures up many delightful memories.   Phelps as King Jamie and Trapbois, the miser, in *King o' Scots* ("Fortunes of Nigel"); as Falstaff in a great production of *Henry IV*, as Sir Pertinax MacSycophant, and in *Manfred*—of which dramatic poem more anon.

Dapper Walter Lacy, our R.A.M. Professor of Elocution, as a vivacious, if elderly, Prince Hal behind the footlights, and one of his students playing in front of them, brought nightly opportunities for chats on the stage. Had I not under his tuition—his phraseology was exuberant—" brought down the house," and incidentally the wings, in the part of the fiery Tybalt on our little stage in Tenterden Street? (We anticipated Shakespearean productions in modern dress.) My fellow-student, Edith Wynne, jabbered Welsh as Hotspur's Kate. Phelps, the great versatile actor, worked up Manfred's tortured soul and agonized visage while slowly pacing the back of the stage with bent head, clenched hands, digging his fingers into his palms, and emitting strange, grunting noises. His wife, a little old lady in black, silently followed close at his heels. Both seemed to be getting into the skin of the gloomy part. Manfred, when in search of the spirit of Astarte, ascending through a trap into Hell, clearly demonstrated that there must be " in the lowest deep a lower deep."

By virtue of a seat at the leader's desk in Drury Lane, I was entitled to be present at the " Actors' Supper " on the occasion of the Shakespeare Tercentenary (Freemason's Tavern, April, 1864). Beginning at midnight, the festivity ended, rather abruptly, some time in the " wee sma' hours ayont the twal." Ben Webster in the Chair, supported by Buckstone and the greater (the unfortunate G. V. Brooke) and lesser lights of their profession.

CHAPTER VI

WORK AT THE ACADEMY AND ELSEWHERE

IN spite of these, for a mere lad, odd but intensely interesting surroundings into which by earliest association I fitted in quite naturally, the more serious and important musical work was not entirely neglected. Besides an excerpt from *Lalla Rookh* for solos and chorus (performed at the R.A.M.), I scored an Overture (rehearsed), upon the merits of which no appeal of mine induced Principal Lucas to reverse his unfavourable opinion—his judgment being a perfectly correct one.

Not many months ago the following notice in *The Theatrical Observer* of March 4, 1864, came under my eye for the first time:

The students of the Royal Academy of Music gave a Concert on Wednesday night, for the gratification of their friends, in the uncomfortable room of the Institution. . . . Several manuscripts by the students were included in the programme. For instance, a Sonata in C Minor for Pianoforte and Violin, by Mr. Mackenzie, the second movement of which may unreservedly be praised, performed by the author and Miss R. Brinsmead.

Towards the end of my scholarship I had to play a rather difficult Concertino with Orchestra by Kalliwoda in the long-since demolished Hanover Square Rooms, a hall with a great history, in which, I believe, Haydn and other more or less eminent musicians of their day had conducted and played.

In a circular space behind the orchestra—uncomfortably small and placed at an inconveniently high level—alone I nervously awaited the approaching ordeal. Enter a white-haired, amiable old gentleman.

" My boy, are you any relation to my late friend Alick Mackenzie of Edinburgh? "

" His son, sir."

Then, after some kindly encouragement and a pat on the shoulder, he told me that his name was George Hogarth. That kind hand was reached out to me from a now distant past. According to Lockhart, Sir Walter Scott selected Hogarth, " a man of business, Writer to the Signet, a gentleman of intelligence whose ability no one can dispute," to prepare the formal contract of 1822 between the publisher James Ballantyne and himself.[1] Lawyer, 'cellist and composer, he had studied music seriously, and as musical critic boldly championed English Opera and native talent. At the time I saw him he had just resigned the secretaryship of the Philharmonic Society after a fourteen years' tenure. Wagner, who in " Mein Leben " persists in calling him Mr. Howard, mentions him—" a worthy and agreeable old man was another person (the only one, he believed) in the circle of my English acquaintances who took the trouble to entertain me."

I know that my performance, beset as I was by hideous nervousness, must have been a miserably poor one; but nevertheless *The Illustrated London News* contained a lenient and kindly notice. *O ! si sic omnes !*

And I am certain the previously-quoted mention of my Sonata and all the fighting paragraphs in *The Theatrical Observer* and many other journals in favour of British art and artists were from the pen of Charles Dickens's father-in-law. I have always been proud of the modest link with a family in touch with the R.A.M. since 1823, when Fanny Dickens became one of its first students. The pleasant legend has it that her famous brother (about twelve) frequently waited in the hall to take her out on Saturdays.

I had the good luck to see the great author on two occasions. Once, in my R.A.M. days, I stalked him closely from Oxford Street to the end of Wardour Street, and noted that—probably in search of material for the concoction of

---

[1] See articles by Charles Dickens, *Examiner*, 1839 (March 31, Sept. 29).

those queer names he loved—his attention was concentrated on the signboards. A waistcoat of assertively reddish hue also impressed me. And again, at a respectful distance, when he visited Edinburgh on a Reading Tour.

Twice I saw Thackeray, at much closer quarters, sitting in the front row of the stalls during the run of *Ixion* at the Royalty Theatre. It may have been the evening when, to an astonished friend's question, " Why, what brings *you* here ? " he replied, " Why, legs, of course." And again at another theatre, the name of which and the attraction have escaped me; but the massive head covered with hair shining like molten silver is not forgotten.

As with very few exceptions all the violinists in Costa's orchestra were past or present pupils of Sainton, an engagement for the Birmingham Festival of 1864 did not surprise me. Rehearsing on the floor of St. James's Hall, I listened for the first time to the wonderful voice of a pretty, black-haired, lemon-complexioned girl of twenty-one, who, after singing one of the solos in Costa's newly-written *Naaman*, was publicly kissed by the usually imperturbable composer. Adelina Patti and I did not meet until we were of a much more mature age.

Our Principal edited and published the *Oratorio*, and great was his joy when informing me of the discovery of what he called a " fine, fat pair of fifths." (The Fifth-hunter's occupation is now gone.) To my thinking there was not very much else of interest to be found in the score.

At the same festival Sullivan conducted his cantata, *Kenilworth*, in which a delightful duet, "How Sweet the Moonlight Sleeps" occurs. The renowned Italian conductor ruled with a rod of iron at Covent Garden and elsewhere, bringing much-needed discipline to bear on the orchestras of the time. The operatic performances under his direction were as admirable as some of his readings of Beethoven and the classics were coarse and mistaken.[1]

[1] I, a modest flower in a large bed of violins, assisted at a slaughtering of the *C Minor Symphony* at Birmingham, when every *sforzato* was delivered with the emphasis and effect of a railway-brake.

And the grim, unalterably stern mask he chose to wear when in command of his forces always appeared to me an unnecessary pose. Festivals of a week's duration, entailing long morning rehearsals succeeded by two equally long performances daily (we being seated on narrow, sharp-edged, sloping stools which left their mark), under the vigilant eye of one who never moved a muscle or permitted anyone else to do so, were severe trials of endurance even to the most hardy frame. But the members of Costa's orchestra invariably comported themselves like well-trained, docile performers on these occasions. While this drill-sergeant's method would not be acceptable now, in justice be it said that the great chief was intensely loyal to their interests, jealous of the reputation of his orchestra, and was, in many respects, the man needed for the hour.

A final engagement affording experiences of a widely different kind came unexpectedly in my way before quitting London. On the site upon which the first Gaiety Theatre subsequently stood, a building was erected and opened under the name of the "Strand Musicke Hall" for the purpose of giving promenade concerts. A very competent band (chiefly recruited from Mellon's orchestra) being engaged, I was chosen to play, not only at the principal desk, but also to fill the responsible post of pianoforte accompanist to the soloists and singers.

A young Italian pianist, Tito Mattei, made a successful debut, and established his home in London.

From the beginning the scheme hung fire. Something had to be done to entice public support, so one "Comique" after another intruded upon the more or less classical programmes, until the enterprise fell from grace and became an ordinary music hall of the then prevailing sort, greatly inferior to the variety entertainments we now know. With some truth, the facetious dubbed it "Ye Sicke Hall."

The orchestra, now doing little more than open and conclude the programme, had an extremely easy time; but a three months' agreement as accompanist kept me at the piano

during the entire evening, compelling my services to the
" Great " Vance, W. H. Stead, " Jolly " John Nash, Arthur
Lloyd, the Sisters Dashwood, and many others of that good-
natured and generous branch of our profession.

These were the days of rollicking ditties, such as, " In
the Strand; " " Slap-bang, here we are again; " " The Perfect
Cure; " " Champagne Charlie," etc., all of which, and much
else of a similarly stimulative nature, it was my nightly task
to thump out while seated *on* the stage.

Only once, on Vance's first appearance, had I to deprecate
the attempts at jocose conversation on the platform, after
which the dignity of the young man at the wheel remained
unruffled. Much was learned when transposing at sight
from quaint MS. copies, or vamping from none.

" It goes like this: Tumtitum, tiddelum. *You* know."
And being quick in the uptake, the most pleasant relations
were established between us all.

After a time, however, amusement yielded to distaste.
The business became irksome; detrimental opinions might
have been formed by the R.A.M. authorities; and, as my
repeated applications for release were ignored, other (more
Machiavellian) means had to be resorted to. So it befell
that memory suddenly failed me and my hitherto valued
adaptability became defective. The compulsory waltz—this
time *The Fountain*—of which portions had to be strummed
during unforeseen delays between " turns," although played
by heart for a month could not be remembered! All without
avail, until a friend pointed to the fact that agreements signed
by minors were invalid. The course being now clear, an
improvised engagement of importance necessitated the sub-
stitution of a deputy for a night, and an organist who could
boast of exceptional inexperience in this class of work kindly
agreed to take my place. My determination to settle matters
assumed an impudent form, when, during the course of that
evening, I casually strolled in, cigar in mouth, took a seat
among the audience, and calmly listened to the results of my
defection.

I am far from being proud of the means by which release was secured, but the fight was won and the place knew me no more. While this brief peep into another section of the profession under its then existing conditions has never been regretted, my friend Walter Bache's singular reason for relinquishing a valuable church appointment on the plea of its being "so d——d demoralizing" may perhaps serve partly as an excuse in my own case.

My happy days at the R.A.M. drawing to a close, an unwilling adieu to London had to be said. But its call was too strong to be resisted, and for several years I returned during the summer seasons to keep in touch with theatres and the Festivals. Thus my name was still included in the orchestral lists of the Handel Festival of '65, and those at Birmingham in '67, '70, and '74.

The only occasions upon which I saw Sterndale Bennett were at the rehearsals and performances of *The Woman of Samaria* (conducted by W. G. Cusins), when the pale and somewhat care-worn looking man responded to the unanimous calls of the audience. His kindly face and modest demeanour clearly accounted for the widely-felt affection he enjoyed and in which his memory is held.

That Bennett could assert himself firmly was shown during the nine critical years of Principalship in which the R.A.M. rose greatly in public estimation, although its financial position may have profited incommensurately thereby.

Let it be remembered that the fast friends, J. W. Davison, W. S. Bennett and G. A. Macfarren were, from early man-hood to their last days, staunch and fearless fighters for English music and musicians when that cause had greatest need of plain speech and sturdy action.

Pleasant thoughts arise when recalling the initial perform-ances of Sullivan's Overture *Di Ballo*, and of the unfairly neglected *Light of the World*. That oratorio not only con-tains much of his very best work—the Overture to Part II is exceptionally good—but is imbued with sincere religious feeling. The whole work had a strange effect upon me, although I felt that the sombre colour of the violas and 'cellos persistently accompanying the voice of the Saviour produced an unnecessary monotony. Disappointed at the limited appreciation it afterwards met with, Sullivan seemed to lose any inclination to devote further time to the strenuous labour which the composition of so serious a work compels. Who shall blame him?

The Italian conductor's impassive face relaxed sufficiently to indicate what was passing in his mind when, at the first reading (in the composer's absence) of Ferdinand Hiller's *Nala and Damayanti*, we had proceeded little more than half-through the long cantata, his increasing impatience broke bounds and with a very audible sigh he turned over the remaining pages yet to be rehearsed. We all thoroughly agreed with him, for even witty, vigorous old Hiller himself could arouse no interest in the tedious work. And once the chief allowed himself a hearty laugh. His intimate friend Schira, a popular favourite, but an extremely excitable man, was rehearsing his noisily-scored *Lord of Burleigh*, while Costa helped from a seat in the gallery. At a point when the din (inappropriate to Tennyson's simple story) was at its height, the enthusiastic composer shrieked: " Fire, gentlemen, fire! " Intense amusement caused a sudden stoppage of our strenuous exertions, and Costa unbent to join in the burst of irresistible merriment. Of the same good-natured composer's opera *Nicolo di Lapi* (at Her Majesty's in '63) wicked wags decided that the best place to hear it was at Charing Cross.

PART II
EDINBURGH

CHAPTER VII

THE transition to what promised to be a much duller life was not made without regret, but depressing forebodings were dispelled by the cordiality and encouragement offered by numerous friends whose goodwill proved quickly helpful.

I realized that, following in my parent's footsteps, a careful study of our national music would be the shortest, indeed the only way to win any degree of popularity at the start. On my own inclinations no tax was needed, for its touching verse and melody always had a fascinating hold upon me, and the results of the preparation soon justified the resolve.

A first and successful attempt in this direction was made at a popular Saturday Night Concert (the programme included the names of Edith Wynne and the admired reader, George Grossmith, the grandfather of the present generation of that family) and was followed by many similar engagements.

That national habit of mind which acts as a discriminating drag upon excessive laudation, and the probability that my interpretations of our " native woodnotes wild " had not yet reached the expected state of perfection are both sufficiently illustrated by the following incident.

Playing at Dumfries, I noticed a burly, good-humoured looking man in the audience listening intently and exhibiting evidence of complete satisfaction. His vigorous applause shed encouragement, and I did my best to deserve his approbation by playing *at* him. At the end of the concert my friend appeared in the ante-room where I was putting my violin to rest. He dealt me a powerfully enthusiastic thump on the back and, beaming with pleasure, exclaimed: " Eh!— but you'll never be a man like your faither! " Incongruity between word and deed, and the characteristic restraint upon exuberant commendation, conveyed one of those wholesome lessons of which I received several.

The manager of the Theatre Royal was approached with a view to the vacant leadership of his orchestra, but my father's old friend, R. H. Wyndham, rightly considered me too young a man for the post, and the long chain of association with the Edinburgh stage was finally broken. The reasonable refusal of an application which, had it been successful, would have altered the course of my life, is now thankfully regarded as providential.

An introductory concert on ambitious lines having now to be given, I imported the Dane, Frits Hartvigsen, a newcomer to London, but already known as pianist to H.R.H. Princess Alexandra, who, in course of time, joined my staff at the R.A.M. A brilliant executant and exponent of his school of pianism, he, like others of his class, shone more brightly as a soloist than in chamber music, although their mentors, Liszt and Bülow, were past-masters in the gentler art in which subordination is an essential virtue.

Opportunities for hearing either chamber or orchestral music were very rare. The annual " Reid Concert," for twenty years treated by Town and Gown more as an occasion for amusement than enjoyment, was yet to be lifted into serious consideration by the newly-appointed occupant of the Chair of Music, Mr. Herbert Oakeley's wise engagement of August Manns as its conductor in '65. A well-meant effort on the part of some enthusiasts was made to found a permanent series of orchestral concerts under the direction of John Hullah with a large contingent of players from London, headed by Henry Blagrove and supplemented by competent local musicians.

With Dr. John Hullah I became well acquainted, and as I was indebted to him, have therefore no inclination to revive impressions of his powers as a purely orchestral conductor. He worked so well and successfully for musical education, the popularization of choral music, and vocal instruction of the masses, that his name deserves reverent and lasting remembrance.

At one of these concerts Joachim, after finishing his own rehearsal, sat down beside me among the first violins and fiddled through a Haydn Symphony at the same desk. We spent that afternoon together, when, meeting by chance in Princes Street, he gladly accepted my offer to show him the superb panorama of the Firth of Forth, the comprehensive view of the city from the Calton Hill, and other beauty spots. Joachim, then at the height of his form and fame, commanded my admiration by his great and pure tone, an exceptional skill in the art of bowing, and the intellectuality of his dignified readings of the classics.

In the same season Clara Schumann came for the first time, with her husband's beautiful *Concerto*. Of that eminent pianist I reserve further mention until later.

In spite of signs of an increasingly satisfactory position, ambition and interest lay elsewhere, and I have a clearer remembrance of my absences than of my stay in Edinburgh at this time. Thus I departed on a visit to Paris, where rooms were found in a centre (Rue Neuve des Petits Champs) from which the City of Light could be explored to heart's content. What if I did, after an hour's violin practice—which brought my landlord to my room with the invariable, " Mais, vous jouez bien, Monsieur "—regularly begin the day with a visit to the Morgue? The gruesome place, with its corpses on stone slabs over which water trickled, the bundles of clothes suspended over each for identification, and the endless stream of people strolling casually in, had a morbid fascination. The day often ended with unwelcome thoughts of it all, for my bedroom contained several of those large mirrors so dear to the French, in which my movements as I lay in bed were repeated all round me in a startling manner; but this did not prevent my return to the grim spectacle on the following morning. Once I thought to have recognized the features of an acquaintance, and so strong was the conviction that I returned to take another look at what I imagined to be the body of Dr. Lyszynski, with whom Chopin lived and by whom he was attended during that composer's depressing stay in Edinburgh in 1848. Fortunately I did not offer any information to the authorities, for I found the good old doctor as lively and well as ever on my return.

I saw much Molière at the Odéon, *l'Aventurière*, with Mdlle. Reichemberg and Coquelin, and, I think, young Sara Bernhardt, at the Comédie.

Also *L'Abîme* (Dickens's " No Thoroughfare ") with Fechter as Obenreizer, and a very French Joey Ladle, in a very dirty theatre. The little box into which I was put soon testified to the presence of undesirable companions, but I sat the play out. The theatres were uncomfortably, uncivilly and very badly managed, and not to be compared with our own. Our playgoers would not have tolerated those chattering harpies, the *ouvreuses*. On one occasion, at the Comédie, my imperfect but polite remonstrances raised a storm of personal abuse from which a judicious retreat had to be made rapidly.

A glimpse of the popular Jacques Offenbach, pince-nez and all, in an open carriage on the boulevards, recalls an amusing evening during the revival of *La Belle Helène*, when Mdme. Schneider was at her daring best.

Of orchestral or chamber music there was none during the summer *relâche*.

The greatest impression was made upon me by a superb spectacular production of *Don Quixote* at the Gymnase. Lesueur, an astonishingly fine actor as the crazy knight, and a little fat Sancho (Pradeau) were inimitable. The length of the play being inordinate, I resolved to return on the following night to see the final tableaux; but, although I took my seat at a late hour, I never saw the end of it. Presumably it finished at 1 a.m., the insatiable Parisians showing no signs of fatigue.

When Irving presented his life-like embodiment of the Don (in a reduced version in 1895)[1] he questioned me on the subject, and adopted certain effective points which I remembered, such as turning over the leaves of " Amadis de Gaul " with a huge sword.

At the Opera (the old house in Rue Lepeletier) I heard Christine Nilsson and Faure in Ambroise Thomas's *Hamlet*, but the ridiculous libretto, with the melancholy Dane's Brindisi and the Ghost's reappearance at the end (among other perversions) completely undermined my appreciative powers. Verdi writes to his friend Escudier: " Poor Shakespeare! How badly they have treated him! There is only one scene between Hamlet and the Queen that is well done and is dramatic and suitable for music. But the rest. . . . mum."[2]

Meyerbeer's *L'Africaine* (another revival) afforded me far greater enjoyment, the performance being an admirable one and the famous turning of the huge ship by the steersman a fine bit of stage engineering.

That master's unfairly decried works, in spite of obvious weaknesses, have always had a warm corner in my affections. In the art of instrumentation, if in naught else, he taught us much more than is now acknowledged.

To my collection of operas were added Halévy's pleasant *l'Éclair* and Auber's *Domino Noir*, well presented at the Opéra Comique. Waiting at the Gare St. Lazare one evening a figure bearing a startling likeness to the great Napoleon strode slowly past me in the dusk. " Plon Plon " looked exactly like an enlarged edition of his uncle, and evidently knew it.

Alas, it was not the same Paris I saw less than four years later, when War and the Commune had done their fell work. Cannon balls embedded in its walls, and the red ruins

[1] So far as I can trace, no dramatic or operatic version of the Spanish masterpiece has been thoroughly successful on the British stage.
[2] The Italian Maestro's letters contain many sarcastic remarks about " La Grande Boutique," as he rightly or wrongly described the French Opera House.

of the Tuileries and Hôtel de Ville were sights to move to tears. With a friend I followed the march of devastation from Spicheren Heights, where the first shot was fired, through Metz, Strasburg, Belfort and Nancy to the still suffering capital.

Rambling backwards to a link with the remote past, in early youth I became acquainted with my father's friend, the youngest and last of an old Scottish family, the Sharpes of Hoddam (on the banks of the Annan). William of that ilk (born 1792), a quaint old gentleman of artistic tastes and the courtly manners of bygone days, saw Sir Alexander Boswell of Auchinleek at a party in his mother's house on the night before he fought his fatal duel with Stuart of Dunearn—almost the last encounter of the kind in Great Britain—in 1822, and, when a lad, had met Sir Walter Scott. Charles Kirkpatrick Sharpe, antiquary, etcher, and musical dilettante, whose name is so closely connected with the novelist, was his elder brother—familiarly called " Cheepin' Chairlie " on account of his high-pitched voice, and, in England, " the Scottish Walpole."

A book of scandalous gossip, " The Diary of a Lady in Waiting " (to Queen Caroline), immediately interdicted by reason of the unwarranted publication of certain private letters, was republished a century after its original issue.

Among the first of these letters are some over the signature of Ch.K.S., and the fact that I was intimate with his brother is a stern reminder of my own advancing years.

It is something, however, to have had the last glimpses of cordial affection between master and man, laird and dependent. This case may have been an extreme example of an odd, but consistently respectful, familiarity often more than merely amusing. Conversations such as this were not uncommon at table.

" Wull! I'll hae anither glass o' sherry."

Came the butler's retort: " Dam the drap mair ye'll get frae me, sir! Ye had ower muckle yestreen."

Which extreme care for his master's health would provoke

the reply: " Speak for yersel! I heard ye turnin' that cellar key ower often this mornin'."

Frequently in the evening the head servants and a couple of gamekeepers joined any visitors, irrespective of their rank, in a game of cards; after which the laird would descend with them to the huge kitchen to see that all were provided with a " deoch an doruis," maybe to listen to an impromptu concert of " auld sangs," or a tune on my fiddle.[1]

Leading me up to Winterhalter's well-known picture, he would say, " Alick, come and hae a look at my cusin the Empress and her leddies." From the Kirkpatrick branch of the family the Empress Eugénie was descended.

But once only, when I spoke admiringly of " Sartor Resartus," did I upset the kind old gentleman's equanimity. Ecclefechan, birthplace of the great Thomas, was the " Town," and stood on the Sharpe family's property. Carlyle's father, the stonemason, had been their tenant, and I gathered that evidently there had been little love lost between them. My innocent remark called forth this outburst: " Alick, don't speak of him! I've seen him ridin' past our windows, pretendin' to read the newspaper on a powny! He's a humbug! Nae man can read a paper on a powny's back! " Thinking it wiser not to pursue the subject, or ask how the offence could affect the author's literary eminence, I held my tongue.

He often spoke of his connexion with the family of the author of " Roderick Random " and his " Auntie Smollett." But Mr. Sharpe, educated for the law (actually once a partner in a Writer to the Signet's firm), was a noted sportsman of the olden time, who bred racers, never betted, and preferred to follow the hounds instead of his profession.

Among other peculiarities, my friend disliked the sight of two explosives: *i.e.* female domestics and loaded guns. There may have been reasons for the strict order that the serving

---

[1] Similar experiences were mine in the North on visits to the Menzies families, when we danced in the kitchen with their devoted domestics, and in a slightly lesser degree a like unconstrained state existed in the oldest *Case Nobile* of Tuscany when we lived there. Certainly all were more contented and happier under these friendly conditions.

maids should remain as invisible as their domestic duties permitted.

Recollecting one day when returning from a shoot that only empty guns were allowed in the house, I stood looking for a cushie to fire at, with my weapon muzzle upwards and at half-cock. A fussy dog pawed the trigger with a result which requires no further explanation. Had my silly head been but half an inch nearer it must have received the charge. The thought of this second merciful escape from death invariably reproduces an accurate imitation of the prolonged shiver which shook me from head to foot. Of the incident strict silence had to be kept, or never again would I have been trusted with a gun; nor did I keenly yearn for the permission.

Either in 1870 or 1871 a very lively gentleman, whose card bore the name Julius Stockhausen, came to see me. The fact that—according to the "History of the Philharmonic Society"—he wrote to the directors that he had asked Beethoven to score one of his larger piano sonatas as a symphony should confirm the famous singer's reputation for high spirits. He was exactly one year old when the great master died.

The object of his visit was to ask me to join him and his pupil Sophie Löwe in a concert to be given in Dunfermline, an offer which I gladly accepted. With three members of the clever Drechsler-Hamilton family I formed a string quartet, and contributed a solo, besides accompanying the accomplished baritone, who did the like for his pupil. Who recommended him to me, or why he chose to appear in the "Royal Burgh" I never knew, but the occasion was an interesting one. Remaining overnight, we repaired to the smoking-room where a number of convivial commercial travellers immediately pressed, unsuccessfully, Herr Julius to "gie them a sang." They eventually provided us with their own versions of national melody and induced him to join them in whisky toddy, which caused him to confide to me on parting for the night that he could "*über die Dächer springen*" (jump over the roofs). Although Stockhausen

must have been an old man at the time, his physical and vocal
agility were alike astounding.

It is now a source of regret that the many concert programmes of this period were not preserved; it never occurred
to me that these records—some of them of an odd kind—
might have any future interest even to myself.

Thus, in far-off Tain, I gave a concert for the benefit
of the Volunteer Band Fund, at which, with the exception
of the local and vocal baker, I was the sole performer.   Beginning with a pianoforte piece, I proceeded to play solos on a
violin borrowed from Inverness; although my own efforts
were unaccompanied, I did the necessary service for the
baker, with the resulting profit of £30 in favour of a worthy
object.

The kindness of some of the inhabitants has not entirely
effaced the recollection of surreptitious drives and stealthily
contrived walks in defiance of strictest Sunday observance.

Although Robert Louis Stevenson's father lived at No.
17 Heriot Row when we occupied No. 41—in ignorance I
must have passed the young student a hundred times—I
recall but a single instance, confirmed by future portraits,
of having seen him.   My attention was drawn to a lanky,
very carelessly-attired figure with a strikingly-attractive,
somewhat tanned face and long straight hair—a decidedly
unconventional, not to say eccentric, ensemble.   To R. L. S.
I shall return in another connexion.

Just opposite to No. 17 resided a brisk little man—almost
a dwarf—whose conspicuously big head was covered by
long white locks: invariably dressed in professional black
with yards of white " choker " wound round his neck.
We all knew him as the famous Sir James Y. Simpson who
introduced chloroform to a grateful world.   He now lives
—in marble—on a beautiful spot in Edinburgh's centre.

CHAPTER VIII

SOME SCOTTISH NOTABILITIES: TEACHING IN SCOTLAND

EXCEPT at the annual concert given by the Philosophical Institution at which the "Monday Pop" Quartet usually appeared, chamber music was hardly ever heard in public. It was my good fortune to be entrusted with the second violin part by Arthur Chappell, and presumably acquitted myself sufficiently well to enjoy that honour as long as I remained in Edinburgh.

Rehearsals with a succession of brilliant artists such as Mde. Neruda, Joachim, Straus, Wilhelmji, Piatti, Hallé, Pauer, Dannreuther and Bache, were sometimes rather perfunctory. Playing with Joachim several times and occasionally accompanying his solos, I became fairly intimate with his broad, imposing style.

Apart from those of his friends Bruch and Brahms, it can hardly be said that he was moved, in public at least, to occupy his classically-attuned mind with the compositions of his worthy contemporaries, such as Dvořák, Goldmark and others.

"Have I ever played Spohr's *Barcarole* here? Yes, it was on last year's programme. Well, let's play it again." And we did!

Very pleasant were the little gatherings which generally ended these evenings, when the habitually silent Piatti brewed punch with solemn care.

"If you could only play the 'cello half as well! Do you ever stop smoking?" asks the Hungarian.

"Yes, ven I sleep," retorts the staid Italian.

My Joseph Guarnarius was an object of much interest to the great 'cellist, who had a keen eye for a fine instrument, and never omitted to inquire after the health of my violin before questioning me about my own well-being.

In chamber music Piatti's noble tone, perfect intonation and phrasing, combined with a rock-like though unostentatious support, was a joy and a lesson to our 'cellists. It may be said truly that he founded a school of playing—much needed in his time—of which the valuable results are still observable. *Nota bene:* Piatti was very sparing in his use of " vibrato," and reserved it for melodic high days and holidays.

A series of classical Chamber Concerts was successfully begun, and afterwards continued (under the management of Messrs. Paterson and Sons) for several years. The arrival of a talented young violinist (Adolf Küchler), with whom I alternated as leader, and the engagement of an exceptionally good 'cellist (Hugo Daubert) enabled us to form a well-rehearsed string-quartet. By means of an occasional visit of Walter Bache we endeavoured to reveal the beauty of Schumann's piano Quartet and Quintet, and of many other masterpieces, for the first time to interested if limited audiences. A competent viola player being less easy to find, I had sometimes to take up that instrument myself, in order to bridge over a difficulty, until the problem was unexpectedly solved. During a summer visit to Düsseldorf, a pupil of Leopold Auer and Hiller was warmly recommended to me as one highly deserving of such consideration and assistance as might perchance come within my ken. I had hardly returned when the Sheriff, D. B. Hope, a firm supporter of our scheme, informed me of a vacancy for an organist and teacher in Dumfries, of which the selection had been left in his hands. Here were two interests which might be served to mutual advantage, and Frederich Niecks was immediately communicated with. Thus Dumfries secured its organist, we our viola player, and the University of Edinburgh a future and very eminent occupant of the Chair of Music.

Flights into the provinces provided experiences, amusing enough after their difficulties had been overcome. On reaching St. Andrews one late afternoon I learned that the pianoforte required for that evening's concert had not arrived; nor could a sufficiently good substitute be found at any of the local dealers. Had not, at the last moment, the amiable wife of a resident University professor generously lent her instrument, the ancient seat of learning would have been deprived of the musical feast we had prepared for it. Being solo pianist as well as violinist, these incidents touched me nearly. Besides playing a Beethoven pianoforte Trio, a Mozart pianoforte Quartet, I travelled on Schumann's *Schlummerlied* and Chopin's *Polonaise in A*. These classics had often to be performed on cottage-pianos, some of which ought to have been afraid to face their makers. But youth dares much.

A greater trial of patience was ours when snowed up on a journey to Inverness, where an afternoon concert had to be given. After many hours delay, made more uncomfortable by pangs of hunger, the train steamed into the station at the hour when we were due at the hall. The public, aware of the circumstance, waited patiently until we had dressed and refreshed ourselves, then received us with encouraging plaudits. Over an hour late, we were about to begin, when a local teacher, who was taking part in the opening quartet, suddenly rose, left his seat, and disappeared from the platform. Time passed; much quite unnecessarily prolonged tuning was resorted to. What had happened? Had he been seized with illness? More tuning! After an embarrassing wait of twenty minutes, our friend appeared as suddenly as he had vanished. Having in his anxiety forgotten his spectacles, he had calmly donned his goloshes, and trudged home through the snow to fetch them without a word of explanation or warning.

On the return journey, a burly native of these parts stepped into our carriage while puffing vigorously at a pipeful of exceptionally powerful tobacco. When the lady vocalist of our party began to show primary symptoms of queasiness, Daubert entered into an amiable conversation with the Highland gentleman and diplomatically offered him a cigar.

" It's a gude ane, an' I'll smoke it the morn! " said the

grateful recipient, as he put it in his pocket without removing the obnoxious pipe. Vain sacrifice!

My travelling companions on a trip to Germany were the distinguished artist Sam Bough and his wife. Sam, a Carlisle man, was what is called a "character." Quick-witted and sharp-tongued, he might well, by right of genius, have filled the Presidential chair of the R.S.A. had it not been for his oddities of manner. He had moved from the Glasgow Theatre to that of Edinburgh as scene-painter—a school in which several great artists such as Roberts and Stanfield had begun their careers.

At Düsseldorf his unusual garb created a sensation among the aristocratic painters when he appeared at their *Mahlkasten* (paint-box) Club in the roughest of tweeds, a large tobacco-pouch dangling over his ample waistcoat, and a broad-brimmed bowler of huge size. It being an exceptionally hot summer, my friend had also inserted a large cabbage-leaf under his hat, and in this guise, clay pipe in mouth, he astonished the inhabitants. The word *Verboten* had no meaning for Bough. In the market-place at Frankfurt he calmly selected a rifle of newest make from the stand facing the guard-house and leisurely proceeded to examine it. The long-drawn, shrill cry "*'Raus*" immediately rang from the sentry-box, and the whole *Wache*, headed by the Herr Leutnant, clattered down the stairs. Only after my lengthy explanation that the delinquent was an eccentric British artist did we escape passing the night in less comfortable quarters than the Frankfurter Hof afforded, and were allowed to go.

An amusing and accurate pen-picture of the "able painter and singular person" will be found in a letter of Robert Louis Stevenson's to his mother (August 5, 1870).[1]

In the morning I met Bough on board, with whom I am both surprised and delighted. He and I have read the same books and discuss Chaucer, Shakespeare, Marlowe, Fletcher, Webster and all the old authors. He can quote verses by the page, and has really a very pretty literary taste. Altogether, with all his roughness and buffoonery, a more pleasant, clever fellow you may seldom see.

[1] "Letters of Robert Louis Stevenson," Edited by Sidney Colvin, New Ed., p. 25

For its humour, the long account of a dreadful dinner(?) at Iona which follows should be read. Referring to a miserable fowl, Bough, who is carving, says: "The strongest jaws in England couldn't eat that leg under twelve hours." And to the landlady, "That fowl is of a breed I know. I knew by the cut of its jib whenever it was put down. That was the grandmother of the cock that frightened Peter."

The Boughs accompanied me to Sondershausen where, Stein dead, the orchestra was under a *Kapellmeister* much less in sympathy with the modernists. Max Bruch belonged frankly to the opposition. With him I conversed much and was sharply questioned about the state of music in London, particularly regarding the Philharmonic, upon which society most German musicians seemed to keep a longing eye.

His *Violin Concerto* (No. 1) had recently met with the success it richly deserves, and the manly "Frithjof Scenes" had already secured fame for him in his own land. When he assured me of his intense interest in Scottish folksong, saying, "*Es hat mich eigentlich zum komponieren veranlasst*" (It really incited me to compose), I hardly realized how much truth the statement contained until I heard the once popular prelude to his own *Lorelei*. A prominent subject in that piece consists of four bars of the second part of "Lochaber no more." As a wide distance separates the Rhine and the Highland moor, the connexion seems a remote one.

And the opening bars of the often sung *Ave Maria* in *Das Feuerkreuz* are clearly recognizable as our old song, "Will ye gang to the ewebuchts, Marion." He told me that he had just indignantly declined a production of his opera *Lorelei* on account of a stipulation that Mendelssohn's well-known *Finale* was to be included.

Apart from his great ability as a conductor, the impression created by Bruch's personality upon me was that of a highly-cultured, musically-gifted man, somewhat cynical of speech and brusque of manner. I was to renew his acquaintance years later, when he received a degree at Cambridge, together with Boito and Saint-Saëns.

A secure position now provided constant occupation and brought me into contact with men of eminence whose friendship I am proud to have enjoyed. Among them the enthusiast for Greek, Gaelic, Scottish music, Burns and Goethe—John Stuart Blackie. I set several of his songs to music.

A little Vocal Club, consisting chiefly of University professors, included the slim, stately octogenarian Sir Robert Christison ("On Poisons"), the ever youthful, genial Sir Douglas Maclagan (Medical Jurisprudence), the burly Rutherford (Physiology) of raucous voice and eccentric manners, and others who sang under my direction, the main purpose being performances of part songs at the annual dinner of our Royal College of Surgeons. Considering the advanced age of some of my singers it was perhaps well that the audience consisted of respectful and admiring friends, but the boyish spirits and infectious enthusiasm of the mature vocalists were perpetual delights to them and myself.

Having promised to sing at a students' University concert (conducted by Sir Herbert Oakeley) at which I invariably functioned as leader of the orchestra, Professor Rutherford came to my house armed with a copy of his song copiously marked with hieroglyphic signs in blue and red pencil. "My danger signals," quoth he. After a satisfactory trial and expressions of unconcealed astonishment at my ability to cope successfully with so mighty a task, he remarked, "For the which I tender you the sum of one guinea." The proffered fee was politely declined. The worthy professor persisted in "tendering," with the result, neither giving way, that he did not gratify a keenly expectant-public on that occasion.

Another time, keeping a promise to play a solo at a students' "Kitchen Concert" at the Royal Infirmary, this strange creature was singing when I entered the large kitchen. Recognizing the words, but not the music, as Wolfram's address to the Star of Eve, I ventured to ask the name of the composer. Closing his eyes, as he invariably did when speaking, he slowly droned in deepest bass: "The vords are Vagner's; the music is mine. I thought them vorthy a

77.

bettaw wendewing!" Which explanation, unequalled for unaffected modesty, completely staggered me.

The conductorship of a very capable and well-supported society, "The Scottish Vocal Association," gave me the chance of introducing Schumann's *Paradise and the Peri*, his *Faust*, some of Bach's cantatas, and works by Beethoven and Schubert hitherto unheard in Scotland.

For one season I also directed a large Tonic Sol-fa Society, but at a hint that an examination for a qualifying certificate from head-quarters must be passed, my services ceased. I had never been unappreciative of the beneficial use of the system—up to a point. But, at that time, injudicious promulgations regarding the future of a new notation in which all music (instrumental, full scores, etc., etc.) was eventually destined to be printed, and other pretentious statements made by too fervent missionaries, retarded the conversion of many musicians. Now that reasonable views prevail, opposition is silent and excellent results are achieved.

My professional work was largely augmented by an appointment in one of the great Merchants' Schools (The Ladies' College) under the exceptional conditions of teaching the piano to eight pupils—seated at the same number of instruments—simultaneously for four hours every morning.[1] With a careful grouping of the pupils at fairly equal stages of advancement, and incessant vigilance—from a certain angle I could observe all the keyboards—the system worked surprisingly well, but imposed an excessive strain upon the nerves and temper of the teacher. Of the unconventional artifices to which I resorted in order to maintain my patience and good humour, quaint legends are, I believe, even yet said and sung in the School.

The Church of Scotland Normal School Training College also engaged me to teach in a like manner. Thus the day's work began with thirty-two, and twice weekly with forty-eight, pupils, before proceeding to other ladies' schools,

---

[1] My friend and headmaster, the late Dr. David Pryde, was the father of James Pryde, the well-known artist.

private tuition and constant public appearances. All this entailed a daily activity of at least ten hours, hasty snacks in cabs between lessons, and insufficient rest, for which I paid the price of gradually impaired health.

During these ten or twelve years the number of pupils passing in and out of my ken was necessarily an exceptionally large one. Long afterwards, when visiting English festivals or conducting my cantatas in the provinces, it was no unusual occurrence for female members of choirs to claim me as their former master.

In my early teaching days a young man, employed in some humble business capacity, wished to take lessons. Finding him ignorant even of musical notation, I asked what instrument, if any, he could play, and I had to admit regretfully that, not being proficient on the concertina, I could not accept him as a pupil. In reply to my request for his name he assured me that it was " Mozart," and that his family came from Australia. Curiosity prompted me to verify the address given me, and I found the illustrious name among the several bell-plates on a house in the Old Town.

Ernest Pauer informed me that, as a boy, he had been taught by Mozart's eldest son, but could recollect nothing about him except a peculiarity in the old-fashioned cut of his trousers!

John Hullah, then a Government Inspector, more than once referred to me in his official reports. " Mackenzie contains in himself the rarest of opposing qualities. He is not only an earnest, excellent and conscientious musician, but he is also endowed with thorough business capacities." With regard to the latter part of the compliment, however, I fear that the good man very considerably overstated his case in that Blue Book.

Some leisure had also to be found for composition, albeit of encouragement there was little. A *String Quartet* was written and performed at our concerts; also some songs and a *Larghetto* and *Allegretto* for Daubert (our 'cellist) were published.

CHAPTER IX

BUT there were bright spots in the monotonous round. One of the most interesting and important periods of my life was approaching when the never-to-be-forgotten contact with two great musicians brought the confidence I needed. The astounding impression made upon me on hearing Anton Rubinstein for the first time is difficult of description. When he rose after completing the first part of the programme, I fully expected him to leave the platform with the Erard grand tucked under his arm, like any violinist with his instrument. His own (unwritten) arrangement of the Overture to *Egmont* and the *Sonata Appassionata* were performances the like of which I have never heard since. His Bach gave me less pleasure, for he adhered to an obstinate conviction that the grand old master's works should be played without nuance or expression of any kind, and I failed to agree either with the dictum or its results. But the Chopin sonata, with his pianissimo conception of the mystical *Finale*, produced an extraordinarily eerie effect. *"Das ist der Wind der über die Gräber heult"* (That is the wind howling over the graves), was his explanation to me at dinner on the same evening at the house of a Hungarian friend and colleague— George Lichtenstein. Chopin's own description: " The left hand unisons with the right one gossiping after the March," is much less fanciful, if not positively unmeaning. The cushion-like pads at the ends of Rubinstein's fingers may have accounted for the rare delicacy of touch and tone exhibited in such pieces as his favourite *Rondo in A Minor* by Mozart; but when in the " 'Ercles vein" he thought in orchestral terms with titanic effect.

On his return visits, being frequently in his company, I became familiar with his firmly-expressed opinions, and still rejoice in the fact that he was invariably amiable and kind to me—although a rough side could be shown when ruffled. To see a collection of albums shot across the room, to the discomfiture of the autograph-hunters, was neither an unusual nor a blameworthy occurrence after a trying recital. A strongly-built, loose-limbed, somewhat ungainly figure, a splendid head—not unlike Beethoven's—covered by a refractory black mane; a disproportionately small nose on a pale, clean-shaven face; and an obstinate-looking mouth and jaw, are my recollections of Rubinstein's outward man. Contrasted with the sturdy frame, his voice was husky and weak; his eyes, with peculiarly heavy lids, were already troubling him sorely. A long, rather ill-fitting black frock-coat and an absurdly little wisp of a necktie complete the picture.

In conversation the composer-pianist showed himself to be an extremely well-read, cultured man of abundant humour; and, while direct, sometimes even to brusqueness, his manners were unaffectedly simple.

"*Sie haben keine Komponisten,*" (You have no composers), said he to me, meaning England! His remark to myself—"*Ich bin stolz Jude zu sein*" (I am proud to be a Jew), explains his personal dislike to a greater composer and his determination to continue a series of Biblical operas and cantatas (*Sulamith, Paradise Lost, Tower of Babel, Moses, The Maccabees*) in opposition to Wagner. That impulsive energy which characterized his playing is reflected in many of his works. Had I not known *Ocean, Don Quixote, Ivan,* and much else of his best before we met? With all my admiration for them, it must be admitted that he wrote too easily, frequently and rapidly to do justice to his genius in every case; but the fact does not excuse the unfair neglect under which many fine works—the beautiful songs and much now quite unknown chamber music—have unjustly suffered for so long.

I can see his fork raised on high with a large pickled cucumber (dear to all Russians) on its prongs, and hear the mock solemn pronouncement:—"*Das ist die hohe Poesie von Goethe!*" (That is Goethe's sublime poetry).

One night I initiated him (with the assistance of the 'cellist, Carl Drechsler-Hamilton) into the mysteries of reels and strathspeys, with the result that on the following evening he rose before the end of the dinner and insisted upon my taking him to the Waverley Market, where the regimental pipers were playing these exciting dances to a Saturday-night audience. In spite of the fact that it rained heavily, he, obstinately disdaining a cab, preferred to take my arm for the whole length of Princes Street and back in the dark. I then realized how dim his eyesight was becoming, when he heedlessly and deliberately stepped into every puddle that lay in his way.

After these exhausting recitals Anton liked nothing better than a quiet meal with cards to follow, and could show a righteous temper if these pleasures were disturbed by the officious or curious. Thus, at the coffee and cigar stage, we were sitting together in a private house, when the street door bell started an ominous succession of gentle tinklings, followed by arrivals and muffled conversations in the adjoining drawing-room.

This bore but one interpretation—an evening party! As the host and some of our table companions—probably "in the know"—rose one by one, I was left with the master and his agent, Levi, who, like myself, perceived and dreaded the coming storm.

"*Das nenn' ich meuchlings ermorden*" (I call that assassination), said Levi, in answer to a growl both loud and deep.

Some time elapsed before Rubinstein could be persuaded to show himself to the company. Presently two daring young women, whose intention it was to perform his charming ballet music from *Feramors*, presented themselves.

"*Spiel ich selber!*" (Play it myself), said the composer

curtly. He did, and soon afterwards quitted the room to resume his cigar in my unworthy company. But the genial spell was broken and he departed early.

In the summer of 1881, when I returned from my first year's stay in Italy to arrange my affairs before settling there, August Manns suddenly appeared in my rooms, the object of his hurried visit being to see Rubinstein, who was passing through Edinburgh on that day.

"*The Tower of Babel* is announced for Saturday next (June 4), at the Crystal Palace, and he declines to conduct because we can't give him a combined rehearsal of chorus and orchestra in the morning. Therefore I had to come here to see him at once, as he definitely refuses to appear!"

Thus the distracted Manns. Here was a pretty coil! Our only chance was to explain to the enraged musician how impossible it would be to comply with his demand and to speak him fair. Even the most enthusiastic members of London choirs may not hang placards in their shop-windows or on their office-doors with the statement, "Back after Choir Rehearsal," as I have frequently seen in German towns. It was a much worried Manns who set out on the errand, but as I had been invited to dine with Anton that night I had a faint hope of rendering some assistance in talking him into reason.

As it fell out, Sarasate was playing on that same afternoon, and we went to his concert before bearding the lion. A memorable day, for I shook hands for the first time with one who became a dear friend.

After some preliminary skirmishing with the angry composer, Manns retired with him to discuss the matter *à quatre yeux*. They emerged presently, having come to an understanding, at least to the satisfaction of the Sydenham conductor; and though some subterranean rumblings, as from the interior of an amiable volcano, were still heard, all was well.

And so to dinner. It was a cheerful Manns whom I accompanied to the railway station before returning to finish the evening with Rubinstein. I only saw him once more,

By chance I occupied a seat immediately behind him and Saint-Saëns in St. James's Hall when Sarasate introduced my *Violin Concerto* (Cusins conducting) to a London audience in 1885; and again I spent a delightful evening in his company at Dieudonné's Hotel. My recollections of the great pianist are of the most agreeable nature.

CHAPTER X

CLARA SCHUMANN, KARL FORMES, AND HANS VON BÜLOW

THE chief exponent of a different school of pianism was Clara Schumann, whose warm tone and dignified interpretations of her husband's compositions I had the opportunity of admiring on two occasions. The privilege of hearing and meeting her (in Edinburgh, probably in 1879) enables me to record the same sense of restraint—almost reticence—which a performance of *Kinderscenen* left upon me.

And I recall how the sad-faced lady unexpectedly announced the title of the final number, " *Der Dichter spricht,*" before playing it. She said little more during the whole evening. Of the beauty of touch and tone, which accorded so well with the poetry of the whole composition, there could be no doubt.[1] But she seemed to be a tired and melancholy woman.

What brought the celebrated *basso profundo* and astonishing raconteur Karl Formes to Edinburgh I know not; but I, with others, passed a wondrously amusing evening with him. We supplied the wonder, he the amusement.

Picturesque even in advanced age, the veteran had been through the American Civil War, discovered Mozart's grave and identified his skull; had fallen asleep one moonlight night at the base of Beethoven's statue in Bonn when the figure descended (like that of the Commendatore in *Don Giovanni*), saying solemnly: "*Formes, mein Sohn,* Du *bist mein Rocco*" (My son, *thou* art my Rocco). These and other veracities made us gasp! We were also informed that he would

[1] The reader is referred to " Robert Schumann " by Frederick Niecks, with a short preface by myself.

85

shortly play Shylock in London, and were favoured with surprising examples of elocution in the English language. True, he did appear as the Jew at the Princess's Theatre for a few nights—with the unfortunate results I anticipated—before resuming the wandering life he preferred.

I always had a kindly feeling towards him, for, though perfect intonation may not have been his strongest point, as Rocco, Beltramo (*Robert the Devil*), and in all his great basso rôles, the actor's powerful characterization was magnificent.

A new appointment as choirmaster (the organ, an instrument with which I struggled ineffectually for some time,[1] being still taboo in our Established and Free Churches) put an end even to my Sunday leisure. An adequate " a capella " choir of about twenty-five voices allowed me to displace the time-honoured, uninteresting Doxologies and introduce fairly difficult anthems. While certainly not diminishing the number of worshippers, our more artistic efforts quickly gained the recognition they enjoyed during my ten years of office in St. George's, Charlotte Square.

In this connexion a weird incident has to be related. In my daily rounds from school to school, I habitually met on certain days and hours a much-employed teacher of French, whose amiable little wife was a member of our congregation, though her husband never attended the services. I was therefore surprised to see him in church at a morning service, and still more astonished at his reappearance in the afternoon. " Why this sudden goody-goodiness? You are overdoing it," was my passing thought.

Meeting him, as usual, on the following day on the Dean Bridge, I stopped him. " My friend, you are going to the devil ! " said I.

Taken aback—as well he might be at the suddenness of so cheerful a greeting—he became pale and, staggering slightly, stammered, " Eh, what do you mean? "

[1] A presumably sufficient reason for the honour of my election to the Presidency of the Royal College of Organists, from 1893 to 1897.

I replied, " You were *twice* in church yesterday! "

With an uneasy, mirthless " Ha, ha! You *will* have your joke," he quickly passed on.

I never saw him again, because not long afterwards he was arrested on the charge of poisoning his wife, tried, and hanged for the crime.

For photographic purposes I happened to be invited to join several of my piano classes one morning at an early hour in Princes Street Gardens. Standing before the camera with my pupils, I saw the black flag hoisted on Calton Jail at eight o'clock at the moment of his execution. The strange coincidence had an eerie effect upon one whose chance words proved prophetic and who was to witness the signal of the wretched man's last moment.

In '74 I left my mother's house to marry and settle in a house of my own within a stone's-throw of the old nest, and during the following summer I joined a party of Düssel-dörfers at Sondershausen, to which I journeyed with my friend Niecks and an *Overture to a Comedy*, which was carefully produced by Bruch's successor, Max Erdmansdörfer. The pendulum had swung back again, for the new Max—a very good, but highly-strung and nervy conductor—belonged to the advanced school, as his programmes showed. As most of my good friends were no more, this visit to my boyhood's haunts was the last.

On our homeward way Niecks and I could not resist the attraction of hearing—for the first time—*Die Meistersinger* at Munich. A splendid performance of a glorious opera.

My youthful activities might have been brought to an abrupt end by an accident—the third—from which I escaped only by a hairsbreadth.

Walking along Princes Street during a violent gale of wind, I saw several cabmen rushing towards me from the rank on the opposite side. Almost at the same moment a stunning blow, followed by a crash of splitting wood, staggered me. A huge board bearing the words " To Let " had been blown down from the topmost story of a high house, and the concussion had shattered it to pieces on my right shoulder The long thin nails, which ripped my coat neatly from the collar downwards and passed within an inch of my temple, revealed the extent of the danger from which I had been preserved. Only the lucky fact that the wood was so completely rotten as to split easily had saved me. After being revived by a friendly chemist I proceeded homewards, and, hardly realizing my good fortune, gave a lesson. The instruction was probably not worth very much!

The incident had its humorous side, however. Acting on the advice of an indignant friend, I discovered the name of the proprietor of the premises and duly reported the information.

"Why, that's my brother-in-law! Make him pay!" cried my friend. The ties of affection were evidently not of the strongest.

Eventually, to save time and trouble, I allowed myself to be appeased by the gift of a new coat, and the culprit escaped very cheaply indeed—so did I!

That extraordinary man, Hans von Bülow, was at the height of his fame as a pianist and conductor when he came to Edinburgh (1875). Brimful of energy, quick-witted, sharp of speech—his short snappy retorts delivered as from a hair-triggered revolver—many-sided, kind and hot-tempered, he could by turns be the high-bred Junker and, a moment later, an amazingly naughty boy. Of that highly-charged and generously-impulsive artist, whose exceptional gifts and characteristics endeared him to many and frightened an equal number of willing admirers, I have much to say in deepest gratitude. Among the audience at his first recital, I rose with a profound sense of admiration of the intellectuality of his interpretation.

Rubinstein could at times behave like a whirlwind; Bülow impressed by a brilliant technique, but even more by the surgeon-like skill with which he laid bare the composer's intentions, while he certainly could rise to moments of great and exciting vigour.

The short, dapper figure with its jerky movements, the somewhat sallow face, pointed goatee and military moustache and carefully-tended short hair, reminded me of a *Garde Offizier en miniature;* assuredly he did not look like a musician. Did he not once twit Rubinstein publicly about his lengthy and unruly locks? Only to receive a recommendation to get his long ears cut. The interchange of such urchin-like pleasantries between artists was not infrequent in those fighting days.

It was not difficult, for instance, to trace the personality of the undersigned " Caligula," but to whom did this enigmatic German trade-advertisement, circulated freely among Bülow's friends, refer?

Es empfielt sich bestens den
P. F. Herren
Musikverlegern, Kritikern, Publikümmern
CALIGULA SEIDENSCHWANZ
entdeckungsreifer neuer Symponiker, auf besondern Wunsch
auch Kakophoniker.

(Roughly translated)
With best compliments to
the Messrs.
Publishers, Critics, Publics
CALIGULA SEIDENSCHWANZ
Certified discoverer of new Symphonies, by particular request
also of Cacophonists.

But when Bülow's folded opera-hat—without which " concertina," as he called it, he never appeared at a recital—was once placed on the pianoforte, a transformation took place: just as his face became rigid on the instant when he lifted the baton before an orchestra: grinding his teeth as the piece proceeded.

Our acquaintance was of his own making. After an inquiry anent local musicians, he sent for me, saying that he knew me already. A greater surprise was mine when he told me that, before leaving Germany, he had been looking at new publications in Leipzig and, seeing a *Pianoforte Quartet* bearing my name, he had brought it with him to London; the fact being that up to the moment of our meeting I had not received copies of that then recently-written work which proved so welcome and helpful a stepping-stone to its composer.

Great was his rage when, later on, he knew that I had paid twenty-five pounds for the privilege of appearing in print. I had no cause to regret it.

"*Schreiben Sie Ihn einen geharnischten Brief, und kaufen Sie es gleich zürück. Ich habe gerade das Geld and Sie sollen's haben,*" he snapped (Write him an armoured letter and buy it back at once. I have the money just now; you shall have it).

But I eluded the generous offer and wrote no " armoured " letter, being amply content with Bülow's assurance that he would play the Quartet as soon as possible. A promise which he, as always, kept at Munich.

On January 24, 1878, he wrote from Hanover. "*Morgen spiele ich in einem Wohlthätigkeits Konzert ein Quartet meines Schottischen Freundes Mackenzie, op.* 11 "[1] (To-morrow at a Charity Concert I play a Quartet by my Scottish friend Mackenzie).

The work was dedicated to Charles Hallé, from whom I had a few words of thanks. Its quick introduction to London I owed to the late Willem Coenen (" Left-hand " Coenen), then a stranger to me. J. W. Davison of *The Times* wrote to that pianist as follows, on March 4, 1875: " With many sincere thanks for the treat given me by his concert at St. George's Hall this evening, and especially for Mackenzie's Quartet."

From this performance, and the publication of a successful humorous part-song, I date the subsequent attention to my early efforts as a composer.

The Franklyn's Dogge was written at the request of a small amateur glee party, consisting of intimate friends. Of

---

[1] *Von Bülow's Briefe,* Band VI.

two versions—one in the Tudor style—the lucky " Dogge," which helped me " over a stile," was chosen by them.

By this time I knew Charles Hallé very well and was to see much more of him. His advent in Manchester, the starting-point of a long-continued 'and highly-instructive series of recitals in the North, is to be regarded as a timely act of providence. No more fitting missionary in the cause of music could have been chosen for the purpose than that calm, strong-nerved man.

A Bülow, not to mention others of lesser eminence, would speedily have worn himself to fiddle-strings in an attempt which Hallé's iron constitution and equable temperament allowed him to accomplish during so many years of splendid educative work at the piano and the conductor's desk.

An engagement as conductor of the Glasgow Choral Union concerts which Bülow had unexpectedly accepted brought us closer together in the winter of 1877. When the orchestra visited Edinburgh every week I was under orders to join him at meals before and after each performance. An exciting time was provided for all concerned, as these exceptionally brilliant efforts were wrung from an orchestra unaccustomed either to the strict discipline or the exacting demands made by a conductor whose sarcastic sallies spared none. The scenes enacted at rehearsals verged on the grotesque; but the redoubtable Hans, however severe with others, had no mercy on his own nervous energy, and lived in a perpetual state of excitement which few men could have endured without serious consequences. But during that season much that was greatly needed was learned by the orchestral players which had a lasting effect upon future generations.

There can have been few conductors with so wide a knowledge or appreciation of the music of every school, country or kind. The same scrupulous care was given to Cherubini's *Ali Baba*, Auber's Overtures, or expended upon the preparation of the solo part of Moscheles' *Fantasie on Scotch Airs* for piano and orchestra (for a single performance), as to Brahms' *Symphony No.* 1—which I heard for the first time under Bülow in 1877. Manns was certainly of that small company of eclectics.

Following the custom of his ex-father-in-law, Liszt, Bülow neglected no chance of furthering the aspirations of young musicians. Thus, he insisted on the immediate acceptance by the Choral Union of a twice-rejected Overture of mine (which he had not seen), and a performance took place in Glasgow on December 1, 1877. Arriving at the final rehearsal, I found that he had so often repeated certain horn and other passages that the orchestra was almost in a state of mutiny which augured none too well for my reception. My nervousness increased when, after more repetitions, Bülow called upon me to take his place at the desk.

" You will conduct it yourself to-night! "

When I pleaded that I had brought no dress clothes (on popular nights they were not worn, nor did I expect to be required on the platform), he wheeled round and called out to a lady seated in the hall: " Has your husband a dress-suit he will lend to my friend? " The good-natured wife of Mr. Stillie, the musical critic of *The Glasgow Herald*, replied in the affirmative, and I had no option but to conduct.

Now as Stillie was robust and round, and I thin and ill, the elegance of the fit of the garments may easily be imagined. But he who must be obeyed seated himself among the audience and vigorously led the applause.

My recollection of that evening is of the dimmest, except for an underlying appreciation of the oddity of the situation which helped to relieve a hideous state of nervousness. *Cervantes* was repeated in Edinburgh two nights afterwards, when Bülow handed the stick to me, while, conspicuously adorned in a bright scarlet Turkish fez, he listened and applauded in a front seat. I have never looked at that piece again, but append the arrogantly-worded "Programme Note" written by myself, as a warning to young composers.

It has no reference to Don Quixote or any of the other literary works by Cervantes. It sprang from the contemplation of the chequered

career of the soldier-poet, a warrior, a prisoner, a pioneer and slave—
a dramatist, romancier and lyric writer—in all of which conditions and
phases of his life, his indomitable courage and cheerful hopeful disposition raised him above the trials he had to endure, infused new energy
and affection in his associates and commanded the respect even of his
oppressors.

Only this, and nothing more!

One afternoon the sensitive Walter Bache arrived at my
house in a state of anxious depression owing to the refusal of
his adored friend and master to meet him. Bülow had
published a series of witty and stinging letters from London
in the *Leipziger Signale*, in which he unmercifully chaffed
friend and foe. August Manns, having had his share of
twittings from the pianist in *The London Figaro*, had thought
fit to issue a saucy pamphlet entitled " Dr. von Bülow's
Prescriptions for the Cure of Anti-Bülowism " by way of
retaliation, and the situation had become awkward for the
friends of the gladiators. Bache's attempts at reconciliation
having failed, I undertook to broach the subject cautiously to
Bülow before the evening concert. My casual remark that
Bache was playing with me on the following day and that
he had arrived was the signal for the expected outburst and
a furious race round the table.

" Friend of Manns "! was the indignant shout.

" A better friend of yours," my venturesome reply.

The storm spent itself, and the welcome invitation to
summon the culprit to the artist's room during the interval
was accorded. All was well, and the affectionate embrace of
the friends was both touching and ludicrous. Bülow came
from Glasgow on the following night merely to join an oyster
supper party given in celebration of the event.

The effect of these, then not infrequent, polemical bickerings which were apt to degenerate into personal abuse—and
to prove contagious—could serve no good purpose whatsoever. Making every allowance for the artistic temperament, I came in course of time to wonder whether it is
worth while spending a brief existence in a perpetual state of
mental excitement, and if the most fervent devotion to our

art really demands these sacrifices of health and friendship. Such primary symptoms as I may have exhibited as a younger man are always recalled with sincere contrition.

During the negotiations over an appointment—held in the following year—as *Hofkapellmeister* at Hanover, Bülow was engaged in another tussle, as I had reason to know. He dashed in upon me with a long letter to his friend the Intendant, von Bronsart, of which I was requested to make a copy without delay. Being engaged that evening at a concert (Pauer, Straus and Piatti) I commandeered the table in the artists' room, continued to write when not required on the platform, and managed to deliver the copy in time. " They are putting on other strings," said Hans to me afterwards; the difficulties had been overcome.

That exciting winter over, the Glasgow authorities again cast about for a German conductor, their choice lighting upon Schumann's successor at Düsseldorf, whom I had occasionally met there.

No greater contrast could have been devised. Julius Tausch, a talented composer (see his *Twelfth Night* music) and admirably-trained musician, was a depressing conductor. The good-natured, rather unprepossessing, silent man was quite incapable of the intrigues imputed to him by Schumann's friends during the latter years of the great composer's life. After the stimulating excitement of the preceding year's tempest, the humdrum season of calm under the new conductor proved utterly devoid of interest.

Tausch was good enough to produce an orchestral *Scherzo* of mine, which also had a hearing at the Crystal Palace in October of that year (1879).

The desire to devote myself to composition had ripened into a decision to leave Edinburgh as soon as I dared risk so important a plunge into the unknown. But overwork had already told severely upon health, and the question was answered by the Faculty of Medicine which ordered a complete cessation of work for an entire year, a disquieting symptom being the strange feeling that things then happening to me had occurred in the same way at some previous time. And the warm encouragement given by Manns, at whose suggestion the first *Scottish Rhapsody* had been written, ended any doubts. That work—my first published score— became a favourite at Sydenham, and speedily found its way to Germany where it figured in a programme of the *Tonkünstler Versammlung* at Magdeburg. Nikisch, who had conducted it there, reminded me of the forgotten fact not long before his lamented death.

Manns, then at the conductor's desk in Glasgow, strongly urged me to adopt the plan (initiated by Liszt and followed by Glinka, Svendsen, Grieg, and others) of working up national material into artistic shape, and he himself did much to popularize these efforts. Although I was the occasional recipient of public and private advice not to meddle with the "auld sangs," my own inclination led me to contribute several specimens of the kind which were not unfavourably received elsewhere.

A voyage to Australia was definitely negatived in favour of a sojourn in Florence upon which my heart was set, and a release for eight months from my public appointments secured the wished-for liberty.

Much of the pleasant life in store for me was owing to the fact that, before my departure, Bülow recommended me warmly to the care of his pupils, Giuseppe Buonamici and George F. Hatton (a son of the composer), requesting them to bring me to his friend Mde. Hillebrand.

The generous pianist visited Edinburgh once more, when I found him calmer and softened in demeanour: even mentioning Wagner's name—hitherto carefully avoided in his presence—and talking of the little fortune he had *zusammen geklimpert* (tinkled together). But he gave his brain no rest. To keep his memory alert he would walk along the train noting the numbers of the carriages and repeating them at the end of a journey. And on this, the last occasion on which I heard him play, he had learned a *Romance* by Sir Herbert Oakeley in the train and played it by heart the next day. Dining together after the recital, when we had emptied a bottle of Burgundy, he, most careful of men, insisted upon ordering and taking a full share of another. That " encore " and the ensuing fatigue of a tiring programme, induced an "exposition of sleep" on the sofa of the smoking-room, while I kept vigil for two hours—to the accompaniment of a long sequence of loud snores—in order to wake him in time for departure. Although he continued to give frequent signs of goodwill, we did not meet again for some years.

A few weeks later I left, with wife and child, for Italy and a new life.

PART III

ITALY

CHAPTER XI

ON our way to Florence the first music I heard in Italy was *Mefistofele* (Turin) and *Aida* (Pisa)— admirable performances in each case. Several subsequent opportunities of rehearing Boïto's opera were taken in hopes of improving a first-formed opinion of its merits. But the early impression produced by the disconnected scenes and mixture of styles remained unchanged.

It was not until 1893 that I met the gifted poet-musician when he, along with Saint-Saëns, Max Bruch, Tschaikowsky and Grieg, received the degree of Mus. Doc. from the University of Cambridge. Truly, a goodly company before whom (in the absence of Arthur Sullivan) I was suddenly called upon to speak—with a too-well-remembered, deplorable result.

Of the first few months, save for the cordiality of the friends to whom I was accredited, the recollection is necessarily confused. All was new, intensely interesting and delightful; work prohibited, the easy life and customs suited my needs and wishes.

Our first rooms, however, were but a few yards from the Teatro della Pergola, and the hideous din made every night by howlings for vehicles and the lusty voices of the good-humoured but noise-loving Florentines in the narrow re-echoing Via (in which Cellini cast his " Perseo ") soon drove us elsewhere. But the temporary discomfort served a providential purpose, for it led to the occupation of a pleasant *mezzanino* immediately below the dwelling of Bülow's friends, the Hillebrands—near to the famous Cascine at the end of the Lung' Arno Nuovo.

On the first afternoon of possession, I laid myself down to enjoy a nap, out of which I was awakened by weird, softly-sustained, very deep and melancholy sounds. Floating upwards, these seemingly unearthly voices continued—ill and nervous as I was—to astonish and agitate me. Was I out of my senses, or had I passed into the Unknown during sleep? If so, these low B flats were certainly not of an angelic kind. "And hark! I hear a singing; yet, in sooth, I cannot of that music rightly say whether I hear, or touch, or taste the tones!" Thus the Soul in *Gerontius*. Presently, the information that my bedroom was situated immediately above the Chiesa Russa, and that the choir was at practice, relieved my perplexity. But this introduction to Russian Church music, and the phenomenal depths to which the singers can descend, was decidedly a fearsome experience.

Popular attention was, as ever, concentrated solely upon Opera (Ponchielli's *Gioconda* the event of the year); excepting on rare occasions a Chamber Concert by Buonamici and the 'cellist Jefte Sbolci, chiefly supported by the British colony and a few Florentine families, there were no musical attractions. Church music was in a deplorably bad state. I listened to an organist lumbering through the Spanish Cachucha, as a voluntary, in the Duomo, and fled!

In the evenings, amusement and instruction were sought in the people's theatres, where the Tuscan equivalent for Policinello and Arlequino, *i.e.* Stenterello, appeared (in his tricorne hat and curly pigtail) in every play, to fire off local allusions and jests in Florentine dialect—period or plot being of no consequence whatever.[1] There was no attempt at illusion. Footmen wandered off and on at odd moments to move furniture; the audible and visible prompter conversed with the members of the orchestra; the double-bass player's bowler hung on the scroll of his instrument, and everybody smoked black cigars excepting the actors.

[1] I frequently saw Landini, the last great "Stenterello," who died an old man in 1884.

How diverting to watch Dr. Dulcamara (straight from Donizetti's *Elisir d'Amore*) selling nostrums and drawing teeth on his caravan in the public square o' nights, the braying of the brass band covering the screeches of the victims to the delight of the crowd. Probably I saw the last representatives of that glib-tongued medical fraternity.

The lovely environs, architectural wonders and art treasures of the ancient city sufficed to keep me busily engaged and entranced.

To Karl Hillebrand and his wife—by a former marriage Mde. Laussot, the early friend of Wagner—we were indebted for so many marks of exceptional kindness that a grateful tribute to their memory must find a place here.

Wagner's twopence-coloured account of his acquaintance-ship with the lady and her family runs through the last twenty pages of Vol. I of "Mein Leben." Capable of great friendships and sacrifices, this gifted woman had, as a girl (Miss Taylor), met her fellow-enthusiasts Karl Ritter and Hans von Bülow (aged respectively 18 and 16) in Dresden; hence her introduction to the struggling composer, who states that, after his flight in 1848, the Ritter and Taylor families combined to offer him " 3,000 francs per annum until the return of better days." [1] When I had the pleasure of knowing Jessie, that excellent pianist and highly-educated musician often spoke warmly of her continued friendship with the Ritters while freely discoursing with undiminished enthusiasm on Wagner's genius.

A reliable witness of the occurrences dwelt upon with so much unnecessary gusto by the Meister was her companion at the time, and who remained in that capacity to the end of her life—Miss Rosa Williams, an intimate friend of ours, who died in December, 1923, at Bournemouth, aged 93. That most trustworthy lady assured me that beyond an intense admiration (*Schwärmerei*) for his compelling genius and an ardent desire to assist his ever-pressing needs, the fantastic insinuations were groundless.

[1] " My Life." English Edition. Vol. I, page 530.

Miss Rosa also spoke of M. Laussot as a kind gentleman and most considerate husband.

The frequently-mentioned Mrs. Taylor, a tall, slim old lady upwards of 80, but still bearing traces of beauty, became much attached to my young wife, who was often summoned by signal-knocks on the floor to take charge of her when in one of those unmanageable moods attendant on senile decay. Jessie's affection for her mother was manifest to us all. I saw my dear friend for the last time when von Bülow's daughter and I sat together at her tea-table. "Mein Leben" was not published until after our hostess's death.

Karl Hillebrand—exiled from Baden in 1849, twenty years Professor of History in the University of Rouen, and exiled from France for being a German—had in his youth taken part in political demonstrations and been imprisoned in a fortress from which he escaped—*via* a drain, I believe. Finding his way to Paris he acted for a time as Heinrich Heine's amanuensis. About that interesting circumstance I was tempted to ask questions, but the whilom secretary, in whose writings there are but few references to the poet, was not to be drawn. Once he mentions himself as having been privileged to penetrate (*dringen*) into Heine's work-room, and that few of his generation had the opportunity of knowing him so nearly, or witnessing the extreme care bestowed on his verses; and again, when expressing at length his admiration for the poet's genius, Hillebrand does not hesitate to point out how much of the *Gassenjunge* (guttersnipe) there was in Heine the man.

The eminent scholar and distinguished man of letters, greatly esteemed in four countries, had a sincere love for Great Britain and its institutions; indeed, was much more like an Englishman than a German.[1] He died of rapid consumption several years before I left Florence.

The Hillebrand salon drew to itself the notabilities in art, science and literature of all nations, and of inestimable value was the privilege of meeting so many eminent men and women

[1] In 1879 he gave six lectures, in perfect English, at our Royal Institution.

which I enjoyed. One day, when the late gentle Henry
James had just left us, my friend whispered, " What a capital
curate he would make."

I believe that the erstwhile revolutionary kept up an
intimate correspondence with the German Kronprinz
(Frederick II) at the time; and when H.R.H. the Crown
Princess (our Princess Royal) passed a winter in Florence
she was a frequent visitor at his house, George Hatton and
I playing *à quatre mains* on these occasions. The Empress-
to-be honoured me by graciously accepting the dedication
of *The Rose of Sharon*, which I was then writing.

Quite unexpectedly I once saw her unfortunate husband
on one of my trips from the Rhine to Schwarzburg. I had
to wait an hour at a junction (probably Lüneburg) before
proceeding. It was late, and the large, dimly-lit station was
empty except for a few officials, when a train consisting of
a couple of carriages steamed in. The stalwart, handsome
Kronprinz, followed by several generals, was the first to
descend. As he was walking briskly away, a tall lady dressed
in deep mourning, whom I had not previously seen, rapidly
approached him. Being but a few yards distant, I heard his
cheery greeting: "*Ach, was bringt Sie denn hier? Ist das bloss
Neugierde oder . . .*" (What brings you here? Is it merely
curiosity, or . . .). The rest was lost as they quickly left.

Similar social enjoyments were mine in the hospitable
Casa Placci—a family with which I was permitted to form
a lasting and affectionate friendship—noted for its artistic
gatherings attended by European celebrities.

There I passed an evening with Salvini, who occasionally
emerged from his retirement to delight Florentine audiences.
In Edinburgh I had seen *Otello*, and his first performance of
Macbetto in this country, and was present at what I believe
to have been his last appearance on any stage, when he gave
a magnificent representation of *Il Re Lear* in the Florentine
theatre named after himself. The old actor's voice out-
thundered the thunder in the Heath scenes, leaving the
impression that it could do more—if it liked!

With the gifted pianist Giuseppe Buonamici—a surname synonymous with his genial, sunny nature—an intimacy was formed which lasted until his premature death in 1914. He was educated in Munich by Bülow (subsequently by Liszt), who, on quitting the Conservatorium, nominated his favourite pupil as Professor; but, greatly to his master's disappointment, the call of the Campanile proved too peremptory for my friend to disobey, and he returned to his native city.

So rare a talent and so bright a mind easily made Beppe a first favourite with all, a fact detrimental to the brilliant European career which undoubtedly might have been his; nor did an easy-going, ingenuous disposition fit him for the exacting life of a travelling virtuoso. In those days—on the Continent at least—success was greatly dependent upon a punctilious observance of etiquette. Cards had to be left or personal visits paid to important critics, and of such "booings" (bowings) as helped Sir Pertinax on his upward way a considerable amount had to be done. So Buonamici contented himself with a numerous but select clientele of private pupils, such as did not mind waiting an hour or so should he be detained in conversation with any attractive dog he might happen to meet and admire, and with occasional public appearances, mostly made at the pressing instigation of his friends.

Possessed of a singularly beautiful touch and velvet tone (the nearest approach to that of Rubinstein in his gentler moods I have yet heard), his playing of Beethoven and Chopin was wholly admirable, and excelling as he did in that searching test of musicianship—chamber music—we could not but deplore a reticence which became almost a platform-phobia. But the artist-teacher's beneficent influence is still at work in Italy.

Wagner's great liking for Buonamici was clearly shown at Bayreuth when the Master noticed him among the audience and helped him with both hands to climb—in full view of the public—into his own loge.[1]

[1] Buonamici appeared several times in London:—Under Cowen's direction at the Philharmonic in 1890 (and previously under mine) and at some recitals here and in Germany, invariably with significant success.

Occasionally, in Buonamici's absence, I conducted the "Cherubini" (a society founded by Mde. Hillebrand), the choir consisting chiefly of British residents with a sparse sprinkling of Florentines. A long absence forbids me to judge of present-day conditions, but with all the advantages of fine voices, keen ears, and an inborn love of the art, it was then very difficult to rouse any interest in choral music.

It was in connexion with this society that the sometimes distressingly candid Bache gleefully announced that he had induced some American visitors to join it, and apologetically added: " They don't *all* sing through their noses, you know! "

One of Cherubini's daughters, a pleasant old lady residing at Lucca, showed me some unpublished manuscripts of her illustrious father.

CHAPTER XII

THE BRIDE: JASON: COLOMBA

THE increasing fascination of my surroundings and improving health clinching the resolve to make Florence our home, I had to return to Scotland, relinquish my appointments, and make the final arrangements for the permanent change. Once more on the road—a couple of days at Verona irresistible—the journey home was broken by a month's stay at Innsbruck, where I completed a little cantata (*The Bride*), which I dispatched to Novello's before moving on to a pleasant little village (Wylderswyl) at the foot of the Scheinige Platte, near Interlaken. Our luggage, inadvertently mixed up with the baggage of a theatrical company at the Austrian frontier (Ala), had disappeared, and for some days its arrival at Innsbruck was anxiously awaited. Frequent inquiries having proved fruitless, great was our joy on the receipt of a notice to claim it. I was escorted to a remote part of the railway-station by an intelligent official who, exclaiming "*Do ischts !*" triumphantly pointed to a truck containing a huge crateful of cackling poultry!

Rising wrath was subdued only by that infinitesimal sense of humour mercifully bestowed upon a few favoured Scotsmen. On the following day our hopes of relief from an embarrassing situation were realized.

Passing through Munich I saw, in a large and beautiful public garden, that gruesome institution in which recently-deceased men, women and children were placed in order to obviate the possibility of premature burial. Behind large, plate-glass windows, like those of any ordinary emporium, the bodies—carefully dressed in their best clothes and their rouged faces fronting the spectator—were seated on chairs, a wire communicating with a bell, which would at once indicate any sign of life, attached to a finger. I am not aware whether this grisly public exhibition is still continued, but I saw it in 1881 and thought it much more horrible than the Morgue.

A gratifying surprise awaited me in London when informed that my cantata had not only been accepted, but had found a place in the programme of the Worcester Festival of that year. Forty-four years later *The Bride* was repeated in the same hall, on the same date, by the thoughtful kindness of Sir Ivor Atkins, on the occasion of my retirement in 1924.

Though against doctor's orders, some work was done during my stay in Florence, for a second *Scottish Rhapsody* ("Burns") had its first performance at the Crystal Palace in March, 1881; and I remember that when the Finale was returned to me by Manns with the remonstrance, "Much too wild," I supplied him with another movement. The discarded piece would probably be rejected as being "much too mild" to-day.

The Bride brought unexpected luck in her train, and I returned to Italy with a commission to write a larger work for the Bristol Festival in the following autumn.

Like King Cole, the redoubtable J. W. Davison held a merry court at Worcester (consisting of his Press colleagues, J. Bennett, Desmond Ryan, W. Barrett and others) to which I was admitted. J. W. D. amused himself at that time by administering "Pills for Professionals" (or some such title) in that crack-brained paper, *The Musical World*, in which the articles and mysterious allusions were only understood by himself and a limited circle of friends. Yet the subscribers seemed to enjoy its literary antics.

I was immediately offered three "pills" at one dose, J. W. D. having them ready in his waistcoat pocket. The first one—I cannot remember the question—was quickly answered. By the second—a couple of bars from an early quartet by Haydn—I was not to be beaten. The final question—certain bars of pianoforte music—proved trouble-some; but, guessing by the style, I made a rapid shot at it. " Dussek, of course," said I, with utmost confidence. " Why, he is one of us," cried the critic, grasping me by the hand, and my initiation was completed. Trivial incidents, perhaps, but they showed that there was some fun to be enjoyed, and that lions and lambs could meet, in spite of differences of opinion, and have a good time together.

My wife's ill-health necessitated a return to the south by sea. She had to be carried on board a P. & O. steamer at Liverpool, and the delightful journey, with its stoppages at Gibraltar and Genoa, enabled the invalid to walk ashore at Leghorn.[1]

Encouraged by recent experiences and offers of work, I gladly resumed the increasingly pleasant relations with my Florentine friends and settled down in our second home. A small return for much kindness was the institution of a Harmony and Composition class to which some young Italian musicians were invited. Our proceedings were certainly of an informal kind, but agreeable and useful to the teacher and his pupils.

An elegant little flask, surmounted by a finely-moulded head of Wagner, which I had bought solely on account of its artistic excellence and regardless of the double meaning attached to the word *Fiasco* (failure), stood on my work-table. My friends, however, failed to appreciate its beauty, and, apprised of an approaching visit from Liszt's pupil, the Roman pianist, Sgambati, I was persuaded to destroy it: an unnecessary sacrifice, since regretted.

For some reason or other Wagner was unpopular, and the lively Bülow, while residing in Florence, had also ruffled tender sensibility by a criticism of Verdi's *Requiem,* for which

---

[1] At that period explosives timed to operate by clockwork not infrequently found their way into the coal bunkers. Two well-known Irish judges, of whom I have most pleasant memories, were enjoying a short holiday under other names than their own. My little success at Worcester seemed to have become known, and I willingly gave short *al fresco* concerts, on my violin, which were well attended by all the passengers and many of the ship's crew.

indiscretion a handsomely-worded apology was afterwards offered to and accepted by the great Italian Maestro.

Jason was performed in Bristol in 1882 with the assistance of that splendid trio of singers, Mde. Albani, Edward Lloyd and Charles Santley.

Hallé's orchestra, travelling during the night from some town in the North, arrived in a thoroughly tired condition and just in time to begin rehearsing a long and exacting Festival programme. My own rehearsal, fixed for the evening, did not commence until after nine o'clock, as Gounod's *Redemption* had taken up the time allotted to *Jason*, the well-prepared and willing choir being completely exhausted by the long day's work.

The members of the band kept going in and out, and the choir gradually dribbled away before my eyes. After little more than an hour I declined to proceed, and in this resolve I was sympathetically supported by the eminent vocalists. The official conductor had already retired to his hotel, where I found him relaxing his mind over a game of cards with the principal violin, Ludwig Straus. Mr. Alfred Littleton (of Novello and Co.) then announced my firm decision to withdraw the cantata from the Festival. Only after many explanations and excuses, and on a promise to be given an hour's rehearsal with the orchestra at the end of each morning performance, did I most reluctantly agree to take the risk.

These perfunctory trial-trips could not be other than unsatisfactory; indeed, a considerable portion of the work was never rehearsed by the choir at all.

The performance, remembered by me only for its painful anxiety, proved a better one than could have been expected; but the cordial reception must have been in great measure due to the sympathetic attitude of the audience and the performers towards a young and comparatively inexperienced conductor under unwarrantable conditions. The representatives of the Press, who had witnessed the scene at the abruptly terminated rehearsal, were neither slow nor reticent in expressing their opinions on the treatment of a new British work.

But the mischief was done, and poor Jason never recovered his lost chance of securing even a tuft of the Golden Fleece.

I was glad to depart for home again. But for the generous hospitality of the Littleton family—the commencement of a long friendship—this, and many subsequent visits to London, must have been fewer, shorter, and much less pleasant in every respect. Before starting work, a short holiday at Livorno proved interesting in more ways than one, as we arrived at the seaport during one of its not infrequent disturbances. Seeing some overturned tramcars and other ominous indications, I strolled out alone in the evening to witness the fun—if any. Reaching the Piazza Vittorio Emmanuele I found it surrounded by troops. All seemed quiet enough, and, curiosity satisfied, I was about to return to our hotel on the sea-front when I was stopped by the military. My request to be taken to the general, who was standing in the middle of the square with his staff, was granted. An explanation, and the mention of Capitano Buonamici (a brother of my friend whom I knew to be with his regiment in the town), was courteously received, and the honour of being escorted home by two armed soldiers was mine. Discretion being the better part of valour, I resolved to be less venturesome in future.

Next day I was shown over the first-built great Italian warship, the *Lepanto*, then almost ready for launching.

A startling letter, containing a commission to write an opera for the Carl Rosa Company, awaited me, and the exciting offer was, of course, eagerly accepted. My two cantatas had induced the librettist, Dr. Francis Hueffer, to suggest the collaboration. I believe, however, that the modest Arthur Goring Thomas, with an unnecessary mistrust of his gifts, or perhaps for some better reason, had previously declined the offer.

Fairly started on the composition, a desire to visit Corsica seized me, and I left home with that object. Why I went to Piombino and crossed over to Elba instead is not now within my recollection. But a few days on the island and the sea-trip from Porto Ferrajo (passing Garibaldi's Caprera and Caprajo) to Livorno provided a pleasant holiday. I saw Corsica—from a distance.[1]

Colomba was, within less than twelve months, written, printed and produced at Drury Lane on April 9, 1883, and followed by six increasingly successful performances with a most efficient cast, which included Mde. Valleria, Mdlle. Baldi (Lady Tosti), Clara Perry (Mrs. Ben Davies), Barton McGuckin, Mr. Ludwig and Ben Davies (under Augustus Harris's stage-management), to all of whom, and their chief, Carl Rosa, I felt deeply indebted.

The author of the book (Davison's successor as musical critic of The Times) could, however, not be congratulated on an equal amount of leniency on the part of the Press. A pronounced predilection for the then by no means wholly acceptable Wagnerian principles had not promoted harmony between himself and his colleagues, and the publication of some songs of his own composition, with an ill-judged preface indicating the manner in which English lyrics should be written and set to music, having further invited resentment, his share of the work had to stand the fire of much unpalatable criticism and frankly derisive reflections on its poetic merits. I thought that the libretto offered many admirable opportunities to the musician, and was more than content.

A preliminary visit from Miss Gladstone—in her capacity of " pilot engine," as she called it—induced her illustrious father to honour us with his presence on the following evening. Called to his box during an interval, he referred in deep and resonant tones to the libretto as " presumably a translation from the German." To my embarrassment, the remark was made in the hearing of the author, who had just entered the box at the inopportune moment. The great statesman generously expressed his approbation of the music, and incidentally informed me that he himself was " three-parts a Mackenzie."

---

[1] A consignment of evil-looking convicts embarked for Capraia, eating on deck from one large dish while closely guarded by carabinieri was not an attractive sight.

A few days later Rosa and I were bidden to breakfast at Downing Street. Arriving early, I was shown into the library where the Prime Minister was reading a Blue Book. Intuitively I guessed him to be looking up some data regarding musical education. Nor was I mistaken, for, when sitting next to him at table, I was questioned about the Tonic Sol-fa method and other educational matters, John Hullah's work being mentioned. That he should spend even a few moments of his time on a subject likely to interest me could only be considered a high compliment. A pleasant recollection is that of seeing him sitting with an engraving of Cardinal Newman's portrait resting on his knees while he addressed the company on the subject of the picture.

When a round of the drawing-room was made under Mrs. Gladstone's escort, among many pictures and interesting possessions shown to me by her was a photograph of a then popular caricature of Landseer's " Dignity and Impudence " (in which the statesman is represented as the big dog and Lord Randolph Churchill as the yapping puppy), and pointed to with the result of eliciting a sonorous grunt from the G. O. M., who was following close behind us. On that interesting morning I look back with pardonable pride and pleasure.

Bülow stated his opinions in these letters (*Briefe*, Band VII).

An die Baronin D.

Avez-vous vu la partition de Colomba *de Mackenzie dont le* World *parle si honteusement ?*[1] *C'est de la bonne musique, parfois originale, toujours (peut-être trop) mélodieuse, très bien faite malgré les longueurs, enfin la meilleure chose qu'un Anglais ait écrit depuis le commencement du siècle. . . . Après* Carmen *c'est ce qu'il y a digne de succès en fait d'Opéra du jour.*

Würzburg, ce 25 Avril, 1883.

An Frau Jessie Hillebrand.

Von Mackenzie's Colomba, *die mich bei erster Lektüre sehr angenehm überrascht hat, bei der dritten jedoch Bizet's frühzeitigen Tod belamentiren machte—im Interesse Merimée's. Dennoch würde ich die Interpretation*

[1] Referring to a depreciatory article by Louis Engel in *The World*.

112

der Colomba auf deutschen Bühnen warm befürworten. Sie ist mir doch sympathischer als . . .

Gurnigl, Juli, 1883.

He laments Bizet's early death, in Merimée's interests: with which I cordially agree.

Suggestions to conduct the opera during the ensuing provincial tour (Marie Rôze, the protagonist), and to visit Hamburg, where a couple of performances took place, could not, for economic reasons, be accepted. Frau Rosa Sucher specially distinguished herself in the title-rôle, and Mr. Alfred Littleton, who was present, reported that the curtain was raised fourteen times. Rumours of projected productions in Hanover, of definite acceptances at Vienna and Zürich, were afloat, and all promised well. Performances at Berlin seem to have been mooted if one could believe this astounding specimen of journalistic accuracy which appeared in a Berlin newspaper on May 29, and was headed " A Mackenzie as Composer."

(Translation)

According to a telegram from Berlin to *The Daily Telegraph*, the General Intendant of the Imperial Schauspiele has accepted Dr. Mackenzie's Opera *Nadeshda* for performance at the King's Opera House in Berlin. The composer Mackenzie is a brother of Sir Morell Mackenzie, the Doctor of our Kaiser, and successor of Sullivan as Director of the Conservatorium of Music in London.

" The crab," wrote the French naturalist, " is not a fish, is not red, and does not walk backwards." At the time, the honour of being a doctor was not yet mine; *Nadeshda* is by the late Arthur Goring Thomas; I am not related to the late Sir Morell's family; nor did I then occupy any official post or ever succeed Sullivan.

Before I had lifted the stick at the first stage rehearsal of *Colomba*, Alberto Randegger hurried forward to my desk with the pleasant news that the Norwich Committee had that morning authorized him to ask me to write an oratorio for its festival of the coming year.

During my stay I wrote, in Littleton's house at Sydenham, at the request of the Philharmonic Society, an orchestral ballade, *La Belle Dame Sans Merci,* which I conducted on May 9, before leaving London.

Bülow must have heard it twelve months later, for on May 6, 1884, he wrote to his sister Marie:

"... *Von Mackenzie habe ich Dir gestern erzählt."* [*The letter alluded to is not in the series.*] *Eine Orchester-ballade von ihm war recht schön and stets originell. Erfolg bedeutend.* London.

Mr. Littleton, senior, wished me to be his guest at the Philharmonic Dinner. Indignant at the objection that, not being a member of the society, I was ineligible, the resolute old gentleman insisted strongly, and I took my seat at the high table on the occasion when the silver-tongued Lord Coleridge occupied the chair.

The author of *Alice in Wonderland* wrote with reference to a musical setting of his book:

Ch. Ch. Oxford,
August 6, 1883.

DEAR SIR,

I write to ask a business question, but must begin by introducing myself. I shall sign my real name, but I have, as "Lewis Carroll," written 2 little books for children, called "Alice's Adventures in Wonderland" and "Through the Looking-glass." It has been suggested to me, as the books have turned out popular with children, to make, or get made, a drama embodying one or other of these books and have it set to music as an operetta. I have enough friends in the stage-world to get it produced. Now, of course, the first question is as to the composer, and not only have I been strongly recommended to apply to you by a friend who is a first-class professional musician, but I have heard enough of your work to feel sure for myself that you are a genuine and original musician, to whom I may with confidence commit the task, if you should ever be able and willing to undertake it.

My one question, this time, is: Is there any chance, say within 2 or 3 years, that you would be willing to entertain such a proposal at all? If you say "No," I need trouble you no further; if "Yes," I will write in more detail.

Believe me,
Faithfully yours,
C. L. DODGSON.

My answer was " Yes;" but only a fragment of one other communication is preserved. The modest author had some quaint ideas about getting the audience to sing or join in the chorus, and I endeavoured to reason him out of the unpractical notion. The fragment referred to contains the last of seven suggestions.

(7) My idea would be to begin with " Alice in Wonderland " and not to mix up the two books. I have other ideas, but I think you will be inclined to say these are quite enough for one letter.

I was ready, but the libretto was not, for the good reason that he who had created Wonderland could not turn it into a play. Nor would he consent to adopt my suggestion to hand the task over to some experienced playwright; and the whole business ended with a letter admitting that my surmise that the task would prove beyond his powers and that he would be compelled to give it up, had proved correct. He wrote:

There is no need for you to answer any of this till you find yourself at leisure and in the mood to write. Meanwhile I will try, when I feel in the vein (there is no use in trying at any other time), to jot down ideas for the visionary and far-in-the-future operetta.

So far as I was concerned the project remained in the future-never-to-be.

A request to write a song for a performance of *A Blot in the 'Scutcheon* in St. George's Hall was readily complied with, and I spent an evening in the company of another author. I was invited to share a box closely draped with muslin curtains, behind which Robert Browning hid himself from public gaze. During the evening he recounted at great length his quarrel with Macready over the production of the play in Drury Lane, the details of which were not made generally known until 1891. Regarding my song, he merely observed that he had set the verses to music himself. As his lyrics are by no means easily dealt with by the musician, and the " Woman like a dewdrop, she's so purer than the purest " had given me considerable trouble,

I still wonder what his musical version may have been like. Except that the great poet's conversation was most interesting regarding the above-mentioned points, I have no further recollection of the meeting.

At the end of an exciting season a short holiday-trip to Paris with Alfred Littleton and Carl Rosa, the latter of whom wished to hear the pretty Opera *Lakmé*, allowed me to meet its composer, Delibes. This big, clumsily-built, plump man appeared to be, except for geniality, the opposite of his graceful and light-footed music. The gentle *Lakmé* pleased me much more than Saint-Saëns' somewhat boresome *Henry VIII* at the Grand Opera.

Subjects from English history on foreign stages invariably provoke unseemly mirth in me. Although the cast was an admirable one, and the *mise en scène* perfect, in this case the cleverly constructed ballet-music (highly effective on the platform) consists of Scottish and Irish tunes non-existent at this period, which seem as incongruous as Robert Volkmann's adoption of the " Old English War-song," to wit, " The Campbells are comin' " in his overture to *Richard III*.

I saw the Italian actor Rossi play " Kean " (in Dumas' absurd drama of that name) in modern evening-dress, with an opera-hat under his arm.

CHAPTER XIII

THE ROSE OF SHARON

RRANGEMENTS were so uncertain that I had failed to secure the delightful abode in Casentino where *Colomba* had been completed; therefore we decided to pass the summer months at Ver sur Mer, a little village in Calvados, in which the arrival of a small piano from Caën created intense excitement.

But after vain endeavours to begin work in the strong sea air, which thoroughly disagreed with me, I suddenly resolved to quit the French coast and risk the heat of the dog-days in our Florentine home. On a previous occasion we must have been among the last travellers to be driven across the St. Gothard before the tunnel was opened to the public. After passing part of an icy-cold night at Andermatt, we started not long after daybreak on August 1, and arrived at the famous Hospice about eight o'clock. The wonderful sight, amid the surrounding ice, of the plain below, the picturesque figures of the good-natured monks—who thawed us with hot brandy and water—and their docile dogs, made up for the discomforts of the long and steep ascent in a somewhat ancient coach. The Devil's Bridge is not to be forgotten.

But the rapid descent down a perilous-looking zig-zag road, stretched out before us like a gigantic pair of lazy tongs, was not without its anxious moments and feelings akin to sea-sickness. Reaching the plain at noon we stood before a welcome *locanda*, refreshing ourselves with cool wine under the powerful rays of the blazing Italian sun, having passed from extreme cold to burning heat within three hours. We had hardly progressed a few hundred yards in the direction of the railway station when one of the wheels of our conveyance came off, and during the delay for repairs we had ample leisure to realize the probable result had the accident taken place an hour or so before.

In a cosy parlour in the hotel at Andermatt there was a piano covered with copies of many operas, and I sat down after dinner to amuse myself. My playing quickly brought mine host—a genial *Schweizer*—who informed me that the inn had been in his family's possession for many years, and that all the great composers and performers who had crossed the Gothard had been entertained in it. He then produced an album and pointed with pride to the signatures of Bellini, Donizetti, Rossini, Cherubini, Meyerbeer, Paganini, and many other celebrities. During the evening an American gentleman joined us, saying that the chief aim of his visit to Italy was to find Wagner and to offer the great composer a commission to write something specially for himself. The bold citizen of the U.S.A. may not have been pleased when I tried jocosely to dissuade him from the attempt, as the Master was notoriously inaccessible and would be likely to vouchsafe a curt answer to the proposal. But he obstinately adhered to a decision of which the result remains unknown to me.

This recalls Wagner's reply to Buonamici when asked which of his compositions he considered the greatest. " Why, the *Philadelphia March !* Didn't I get the most money for it ? "

Adapting ourselves to a new mode of life, we enjoyed the experiences and peace of these scorching summer months during which only those natives who are compelled to forgo the relief afforded by *villegiatura* remain in the towns; perhaps the truly Oriental temperature aided the rapid progress of a work wherein Solomon plays so conspicuous a part.

The year 1885 promised to be a significant one in the history of British Opera, inasmuch as Stanford's *Savonarola* saw the light in Hamburg, his *Canterbury Pilgrims* in London (April 28) during the Rosa season, while Goring Thomas's *Nadeshda* was in the making. And I was called to Darmstadt, *Colomba* having been commanded to make her appearance on the occasion of a Court wedding—not as a *Fest Oper*, as the

Hessian Court was in mourning—on April 29. How much of that honour I owed to Bülow I never knew.

Hofkapellmeister Willem de Haan and the company took great pains with the production, and a pleasant time was provided for me in the stiff and rather dull Residenz-Stadt. An excellent orchestra and willing singers gave of their best. Unfortunately, the principal tenor (the Orso of the cast, appropriately surnamed Bär) happened to be " vocally indisposed " as the announcement ran ; the Hof Theater Direktor, with whom I had one brief interview, objected to animals on the stage, and made Colomba, accompanying mule-bells notwithstanding, enter on foot.

With the exception of one local newspaper, the Press opinions were of an extremely unfavourable nature. One of them laid special stress on the " glacial silence " with which the work was received, and considering the well-known fact that applause was officially *verboten* in the presence of the Court, the benevolent nature of the statement was fairly obvious.

At the second performance, when no such restriction was imposed, the outbursts of appreciation bestowed upon the vocalists—and just at the least expected moments—surprised me by their warmth. Another critic kindly stated that the composer, *"Ein Mann mit spärlichem Haarwuchs"* (sparse growth of hair), occupied a box.

After calling upon every member of the cast, I came away awe-struck by the sense of order and etiquette prevailing in the theatre. From the Grand Duke I received the Gold Medal for Art and Science.

It was pleasant to meet courteous old Louis Schloesser, the long-retired *Kapellmeister*, to whom I was recommended by his son Adolf (an esteemed piano teacher resident in London). He had been sent as a young man to Vienna with Darmstadt's subscription [1] to the publication of the *Missa Solemnis*, an *Overture*, and the *Ninth Symphony*.

---

[1] The list of subscribers includes the names of three London publishers " Herren Boosey et Comp., J. Cocks et Comp., R. Wessell et Stodart."

Beethoven, in his most agreeable mood, invited him to dinner at home and made the coffee himself. The fine old gentleman described the interviews graphically, and proudly produced the MS. Canon which the Master had presented to him as a parting gift.

Two performances of my opera had been announced at Drury Lane, but the only rehearsal was so hurried and unsatisfactory that the Fourth Act had practically to be read at sight by the orchestra on the first evening. The performance was therefore an indifferent one (Marie Rôze good in her part), and its repetition was withdrawn by reason of my departure from London. The action may have been a hasty, perhaps reprehensible one; but I had already spent so much time and money in going and coming on its behalf—although I was glad to have received £100 for writing it—that I could not afford further hindrances to the completion of my oratorio for Norwich. The end, however, was not yet; as I was speedily recalled by an announcement in the prospectus of the Royal Italian Opera, Covent Garden, to the effect that "Mr. Mackenzie's Opera *Colomba* is in active preparation and will shortly be produced. Characters by Frau Pauline Lucca, Mde. Laterner, Miss Gertrude Griswold, Signori Novara, Monti and Mierzwinski." An excellent translation into Italian had been made, and it became my urgent business to coach the principals at the shortest notice.

When I called upon the clever and vivacious Pauline (a typical Viennese) it was at once apparent that any hopes of getting her to study the part were of the faintest; nor did I see her again. Mierzwinski, a huge fellow with a chest full of high C's which he never tired of bellowing out to me in order to waste valuable time, proved utterly hopeless. After many attendances on him he did not get beyond his first scene, but it was not wise to relinquish the disheartening —not to say degrading—task until, after repeated and fruitless visits to the management, I finally threw up the sponge and retired from the Ring. Thus, *Colomba* made her only appearance in the prospectus.

Leaving Bülow one day, after lunching at the Café Royal, to rehearse with Mierzwinski, who occupied rooms over a Bible Repository in the corner of Air Street, my quick-witted friend rapped out: "*Kaufen Sie eine Bibel, schmeissen's ihm am Kopf*" (Buy a Bible and throw it at his head)—a piece of advice which I was sorely tempted to follow. On our way we happened to meet Richter, between whom and Bülow only a cold sign of recognition passed.

A pupil of Buonamici, Struvé by name, and I believe of Welsh extraction, was also taking lessons in composition from me. This young amateur lived with his mother, and I saw a good deal of the amiable couple; a little dog, Fido, completed the family circle. On the day previous to one of our many departures for England, the young man confided to me that he had been seized by the obsession that he would soon meet with a violent death. During a walk to San Miniato I alternately beseeched and bullied him in a vain endeavour to cure him of the absurd premonition which so strangely depressed him. Presently he offered a cordial invitation to join him and his mother at Casamiciola (on the small island of Ischia near Naples), where they intended to pass the summer. The suggestion suited our plans admirably, and arrangements were made to meet at the " Piccola Sentinella " at a certain date. With another warning against Celtic gloom we parted. It happened that business detained me a week longer in London than I expected, and on the very morning of our departure from Sydenham I read the headlines: " Great Earthquake at Ischia." The meagre details available were sufficient to convey the fact that the catastrophe had been fatal to many, and we soon learned that the hotel had been completely destroyed with all its inmates except one.

The guests had assembled in the salon after luncheon and, as usual, Struvé had been asked to entertain them with music. Complying, he began to play Chopin's *Funeral March*, whereupon a male visitor rose, saying, as he went into the garden, that he declined to be made miserable.

Immediately afterwards the whole building collapsed, burying all but the fortunate man. My poor friend was found dead with his skull cleft by a large piece of stuccoed cornice, his hands spread over the keyboard. Death must have been instantaneous. Fido was discovered alive under a large stone in the garden. The disaster occurred on July 8, 1883, all being over in about seventeen seconds. I have seen several accounts of this, but none of them stated the happening quite accurately. Had we not prolonged our stay in London by a few days it is certain that we would have been among the victims. Many years afterwards I saw Ischia, but could not prevail upon myself to set foot on it. But what of the speedy verification of my pupil's forebodings, so convincingly stated to me on that morning on the Piazza Michael Angelo?

Portions of *The Rose* arriving at intervals (I never had a complete libretto handed to me in my life) the oratorio was delivered in good time. In selecting the Song of Solomon, Joseph Bennett chose a fascinating subject; its much-disputed spiritual significance attracted me in a lesser degree than the glowing imagery of the Eastern love story.

Thirty years later the Prologue suggesting the parabolic character of the drama, the Epilogue pointing its moral, and much else, were eliminated.

In connexion with the work there was trouble from the beginning. A serious disagreement arose when I informed Hueffer of my intention to write with Bennett. They differed hotly on the Wagner controversy—then at its height—as well as on other matters; and, although I did not take the faintest interest in their bickerings, or knew either of them well, my collaboration was deeply resented. For the part of the Sulamite, a young singer, Miss Emma Nevada, had been selected, with whom I rehearsed in Paris on my way to England, where a success which eventually influenced my intentions and prospects awaited me.

The girlish simplicity of Miss Nevada's voice and her unaffected interpretation of the part were admirably fitted to it. But in spite of the announcement of an exceptionally fine quartet of principals (Mde. Patey, Edward Lloyd, Santley and Thorndike) the inhabitants of Norwich, probably influenced by unfavourable judgments passed on the work at choral rehearsals, evinced a disinclination to invest in seats for the performance. But after reports on the orchestral rehearsal in London (at the R.A.M.) and the result of the general rehearsal at Norwich, the temperature rose suddenly from zero to summer heat; a crowded hall and a converted and enthusiastic choir rewarded me with warm-hearted ovations. The extraordinary scene when the last note had sounded, during which I was pelted on and off the platform with roses, roses all the way, is unforgettable.

Many Festivals, of happy memories too, which I have attended in various capacities have been made uncomfortable during the preliminary stages by hasty, ill-formed, prejudgments and unnecessary gossipings as to the comparative merits of new works written for the occasion. And some instances are not unknown to me in which the unfair results of an objectionable habit have not passed off so harmlessly to the composers as they did in my case.[1]

On the comments—not made by the Press—passed at the time upon the character of the subject, Bennett wrote at the end of his life:

I refer to passages alluding to the numerous wives and concubines of Solomon and the strong expressions of Eastern love-passion with which the original abounds. It did not occur to me that these, having a place in a Book which we are taught to read, study and reverence, would be condemned as "improper" elsewhere. Yet so it has turned out, and the neglect of Mackenzie's music is attributed by many who admire it to the Nonconformist and Evangelical conscience. But there is nobody in the world more silly than your religious prig. He belongs to the people included in Carlyle's "mostly." [2]

When Bache once spoke of the musical settings of these passages as "sugary," I replied that I meant them to be as sweet as I could possibly make them.

[1] Stanford's beautiful *Elegiac Ode* was first heard in this Festival.
[2] "Forty Years of Music" by Joseph Bennett, p. 382.

On his way from Norwich Bennett paid a visit to his friend Davison at Margate, in which I joined him; and as neither of us saw the retired critic again, I am glad of the pleasant recollection. Remaining there for several days after Bennett's departure for America, meetings with the old Bohemian, who rejoiced in any British musical success, were frequent. I found him usually at noon in the " Bottle and Jug " department of his hotel, standing before a plate of oysters, incessantly conversing with the customers. This to a jug-laden maid: " Susan, let me introduce you to the composer of *The Rose of Sharon*. Nothing like it since *Elijah!* "

Susan, who had probably never heard of Mendelssohn or the Sulamite, would grin pleasantly and be " glad to meet you, sir."

Sometimes, not without malicious intent, I ventured to introduce Wagner's name; invariably calling forth forcible expressions of a desire on J. W. D.'s part for the assistance of the police. But the ever-present twinkle in his blue eyes showed that my motive was quite obvious to a bird not easily caught with chaff.

In little more than a month the first London performance of the oratorio took place with the assistance of the Sacred Harmonic Society's choir and the Norwich principals ; the cordial reception, leading to another one at the Crystal Palace on November 22, when Miss Nevada, being indisposed, was replaced by Mde. Albani. A very large audience attended, and although the prices were raised considerably, hundreds were unable to gain admission. Shorn of a prosy Elder and several unnecessary numbers, the dramatic action gained in conciseness; in a completely revised edition (published in 1910) with the omission of Prologue and Epilogue, some of the words rewritten and a new Part IV, any suggestion of a religious basis disappeared.

CHAPTER XIV

LISZT

IN search of Chopin lore, at the bidding of Frederick Niecks on returning to Florence, I sought out the once popular pianist, Adolf Gutmann—said to have been the Polish master's favourite pupil and in whose arms he breathed his last. Dining with the amiable veteran on several occasions I heard much of interest and was able to arrange an interview with the author of the now famous " Life of Chopin." Gutmann occupied his leisure in painting on silk by a process of his own invention, and had in his possession the carefully-preserved tumbler from which Chopin took his final drink; the faint mark of his lips being pointed out to me as I reverently held the glass. Whether it could, like Rizzio's blood-stains, be subjected to occasional renewal, I am not sufficiently ungrateful to suggest.

With another frequently-mentioned pupil, Mde. Vera Rubio, who furnished valuable information in connexion with the biography, I also became acquainted.

But frequent opportunities of meeting Liszt remained the chief privileges of this time. Our familiar signal-knock served both as an announcement of his arrival and a summons to join him at early dinner. The lapse of twenty years since I had seen him had changed the slim, erect figure to that of a bent, round-shouldered, stoutish old man, while the broadened features, with heavy bushy eyebrows, still retained the keen, alert look of former years.

Our first meeting was not a fortunate one for me, and its record here may serve to illustrate at least one side of his much-discussed and often-maligned character. Seated opposite to him I happened to tell a musical anecdote to my table-neighbour in which Tausig's name was mentioned among others, when Liszt rather snappily said: *"Nein! Das hätte der Tausig nie gesagt"* (No, Tausig would never have said that). Our host, Hillebrand, intervened with the explanation that I had never suggested any such thing. Whereupon the master, leaning across to me, remarked, *"Verzeihen Sie, ich bin etwas taub"* (Pardon me, I am a little deaf).

But afterwards in the drawing-room, where he played to us, he seemed upset and cross. I must confess that I committed a mistake in conveying a request from my friend Niecks for the favour of an interview with reference to certain points in Chopin's life. I ought to have waited for a more propitious moment, as my tactlessness only drew the brusque refusal, *"Ich habe schon genug davon gehört"* (I've heard enough about that), and an unmistakable indication that the whole subject was distasteful to him. The rebuff was deserved.

Having been invited to supper, I felt obliged to tell Mde. Hillebrand that I could hardly count myself a *persona grata* and therefore begged to be excused. My surprise was great when, later in the evening, an urgent message was sent to the effect that Liszt wished me to come up at once. Immediately on arrival he had inquired for *"der Schotte,"* and desired to see some of my work.

"Yes, certainly, Meister; but after supper."

But the postponement did not suit him, and, a fourhand edition of my *Burns* having been produced, he sat down to play it with Buonamici (or Hatton) before being dragged off to table. I was then sent for, and, the meal over, the reading of the piece was resumed. All his amiability returning, he declared himself extremely pleased. Pointing to a passage of exceptionally Scottish flavour, he said, *"Ich habe viel dererlei gemacht, aber doch nicht dieses"* (I've done much of this sort of thing, but not that). Asking for an orchestral score, his promise to send it to Budapest was kept; but I was led to believe that annoyance at the neglect of his suggestion of a performance prevented him from paying his annual visit to that city in the following year.

In a letter, written on the following day to Fürstin Carolyne Sayn-Wittgenstein, he ignored my blunder.

Autres invités de la soirée d'hier: Mr. Mackenzie, compositeur écossais—son opéra Colomba, *d'après un nouvelle de Mérimée, et une cantate de lui ont été très applaudis à Londres.* (Florence, January 27, 1885.)

Between dinner and supper he had taken himself to task —as I knew later to be his habit—for loss of temper; some cases came under my own ken. Thinking that he had been quick-tempered with a somewhat eccentric violinist then living in Florence, the old man mounted many flights of stairs to appease his conscience by making reparation. And again (at Westwood House, Sydenham), when a talkative pianist had ruffled him, he abruptly left us. I silently followed him to ascertain whether he had gone to his room and saw him gazing out of a window half-way up the staircase. After a few minutes' reflection he slowly descended and joined us as if nothing had happened to upset him.

My own lapse proved a blessing in disguise, for not only did he grant a prolonged and profitable meeting to Niecks at Leipzig, but when his devoted pupil Bache—who had met with a previous refusal to visit London—invited him to hear *St. Elizabeth* performed at the Novello Oratorio Concerts, he wrote: "*Mackenzie: ich schulde ihm etwas*" (I owe him something), and came, after a forty-five years' absence from England.

Surely penance for a momentary show of irritation could no farther go!

One late afternoon I slipped noiselessly into the room just when he had begun to play one of the later sonatas by Beethoven from memory in the twilight when only Mde. Hillebrand was present; after which I had reluctantly to take the left-hand part in a piece with which he wished to become acquainted.

Much interesting information was given about the newer Russian composers, then almost unknown in Western Europe, of whom he had a high opinion: of the pioneers Balakireff, Rimsky Korsakoff, Borodin, Cui and some others he explained that they were army officers and chemists by profession. Liszt was not only keenly interested in national musical idioms of every country, but persistently urged their use in composition. Accompanying him to an early train to Rome, I was glad to inform him of a performance of his *Psalm XIII* in the North of England (by an enthusiast, the late Nicholas Kilburn). He quoted, with a cynical smile, its opening line: " O Lord, how long? " referring to the tardy acceptance of his compositions in this country.

For consumption on these journeys certain special sandwiches were made by Miss Rosa Williams. Following her to the kitchen, he would ask, with a chuckle, for them to be given to himself and not to his man-servant. The service of a valet was, he told me, the only luxury he could afford. These trivial touches exhibit the contrast between the natures and habits of Liszt and Wagner. In old age the former travelled modestly, his food in his pocket; while the other disdained the accommodation of a first-class carriage. To Buonamici, Wagner once exclaimed: *"Verhelfen Sie mich zu einer Ohnmacht! Man kann mir keinen Salon-Wagen geben"* (Help me to faint! They can't give me a saloon carriage), and preferred to postpone his departure until the following day.

CHAPTER XV

THE SIMPLE LIFE IN ITALY: SARASATE

SEVERAL delightful summers were passed in a picturesque village about thirty miles from Florence, Borgo alla Collina, in Casentino. I rented an old castello by the kindness of the owner, Signor Nardi Berti, for a mere song. The fortified house—its walls more than a yard in breadth, and an ugly spiky oubliette in the cellar—stands on the field where the battle of Campaldino (in which Dante took part) was fought in 1289, and overlooks the beautiful valley as far as Arezzo. It had been presented by the Republic of Florence, some sixty years after the poet's death in 1321, to one of his first commentators, Landino, to whose mummy, preserved in the church opposite, respectful visits of courtesy were duly paid by me.

On one side of the Apennines lies Vallombrosa and the hill-crests topped by the ancient towns of Poppi and Bibbiena (scenes of Cesare Borgia's triumphant exploits); on the other side Calmaldoli and the magnificent monastery of La Verna —the Sacra Monte beloved of St. Francis. Above the Hospice, from the highest point (La Penna) of the Apennines, I have seen the glistening shimmer of the Mediterranean and the Adriatic at the same time.[1]

It may be that I was unfortunate in my search, nor do I presume to speak of later days, but it was at that altitude that I heard the only worthy attempt at an adequate selection, or a reverent performance, of Church music. When I met the young organist, Padre Damiano, in his carpeted cell,

[1] At the foot of the mountain lies Fonte Farnete, a country residence of the ancient Corsi-Salviati family, whose friendship and generous hospitality we enjoyed there and in Florence for many subsequent years.

containing a piano and other unusual comforts, he was dying of consumption, and this pupil of Rheinberger at Munich did not live for many months longer.

The joy of living in such beautiful surroundings was enhanced by the good nature of the Contadini. Working around me in the fields and vineyards while I wrote in a narrow tower, they would hush down their singing—sore deprivation—with a *"Zitti! Il Maestro scrive"* (Keep quiet; the master is writing). Frank, considerate treatment soon earned their good-will and readiness to accept *"la famiglia Inglese"* as of themselves, though the same cordiality was not extended to the inhabitants of some of the neighbouring villages; but in spite of whispered warnings this did not deter us from exploring places into which few of our own villagers cared to enter. Old feuds seemed to breed an habitual cautiousness of speech.

In the summer of '85 Italy was visited by a furious outbreak of cholera, during which the King and Queen distinguished themselves by dauntless courage. Raging from Spezzia to Sicily, the epidemic assumed disastrous proportions, with the usual panicky results. The ignorance of our peasantry manifested itself in the revival of a traditional distrust of the physicians, who were popularly supposed to carry some drug wherewith to make a speedy end to the patient's sufferings. Broken windows and other disquieting compliments were not uncommon, and in our neighbourhood small bottles containing a pink liquid, blessed by the Pope, had a vigorous sale and seemed to be the only precautions taken or believed in.

A suspicious case occurring in our dwelling, a medico had been summoned without our knowledge. He had come, seen, ordered poultices to be applied, and departed—not to return. Finding a bevy of chattering crones hanging these potent remedies out of the window to cool before application, my wife ordered them off the premises and took charge of the exhausted patient. A goodly covering of mustard leaves and a glass of whisky and laudanum worked miracles. But the old woman's recovery (wife of the *custode* in our service) became the cause of frequent requests, on slight ground for immediate apprehension, for doses of the wonderful elixir which had saved Sorra Julia's life.

The simple habits of the natives were amusing, albeit at times of an embarrassing kind. Whole families—masters and servants—were accustomed to bathe (?) in the inch and a half of water provided by the Arno in summer, and these annual occasions were prolonged picnics enjoyed in primitive fashion. On our daily walks at sundown we frequently came upon these *al fresco* parties, when there was no escape from an interchange of friendly compliments. Once, espying a portly figure clad only in a huge straw hat standing in midstream, we made a vain attempt to slink past unnoticed; but the loud *"Buon giorno, Signori,"* punctuated by much bowing and doffing of the headgear, had to be as heartily reciprocated.

Disturbed one morning by voices in the immediate vicinity of my tower window, I saw a number of men busily engaged in turning up a drain, in the great heat of that summer, under the direction of the burly *Sindaco*. Addressing them solemnly, I requested them to choose some safer season and retire. The order was instantly obeyed, and with many *"Saluti, Maestro,"* the chief magistrate and his men departed. Forty years ago the childlike ignorance prevailing in these regions was wonderful. My chief concern was the possibility of our servant's illness being reported, in which case a cordon might have been drawn round the Borgo and an indefinite detention have prevented me from leaving in time for the Birmingham Festival for which I was finishing a *Violin Concerto*. But nothing happened.

The course of the Sulamite's true love was not running smoothly. Her next appearance, at the Albert Hall during the winter of 1885 under the guidance of Mr. Joseph Barnby, brought important consequences with it. Without doubt the choral and orchestral demands had been—as the popular conductor afterwards admitted to me—underestimated; nor was the selection of the principal soprano a happy one for the part. The general result therefore was so unfavourable that unfulfilled expectations caused the performance to be freely condemned.

The work was evidently destined to be unsuccessful at the Albert Hall, for, on the only other occasion it was given there, instead of an audience a dense fog, which prevented the performers from seeing the conductor, filled the hall.

It being deemed necessary to recover past impressions, I was suddenly summoned to conduct a repetition of the oratorio, for which Mde. Albani, Hilda Wilson, Lloyd and Santley had quickly been secured. Mr. Eaton Faning had carefully prepared a choir and the former success was repeated a month later.

But for the mishap at South Kensington, Novello's Oratorio Choir would probably not have been revived, after the lapse of a decade, under my direction.

Sarasate's approval and acceptance of my *Violin Concerto* had now to be secured, and to it I owe the beginning of a friendship which lasted until his death in 1907. His MS. part propped up on the mantelpiece, we ploughed through the first reading with few stoppages. *"Je suis myope,"* was his only excuse for crying a halt, sight-reading being amazing and technical difficulties non-existent. Unreserved satisfaction having been expressed, we proceeded to a second and more careful trial. On the eventful evening at Birmingham an unduly prolonged programme brought on a new, full-blown *Concerto* at a very late hour and displeased the usually placid artist so much that a refusal to play was gradually coming within the range of possibility—the only occasion upon which I have known him to show signs of irritation. Richter and I exerted the blandishments of our persuasive tongues to prevent impending trouble, and friend Pablo's habitual good-humour was eventually displayed in my favour with gratifying results then, and shortly afterwards in St. James's Hall when Cusins conducted.

To know Sarasate was to love a simple-minded, unaffectedly modest and generous artist. There cannot be many with a greater claim to speak of his gifts and character, for I enjoyed an intimacy which revealed the estimable qualities of the musician and man.

Easily pleased as a child, in spite of all temptations quite free from vanity, living for his violin alone, he disliked " Society," and his joy was to entertain a circle of congenial friends and compatriots; the more the merrier.

A very much more cultured musician than some of those who dubbed him " Prima Donna " were capable of judging, his favourite recreation was chamber music and quartet playing; but, aware of limitations and his own métier, these pleasures were mostly reserved for private enjoyment. In my opinion, Sarasate left a deeper mark upon violin playing than any other performer of his day.

The more laboured style of the North German school at times provoked gentle ridicule from one whose outstanding qualities were an entire absence of effort, a fascinating natural grace, and unfailing certitude of intonation. In this latter accomplishment Lady Hallé was equally distinguished. An opportunity of realizing the phenomenal ease with which all this was achieved was mine when, at his invitation, we enjoyed a fortnight's companionship at Frankfort, where he introduced my *Pibroch* to Germany under the composer's direction. Occupying a couple of bedrooms leading to a circular sitting-room, we were so constantly together that there could be no question of practice without my knowledge. During the two weeks his violin-case was only opened twice: once to put on a new E string before leaving for rehearsal, and again to assure himself that all was well on the evening of the performance. Five minutes sufficed on each occasion; serious study and practice were confined to the leisure of his summer holidays at San Sebastian. A method not to be recommended for adoption by less agile-fingered instrumentalists.

The conductor of the Museum Concerts at Frankfort was then either about to resign, or had already done so, which fact was made known to me when a resident delicately suggested that any pretensions on my part towards the occupation of Herr Müller's position had better be at once relinquished. The Principal of the R.A.M. was, however, able to assure the tactful counsellor that his aspirations did not presume to venture on so high a flight.

Don Pablo, ever ready to encourage the young, gave up an evening to my students. On mounting the platform their enthusiastic greeting and the sight of so many eager young faces impressed him so much that he began my *Concerto*—accompanied by myself—an octave higher than written. Aware that it would be impossible to proceed beyond a few bars, I deemed it wiser to let him continue until he came to the inevitable grief which awaited him. That happened quickly, and amid much laughter, in which we both joined, a fresh and safer start was made.

I was not present when something similar (again in a piece of mine, *Pibroch*) occurred at a Norwich Festival. Gazing round the beautiful St. Andrews Hall, he abstractedly started off in the middle of the first movement and all came to a sudden stop. Calmly walking to the conductor's desk (Alberto Randegger) to glance at the score, with a quiet "*Tiens, tiens!*" and a smile, the performance was resumed at the proper place—the beginning.

This Scottish suite, written at his request and produced at the Leeds Festival of 1889, became a favourite show-piece of the great violinist and was played by him in many countries —Mexico in 1890 (on the same programme figure Don Francisco Eugenio D'Albert and Mde. Berta Marx), and in Paris (*mirabile dictu*) with Colonne in 1894.

PART IV

LONDON

CHAPTER XVI

THE NOVELLO CHOIR: DVOŘÁK: GOUNOD

HARKING back to '85, the scheme of a suggested resumption of the Novello Choir had matured sufficiently to lead to an offer of its conductorship. After due consideration of a proposal necessitating a permanent removal to London, it was, not without diffidence and hesitation, ultimately accepted.

In this connexion my wife had a strange tale to tell. One evening at a late hour a female servant arrived unexpectedly. She was greatly excited and imbued with the conviction that, although every arrangement had been made, we would return no more to our summer home in Casentino. The poor girl—a beautiful specimen of the Tuscan peasantry —had, impelled by a desire to see us once more, trudged thirty miles over the rugged Consuma Pass with baskets of fruit, pigeons and other presents to bid farewell to her *Padrona*. My wife, ignorant of the impending change, endeavoured to assure the faithful Maria that there was no reason whatever for all her agitation; but nothing could remove the idea from the girl's mind. After a few days' rest and many affectionate *addios* she returned to her home. Her premonition was correct; our last visit to Borgo alla Collina had been paid.

When we were settled at Lower Sydenham, opposite to the " Wooden House " occupied by Mr. George Grove, the first Director of the Royal College of Music, a busy time began. With " G," always brimful of schemes for the success of his beloved school, an intimate friendship developed.

Among " Grove's young men " were Parry, Stanford, Franklin Taylor, and others rapidly justifying his confidence in them.

Dear old Charles Ainsley Barry (" C.A.B." of the Crystal Palace programmes), whose gruff, staccato utterances belied a good-humoured and generous nature, lived near; my friend Manns within easy hail; so our surroundings were of the pleasantest. Rehearsals, with a newly-formed and devoted choir, of new and standard cantatas and oratorios —a congenial occupation bringing me into contact with many prominent artists—had their responsibilities as well as pleasures. This list of works performed during the following seasons furnishes proof of our combined activities:—

Rose of Sharon, Redemption, Mors et Vita, Patriotic Hymn, Stabat Mater, Spectre's Bride and *Ludmilla* (Dvořák); *Water Lily* (Goetz); *Story of Sayid, St. Elizabeth,* and *Psalm XIII* (Liszt); *Sleeping Beauty* (Cowen); *Calvary* (Spohr); *The Ninth Symphony, Light of Asia* (Dudley Buck); *Judith* (Parry); *The Dream of Jubal, The Golden Legend, Third Messe Solennelle* (Gounod); *Messiah* and *Saul.*

To which may be added Wagner's *Holy Supper of the Apostles* (prepared, but withdrawn) and several noteworthy orchestral works. The series of concerts, given with the aid of the most eminent vocalists and the best orchestra procurable, were interesting and expensive ventures.

For Pan Antonin Dvořák, whose genius was first fully revealed in his *Stabat Mater,* much was done. I conducted the first London performance of *The Spectre's Bride*[1] and prepared *St. Ludmilla* to appear, under the composer's baton, after her debut at Leeds. Far from shining at the desk, the composer was a singularly uninspiring and helpless conductor. The oratorio, while containing much fine music, had less of the genuine Dvořák in it than we expected, and

---

[1] The translator (a Bohemian) had, after careful consultation with the English Dictionary, selected *The Bridal Shift* as its title, but the one chosen was considered more suitable

the subject proved utterly uninteresting to the British public. The sensitive Bohemian master took its unfavourable reception so much to heart that it was only under pressure that he kept his promise to conduct it at the Crystal Palace. At a memorable meeting at the Café Royal he flatly refused to appear at the desk, saying that it was my business, but that he would occupy a seat in the hall. Equally firm, I declined to take his place unless armed with the excuse that he had left London; that the public wanted to see him, not me, etc., etc. This reasonable condition did not please him either, but, eventually yielding to our wishes, he appeared as announced.

During frequent walks and many pleasant hours in his company I found the gifted musician to be well-read in German and his native literature (about the latter I gathered much useful information), and, while extremely simple in his habits, in many respects uncommonly shrewd, as peasant natures often are.

Inclined to keep long silences, at times abrupt, but always revealing that childlike disposition exemplified in so many of his best works, anyone less fitted to occupy so important and diplomatic a position as the Directorship of a Conservatorium, such as he held in America, could hardly be imagined.

Of his taciturnity we had an amusing example at Birmingham. The committee, in their admiration, thought that a larger sum than the original commission had promised would break the silence; but the cheque was placed in his pocket without a word, or even being looked at.

Dvořák's inexhaustible flow of ideas, the ease with which he shakes countless little melodic episodes, as it were, out of his sleeve is astonishing. He told me about his habit of writing and scoring forty bars daily. " That makes about three hundred bars weekly." While doubting a strict adherence to the prescribed number of bars, I have often fancied that I could detect the points at which he had stopped and resumed.

That he could be obstinate to his own disadvantage I

knew. I pointed to a difficult cadence (in *The Spectre's Bride*) given to the second flute, while the presumably superior player has the pleasure of listening to it, and begged in vain for the needed alteration. A stroke of the pen would have sufficed, but "*Es steht geschrieben*" (It is written), was the reply.

An impartial study of Dvořák's music brings out the fact that his best works are those in which he speaks in the naïf idiom of his country. To our credit, be it said, his merits were recognized in England at an early stage in his career. In 1884 Pan Antonin wrote, *inter alia*, to Mr. Littleton: "That you have bought the new oratorio *Life and Death* for the nice sum of 100,000 franks, I get from the Wiener and Prague papers only yesterday. Pray do not pay Mr. Gounod, who really does not need it, so immense sums, for what would be left for me?"

Before *Mors et Vita* reached the Metropolis, I accompanied Alfred Littleton to Paris on a visit to its composer. Written for the Birmingham Festival, it had been performed there under Gounod's direction when disturbing circumstances marred his pleasure; the responsibility of the London production therefore became mine.

During an evening spent in the spacious house of the always excitable musician, I requested to be shown the original MS. score of *Faust*, and he willingly turned over the pages of that delightful opera. Arriving at Mephisto's entrance, he jokingly remarked: "*Je sens le souffre toujours*" (I always smell sulphur here), and not without justification, for, although produced by the simplest means, the effect is a weird one. My early acquaintance with the opera at Sondershausen and its first performances in London were of interest to him. My recollections are of a very handsome studio containing a large organ, on which he improvised; in the middle of the room a writing-table with a small pianoforte keyboard attached, and a tiny, dark bed-closet used by him in order not to disturb the household by his habit of rising early to work.

Notwithstanding an evidently impatient temperament—
"Où est ma femme, je demande?" when Madame Gounod
was a few minutes late for dinner—and thoroughly conscious
of his fame, he was a fascinating host of charming manners
and speech in four languages.

In a weak tenor voice, but with dramatic effect and facial
expression, he sang to his own accompaniment some Nor-
mandy folk-songs, concluding with an exceptionally grisly
one about a *"Tête qui r-r-r-roule,"* while his eyes, to make
our flesh creep, rolled terribly.

I heard two operas of his which were running at the
same time—the long and rather wearisome *Tribut de Zamora*
at the Grand, and the charming *Philémon et Baucis* at the
Opéra Comique.

CHAPTER XVII

AN UNFORTUNATE OPERA: LISZT

WHEN Carl Rosa suggested another opera, feelings of grateful sympathy with the author who had given me my first chance induced me to disregard promptings of caution and advice and turn again to him for a book. "You are playing the Good Samaritan," said he plaintively.

An ominous cloud hung over our *Guillem de Cabestanh* from first to last. There were early signs that the librettist could not reckon upon leniency, and a rather gruesome story (Hueffer was an acknowledged authority on Troubadour lore) told in an obviously Wagnerian manner, with its long silences and gazings, afforded fair game for the merciless. Even now I am not convinced that the book merited the slashing onslaughts and ridicule it provoked, though the effect of a bright and spirited Act I was nullified by a succession of gloomy scenes.

The *Sanh del Trobador* was treated symbolically as a vintage, and neither the lover's heart nor blood was served at supper as the facetious declared.

"Why on earth did Mr. Mackenzie accept such a book?" asked *Punch*. The question has now been answered, and in fairness to myself the course of the tragedy, enlivened by a few welcome glimpses of humour, should be recorded.

On Rosa's taking possession of the theatre, his company met to read the opera in the large saloon (refreshment lounge) at Drury Lane. The first comic incident began with the discovery that the long-disused grand pianoforte was so much out of tune as to be only serviceable in the lower octaves, treble and bass differing by nearly half a tone. After a few ineffectual struggles, a rehearsal being impossible, we all departed; but not before Augustus Harris had reprimanded a member of his staff for neglect of duty; my own surmise being that the delinquent, like most scapegoats, was an innocent animal. My ardour had also been damped by the producer's questions as to the nature of the plot, its period and costumes. The book, like the piano, had evidently not been opened.

My chance came. Harris was kindly assisting me to pass to the stage through the dark theatre, when I stopped at a room whence issued the sound of a soprano voice accompanied by a well-tuned instrument. I could not suppress the remark: " So that's where you keep the national piano! " The impertinence fairly roused the good Harris, who loved to call Drury Lane the " national " theatre; and still more raised his anger because the unseen player was rehearsing a Frenchman's opera, *Frivoli*, which was to occupy the stage at the end of the Rosa season. My sarcastic sally provoked the outburst: " I've apologized! No man can do more! "

Young composers! Forbear to be funny with your managers!

The incident passed off harmlessly, however; my long future relations with " Gus " were of the friendliest and pleasantest, and I have good reason to know that, had he lived, British Opera would have had a liberal and powerful supporter. He had already shown his interest by producing three operas by that zealous worker in our cause, Frederic H. Cowen: *Thorgrim* at Drury Lane, 1890; *Signa* (in Italian) at Covent Garden, 1894; and *Harold* (in English) during the Italian Opera Season of 1895, with Mde. Albani as Edith.[1]

My music was not of the easiest, short seasons necessarily mean a limited time for preparation, and we were being persistently disturbed by ballet rehearsals at the back of the stage. A *Jeu de Paume* evidently called for much very noisy practice which impeded progress to so great an extent that I had seriously to warn all concerned—including the

---

[1] Shortly before Harris died I discussed, at his bedside, an English version of *Le Luthier de Crémone* upon which I had already begun to work. Unfortunately the only copy of that translation was irretrievably lost.

author—to the effect that no further interruptions would be tolerated. But we had not proceeded far on the following morning when the infernal " pom, pom, pom " of the battledores recommenced. Patience now completely exhausted, I rose, threw my baton at the offenders, and delivered certain drastically expressed opinions.

The hard-working principals, though equally irritated, were nevertheless anxious regarding any possible consequences of my action. There are, however, reasonable limits to the endurance of the most complacent composer, and these had been far overstepped. The cast worked loyally for me, but at the end of the dress rehearsal I knew that a work, over which I had taken great pains for many months, was doomed, and when the curtain fell on the memorable night congratulations were conspicuously absent.[1]

Verdi's *Il Trovatore* was performed at Covent Garden on the same evening! Whatever shortcomings—doubtless many—may have been mine, few if any of the scorchingly critical gibes were specially aimed at the composer, and I sincerely regretted the resultant break with my collaborator, whom I met no more. Thus ended a nauseating experience which deterred me from any further operatic attempts for long.

A couple of years later, Carl Rosa openly admitted to me that my attitude had been thoroughly justified, though he opined—as I did—that the *modus operandi* was perhaps not of the wisest. And only a month before his lamented death (at Paris in 1889) my friend asked me to rewrite the Finale to Act III in view of an immediate revival of *Colomba*, which, alas, was not destined to take place.[2]

Roughly computed, Rosa produced, in addition to many familiar operas and the four earlier ones of Wagner, fourteen

---

[1] The next performance was cancelled on account of Mde. Valleria's indisposition, and only one other took place.

[2] The suggestion was adopted and a complete revision of the opera, cleverly reduced to three acts by Claude Aveling, was published and excellently performed by the students of the Royal College of Music at His Majesty's under Sir Charles Stanford's direction in 1912.

operas not previously heard in our tongue, and commissioned seven new works by young British composers within ten or eleven seasons. This ceaseless and successful activity has rightly earned the grateful remembrance his name invariably awakens.

To the timely, practical encouragement of three Germans —Von Bülow, Manns, and Rosa—I owe whatever recognition has come to me.

The Austrian critic Dr. Eduard Hanslick, visited London and, when hospitably entertained by George Henschel, met a few native musicians. The gist of his impudently-expressed opinions is conveyed in these few scraps from articles which appeared on his return to Vienna:

> Sterndale Bennett was a slack unenergetic conductor; Arthur Sullivan his successor, is altogether a drowsy fellow, etc., etc.
> The Philharmonic seemed to me to deserve no more praise than it did twenty-four years ago. The Albert Hall Orchestra (*sic*) is conducted by a pedantic gentleman, with grey whiskers, black coat and white tie. He looks exactly like an English clergyman and also conducts very piously.

Of Sims Reeves he wrote:

> When I heard him in '62 I was told that, although no longer having a voice, he still sang well. One can easily imagine what his voice is like after another twenty-four years.

He characterized us composers generally as " amiable, distinguished and well-educated gentlemen . . . some of whom assisted me in a very sympathetic manner. Cowen and Stanford have written music of moderate ability, a good school, taste in tone-picturing, and great ability in orchestration."

I was less favourably treated, probably owing to the obnoxious odour of Wagnerism he may have nosed in the *Troubadour*, the only work of mine our friend had heard at the time.

Then followed some strange statements. " The patriotic side of the English honours and rewards native productions the most . . . Richter produced the *Ninth Symphony* and

The Spectre's Bride for the first time in London." The latter statements are worthy of Münchausen.

Attributing all that was musically good to the influence of Hallé, Manns, Richter, Ernst Pauer, Wilhelm Ganz, Wilhelm Kuhe and Carl Rosa, he ended an exhibition of ill-manners with: " The same may be said of the German critic of the mighty *Times.*"

The Viennese sage might easily have added several names to the list of German musicians whose helpful influence in those days " nobody can deny," without emphasizing British inefficiency so fervently, and the incident is mentioned here only to illustrate the kindly estimate of the honest endeavours then being made to redeem our musical character (1886).

At the Leeds Festival in October of the same year Sullivan's cantata, *The Golden Legend,* made the instant and popular appeal it richly deserved. His simple-minded Elsie put both Dvořák's Bohemian saint and my Arab chief into a modest corner. As on the first occasion, despite present-day opinions, I never hear the touching Epilogue (and other portions) without a moistening eye; nor am I in the least ashamed of the fact.

It became my immediate business to prepare the work for its first London performance by our choir, and thus began an intimate friendship with the composer, who conducted on the occasion. With chuckles he told me of his (pretended) difficulties of avoiding Savoy habits and of resisting the temptation to follow up Elsie's statement: " I come not here to argue, but to die," with such choral responses as " She comes not here to argue."

I was once conducting the cantata when young Madame Nordica, whose sense of time was not then so reliably developed as later, calamitously tripped in the simple passage, " My life is little, Only a cup of water." Some years afterwards the fair Lilian observed me among the audience, listening to the work at a Festival at Cardiff (Barnby conducting), and promptly repeated the mistake at the same place. Meeting that night at dinner in the house of my old friend,

Samuel Aitken,[1] she protested that I had hypnotized her. We agreed that, in order to prevent future slips, that cup of water must be fortified with alcohol of some kind.

Mdme. Nordica, gifted with a voice and disposition of equal sweetness, became, by perseverance and hard study, celebrated on the Wagnerian operatic stage. While the hearty reception promised greater prosperity than my cantata ultimately enjoyed, the *Story of Sayid* brought me much pleasure at Leeds, when I was admirably assisted by Mdme. Albani—ever ready to give of her best in aid of a new work— and Barton McGuckin in an arduous tenor part. But when no fewer than three lengthy choral novelties are produced in one week, it is a reasonable assumption that the chance of success for more than one of them is improbable.

* * * * * * *

These two letters to me announced Liszt's visit:

"*Hochgeehrter College,*

Herzlichen Dank für Ihre wohlwollende Gesinnung und Fürsorge. Mit vollsten Vertrauen erwarte ich davon eine günstige Aufführung der ' Eliza-beth' in London am 6ten April. Ein paar Tage früher wird das Verg-nügen haben Ihnen persönlich zu danken.
                              Hochachtungsvoll ergebenst
                                        F. LISZT."
30ten März, 86
München.
"*Sehr geehrter Herr und Freund,*

Es wird mich freuen Samstag Abend mich einigen wohlwollenden Gesinnten vorzustellen. An Walter Bache telegraphier ich übermorgen die Stunde meiner Ankunft in London, Samstag den 3ten April" (1886). *Paris.*

His arrival signalized an exciting fortnight such as musical and unmusical London has rarely witnessed. The populace caught the fever and, crowding to catch a glimpse, perhaps hardly knowing why, of the " Habbé," lustily cheered him whenever possible.

Just as remarkable was the revival of unreasonable prejudice on the part of those to whom the very names of

---

[1] Who, years afterwards, became an energetic Hon. Secretary of the Associated Board and Hon. Treasurer of the R.A.M

Liszt and Wagner were anathema, on an occasion which appealed so strongly to us younger men as a momentous event in our lives.

The determination to honour the old master was carried out to the full. On the evening of his coming he was taken —on the way to Westwood House, Sydenham—to the final choir rehearsal, when, tired as well he might be by the journey from Paris, he immediately sat down at the pianoforte to improvise on the phrases which had been interrupted by his entrance. His first notes after an absence of forty years.[1]

A series of fêtes followed—not only in Mr. Littleton's hospitable home, but elsewhere—at all of which he displayed an imperturbably calm amiability and dignified demeanour toward everyone. We knew that he had been subject to tearful fits of melancholy, was in danger of dropsy and total loss of sight, but of these gloomy forebodings he gave no sign; indeed it was difficult to prevent him from overtaxing a waning strength. Young Bernhard Stavenhagen was his travelling companion.

Present at a brilliant reception given by Walter Bache, I had the satisfaction of seeing Joachim shaking hands with his now aged former chief at Weimar, after many years of separation and dissent. They had, however, met for the first time at the Bach Festival in Eisenach two years previously (1884). But the moment was a memorable one for those who deplored a cleavage as unnecessary as useless. *Das Judenthum in der Musik* was, more than once, responsible for much mischief.

An audience of the élite of our profession (Hallé, Piatti, Manns, and many others) listened to a programme of special interest, to which the honoured guest, forgetting his decision not to play in public, added performances of several items with unexpected vigour.

We had the pleasure of hearing him play frequently in

---

[1] Enthusiasm manifested itself in various ways. In connexion with this occasion it was reported that an excited member rushed into his club exclaiming, " He played! " And on being asked what had been played, replied, " Why, Bechstein, of course! "

private, notably on one Sunday evening when he gave a brilliant Recital (no less!) when Henry Irving and Ellen Terry came to Westwood House. To our surprise and amusement the first piece was Cramer's little *Study No. 2 in D*.

Those present could truly say that they had heard Liszt, for probably this was the last time he ever ventured on so long and physically exacting a programme: and much more than mere flashes of his former supremacy were exhibited that night. All this in return for an invitation to *Faust* and supper at the Lyceum Theatre, when the lateness of the hour prevented him from playing. I preserved a scrap of paper on which the intensely impressed actor hastily pencilled these words for my interpretation:—

To Dr. Franz Liszt (the Master)

Will you let me send you a trifling souvenir in remembrance of the glimpse you have given me of Olympus?

Your devoted servant

18 *April*, 1886. H. IRVING.

God bless you, Master!

On one of those few free evenings spent over " Whist mit Conversation," as he called it (" Little Madame Mackenzie " usually his partner), he told me of a game he once played with Adolf Henselt, who annoyed him by continually drumming with his fingers on the table. After repeated remonstrances the pianist stopped and explained that he was writing an arrangement of his celebrated *Si j'étais Oiseau* for the left hand alone and had just finished it!

Liszt's old mischievous trick—known to most of us— of leading an unsuspecting pupil to the piano after an exceptionally jovial dinner and insisting upon a performance of some difficult piece, had also to be played here. Excuses unacceptable, to hear was to obey and there was no escape from the ordeal. Listening to the victim he would chuckle heartily, while interjecting ironically appreciative remarks on the excellence of the rendering. Buonamici had told me of his unfortunate experiences, and on the present occasion Bache was led to the sacrifice. The wary Master, however, was not to be trapped, for he invariably rose early from table and withdrew to his room, for a short nap, when he meant to play after dinner.

While he was playing *en famille* to us one night, Mdme. Munkákczy, his Parisian hostess and wife of the famous Hungarian painter, continued to express her effervescent feelings of delight in whispers so loud and deep: "*Ah! que c'est beau! Ravissant!*" etc., that I, sitting beside her with my open penknife predicted her approaching end, to the amusement of the tittering children. Jolly Madame—not without some scathing remarks, " Mais, I be not Ingleesh! " —had to succumb to my murderous threats and keep silent.

Presently an elderly, well-nourished Hungarian lady of high degree sang to us—but with untoward results. Too strenuous exertions in doing justice to her upper register caused a beautiful necklace to break bounds, scattering the pearls about the room. The sudden end of the song and the sight of the boys and girls scrambling on the floor to recover the gems was a source of ill-concealed enjoyment to Liszt, who was in one of his naughty, boyish humours, when he could play his part in a children's hour with the youngest.

I cannot help attaching a strange significance to a visit to the R.A.M. in which his name was not then held in the highest estimation. Honoured by an invitation to be present (except at an orchestral rehearsal of the *Rose* I had not been within the walls of my Alma Mater for more than twenty years), I experienced some satisfaction at the raid upon its peace of mind, and on the foundation of the Scholarship which, as the programme stated, "has been initiated and will be presented to Dr. Liszt by Mr. Walter Bache." Edward Dannreuther and I, with Principal Macfarren, adjudicated at the first competition in the following year: a duty to be mine on many subsequent occasions.

The programme consisted of the following works: *Goethe Festival March* (Liszt); ·*Caprice in E* (Sterndale Bennett; Miss Dora Bright); *Concerto for Violin* (Mackenzie; Miss Winifred Robinson); *Concert Study* (Liszt; Mr. Septimus

Webbe); Overture *John the Baptist* (Macfarren). Conductor: Mr. William Shakespeare.

Liszt then played to the delighted students his own *Chant Polonais* and *Cantique d'Amour*. The function of that afternoon left its uneffaceable traces.

St. Elizabeth [1] attracted a large audience, including the Prince and Princess of Wales, to St. James's Hall on April 5; but, except for the fact that the unusual height of one of the soloists caused my baton to come into contact with her head-gear with unexpected consequences, only a dim recollection of that exciting performance remains. An anxious conductor had to thank the successful efforts of Mesdames Albani, Pauline Cramer, Messrs. Santley, Vaughan Edwards, and others, and the enthusiasm of a fine choir for the satisfactory result.

On the previous day the composer attended the general (public) rehearsal, making but one suggestion towards the end; nor did he indicate any further wishes to me in private. Considering the difficulties and the electrical state of the atmosphere a much less public preliminary trial would have been advisable, for he must have had many a fault to correct. Regarding the second performance memory serves me much better. Rapidly-made arrangements for a repetition at the Crystal Palace—necessitating a renewal of choral rehearsals— gave opportunity for a more perfect rendering of the work before an immense crowd of listeners on April 17. In more than one book it is erroneously stated that Manns conducted. On the platform, when responding to the last of many ovations and shaking my hand, the courtly old man whispered to me: "*Nun am Ende hätten Sie das selbst besser gemacht*" (Well, perhaps after all you would have written it better yourself). While thoroughly disagreeing with the kindly remark, the compliment was cordially appreciated, for Liszt was always most gratefully cognisant of anything done on behalf of his works.

[1] Written for a Festival held at the Wartburg in '67, but had its first performance at Budapest two years earlier. An English edition with a translation by Constance Bache was published expressly for this occasion by Messrs. Novello.

In my wife's copy of the oratorio he wrote:

And a letter to the Fuerstin Wittgenstein contains the following:

Bulletin : Magnifique exécution de l'Elisabeth avant-hier à St. James' Hall. Entre les 2 parties le Pce de Galles est venu dans la chambre des artistes, et m'a reconduit dans la salle, pour me présenter à sa femme et à sa belle-sœur la Dsse d'Edimbourg. Hier, à 3h... la Reine m'a fait commander à Windsor.... pour Dimanche prochain je suis invité à dîner chez le Pce de Galles.... Une 2e exécution de l'Elisabeth est annoncée pour Samedi, 17 Avril, au Crystal Palace. J'ai promis d'y assister. Le personnel chantant et exécutant sous l'excellente direction de Mackenzie, sera le même qu'à St. James' Hall.

Avril 8, 1886

Ever remembering my *faux pas* at our first meeting, I abstained from asking questions, but during these opportunities of being so much in his company many incidents and anecdotes, chiefly of a humorous kind, were offered by himself. Few may know that one of the principal subjects of the popular *Les Preludes* is by Rossini: I think it appears in *La Donna del Lago*, but its Italian character is obvious enough. " I adopted it to please him," said Liszt. *"Immer die Andern sich ärgern lassen!* " (Always let the others get angry), was the sound advice offered with a kindly grin when I had expressed annoyance at something.

Referring to composition he told me, " If I do any more now it is always in the early morning hours." As a rule he rose even then at a very early hour and was about before anyone else. One morning, long before breakfast, we met in the spacious music room leading to a conservatory in which stood Roubiliac's famous statue of Handel. *"Ach, der Alte!* " (Oh, the old fellow!), was his cheerful greeting, " I used to play a fugue of his—in G Minor. H'm, let me see," and, sitting down, he began to play it to an audience of one. It was my last chance of hearing him.

Nothing can be further from the truth than the amiable assertions made that we hastened the end by subjecting him to all this fatigue. Far from harming him, the visit provided the last happy weeks, and the final blaze of triumph in a uniquely successful life, and, dying man as he was, he either forgot or ignored his ailments and troubles while here.

Had he not been induced to revisit Paris and include three towns on his homeward way before reaching Bayreuth, the end might perhaps have been postponed for a brief space; but, already doomed, he was assisted to a performance of *Tristan*, and death came barely three months after he had left us with the words, " I am coming back next year."

The great pianist, retiring at the height of his fame at the age of thirty-eight (in '47 he appeared on the platform for the last time for money) to devote himself solely to his art and the service of others; who had spent thousands in charity without a thought for himself, was of the simplest and most self-denying habits.

On principle he smoked cheap cigars, drank rough inexpensive wines, and could not have been possessed of more than between three or four hundred per annum for his own personal wants. When Beethoven kissed a prodigy at Vienna he could not guess that his own monument was to be erected at Bonn, chiefly—one might say solely—by that boy's unceasing exertion; or that his works would be carried from country to country by the little hands he had admired.[1] In like manner all the great composers owed much of their popularity to an unselfish missionary who had to wait longest for an appreciation which he was bent on securing for others. Even now the familiar parrot-screechings (blatant, incoherent, tinsel, etc.) are still heard from those who will not, or cannot, know how greatly and in so many directions our art is his debtor, or how much he has taught generations of musicians. I hold that reverent opinion—and in tolerably good company, too. The knowledge that there can be but few musicians now alive whose privilege it was to come under the spell of his influence induces me to dwell so long on the subject.

I complied with his request to send a copy of my second opera, with the chief themes marked; and learned that the beginnings of a Fantasia (or Transcription) were the very last notes written by his hand.[2]

[1] Doubts are cast upon this story: but on page 124 of *Thayer's* "Life of Ludwig van Beethoven," Vol. III, it is stated, " So the world has believed on the authority of Nohl, who got it *from Liszt himself.*" Sufficient for me.

[2] One of the few copies extant of his death-mask, given to me by Miss Margaret Bache, was presented to the R.A.M.

CHAPTER XVIII

THE ROYAL ACADEMY ELECTION

THE season's concerts of 1885 were conducted by *Dr.* Mackenzie: the University of St. Andrews—the oldest in Scotland—having once only exercised its prerogative of granting a musical degree. Since its foundation in 1411 I became, so information ran, the second recipient of the honour after a lapse of many centuries.

A commission to write an Ode for the Crystal Palace in celebration of Queen Victoria's Jubilee now occupied me; and the attempt to make its performance possible in every part of Her Majesty's Dominions on the identical day was accomplished. That it could be written, printed and dispatched in time to be given simultaneously in Canada, Australia, Trinidad and Cape Colony seemed no mean achievement on the part of the publisher and authors. Mr. Manns undertook the preparation for home consumption, and secured an excellent performance at Sydenham; but London offered greater attractions on the great day, and the concert was not largely attended. Cannons were to be fired in the grounds by electric communications from the conductor's desk. The buttons were pressed at the proper moment, but the guns did not always respond at the places marked in the score.

"Save me from my friends," rose to my lips, when a prominent and kindly musical critic requested—in the course of public duty—to know why Manns had conducted the Ode while the composer was present among the audience. Whatever may have happened to delay the salvo at the performance, Manns now fired off his guns with amazing promptitude at me.

Early in the forenoon an indignant letter, sarcastically urging a better control over the indiscretions of my friends, reached me. Never having expressed a wish or any claim to conduct, and more than content to leave all in Manns's experienced hands (moreover, it was *his* choir, not mine), my withers were unwrung. I resolved to beard the lion immediately, and within half an hour I traced him to his lair, or garden, where he was pacing up and down " nursing his wrath to keep it warm."

To disclaim any act or part in the imaginary conspiracy was an easy matter; and soon we were toasting each other in the big-hearted German's best Rhine wine. Of the many future occasions upon which I was to deputize at his desk at the Saturday Concerts during his illnesses, we guessed nothing. While of a highly-strung, nervous disposition and extremely touchy regarding any fancied slight upon his justly-attained position, Manns was equally quick to understand and forgive offence when approached openly and fairly. The cordiality of our long intimacy was never again disturbed.

Congenial and interesting as these occupations and useful experiences may have been, the call of the South had to be obeyed. How often was my nomadic family dragged across the Alps during the years? Once more the tent was folded and pitched again in Florence. Many friendly welcomes, the resumption of a pleasantly independent life, and undisturbed work, were the attractive lures.

The Novello Choir—my only tie—was placed in Randegger's safe keeping. *L'homme propose et compose, mais* ——! The desired agreeable change—but for the uncomfortable interlude of an earthquake of some violence—had not lasted for more than a few months when the news of Sir George Macfarren's death reached me. None can fail in respect for the talent, erudition, and courageous industry of one whom the affliction of blindness compelled to dictate every note and word of his numerous compositions, books and lectures. That additional strain, imposed upon an indomitable energy, coming as it did, in later life, must have proved trying even to exemplary resignation and patience.[1]

A great teacher, those who knew him well invariably spoke of him with affectionate admiration and gratitude. I was only acquainted with a thoroughly earnest, rather stern man, slightly impatient and obstinate. The firm Radical—as the term then went—in politics, and the staunch Tory in music, seemed an incongruous combination. Strictly consistent, however, was the sturdy adherence to that manly and cheerful British spirit which distinguished his music from first to last. Something of the wholesome Macfarren touch might, in addition to all we have since learned, not be amiss to-day. Macfarren was too fond of the school in which he had been educated to permit it to be wiped out at a time when fortune seemed to be inclined to smile on it, and vigorously continued Bennett's championship with increasing success against heavy odds.

Without aspirations in any such direction, until communications from friends urged immediate consideration, no thought of succeeding so eminent a scholar and teacher or of filling so prominent a position ever crossed my mind. Shrinking from yet another change, I passed some anxious days before resolving to take my chance of success in what I fondly imagined would be a privately-conducted election to the vacant Principalship. Not so. If he had foreseen the unenviable degree of publicity attached to the candidature, Whittington would not have turned again. Press and public took an unexpectedly lively interest in what became a neck-and-neck race between a popular favourite (Joseph Barnby) and a " dark horse " known only as a composer and conductor; my fitness to preside over an institution—itself subjected to vigorous criticism—was freely discussed and questioned in articles short and long.

[1] Barely a year prior to his death a new Overture, *Kenilworth*, was played at the Philharmonic, and during the following season (1888) another, *Romeo and Juliet* (posthumous) was performed by the old Society which he had served so devotedly.

On my way Londonwards *La Scala* was visited, when I met the famous conductor and friend of Boito, Franco Faccio, who took me behind the curtain before it rose upon a gorgeously-equipped ballet. A rare sight. It was then the custom in Italy to interpolate a ballet *between* the acts of any opera!

During the period which elapsed before the R.A.M. Committee's decision, the Novello Choir was again entrusted to me and helped to distract my attention from the discomforts of the situation. The fourth concert had been announced without a conductor's name for Feb. 22, 1888, but I was glad to undertake the duty. As it fell out, the date proved to be that of the election; and two hours after the event I was greeted by a splendid ovation from choir and orchestra when appearing to conduct *The Golden Legend* in St. James's Hall. In view of the performance I had, in dumb show, to beg the choristers to spare their larynxes! The vigorously conducted battle between the supporters of both candidates was over. That so much heated feeling could have been engendered surprised me; but the R.A.M. seemed to be considered fair game for such sarcastic references as " Spring cleanings," " Augean stables," and similar pleasantries.

A promise made to myself that, so far as in me lay, it would be my endeavour to prevent the possibility of so undignified an election ever occurring again, has been kept. My retirement and the choice of a successor in office—solely the responsibility of the R.A.M. authorities—were announced simultaneously.

After four consecutive seasons, of which I conducted " three and a bittock," the Novello Concerts came to an end, the Albert Hall authorities having undertaken to " produce a certain number of new works "—those in point which would have been given at St. James's Hall had the concerts continued. Thus the official statement in the *Musical Times*. After a performance of Handel's *Saul* I most regretfully parted with a devoted body of amateur vocalists who had eagerly done the State some service. But not before having had the gratification of preparing and presenting *Judith*. It was at Parry's suggestion that the London performance was entrusted to me; and although I never quite succeeded in taking the *tempi* fast enough to satisfy the impetuous composer (this was perhaps the Welsh part of him), the English masterpiece had to be immediately repeated at Sydenham. In *Blest Pair of Sirens*, immortal verse is wedded to music such as none but a British musician of highest attainments could have produced. The oratorio showed the rapid development of that noble speech which remained peculiarly Hubert Parry's own. Neither in it nor in *King Saul* is there any attempt to tinge the old Eastern stories with local colour. Judith is a British heroine, and Meshullameth's delightful children are Gloucester born and bred.

Using the word in no narrow, but in its most liberal sense, I claim him as a foremost Nationalist in music. It is not premature to indicate what the ultimate position of so complex a personality as Parry the musician, poet, thinker, historian, teacher and idealist must be.

The life-work of one who, instead of bidding for a more easily-won popularity preferred to stand aside from the crowd, must needs wait for that full recognition which its very steadfastness of purpose is bound to secure for it. It is one thing to have won a distinguished name, quite another to be rightly comprehended. As yet he is known and understood by the comparatively few. As the natural result of dissimilar training our musical views and tastes differed considerably, but I look back upon a very long and harmonious association with the utmost satisfaction and pleasure.

Four young musicians—Parry, Stanford, Cowen and I—representing as many nationalities, were at work on widely differing lines.[1] Whether with exactness or not, it has been said that through all my efforts at composition the Scot keeps peering out. If that be so, he obtrudes his presence

---

[1] None of us thought it advantageous to decry the works of our predecessors, or, like W. S. Gilbert's Coster, to dance on our mothers.

either unwittingly or beyond control.   When I did write in the Doric I meant it; and have contributed more than nineteen works to its native list.

But, with all my admiration for Parry's idiomatic consistency, I still hold the opinion that any chosen subject should appropriately be coloured to match its peculiar characteristics.

CHAPTER XIX

ON DUTY AT THE R.A.M.

WHILE this is not a history of the Academy, its interests entered so intimately into my life that this story might well end here were not some of the conditions under which I began work in it set down plainly, if reluctantly. I have outlived all but one or two of those who took a more or less active part in the events of those early days.

The late Sir George Lewis at the time correctly described the Academy to me as " a Professors' Club." Dating from 1868, when the entire teaching staff wisely sacrificed its claims to remuneration for a term or two in order to stave off inevitable collapse (Principal Bennett nobly refusing any salary until better days), a purely supposititious prerogative to meddle in the management had been established and still remained unexploded. Nor were all the students inclined to be tractable. Asking, on my first visit, to be shown to the Principal's room, the Secretary informed me that there was none such, and that there would not really be very much for me to do. Not sharing that opinion I proceeded to select a modest room adjoining his office and had it fitted up for my use.

Every inch of ground had to be contested; but a prolonged contention for discipline and order was unavoidable. Such changes as were deemed advisable were introduced cautiously and gradually. So many rooted habits, dissensions and wilfully constructed obstacles had to be overcome that courage not infrequently almost deserted me; and little or nothing could have been achieved without the invaluable confidence and friendship of the Chairman of the Committee of Management, Mr. Thomas Threlfall, who not only laboured incessantly, but loyally assisted my every step. Whatever place in public estimation the R.A.M. now holds, it undoubtedly owes as much to him—from stormy '88 to prosperous 1906, when we sustained a very great loss in that year by his death—as to any other man's exertions.[1]

Recognizing that much of the prevailing unrest had been constantly arising at rehearsals when students tried their wings to orchestral accompaniment, I stipulated that my duties were to include the conductorship, as that office provided the only artistic link between pupils and Principal, and the best opportunity for observing talent and its progress. Furthermore, the professorial habit of interference at rehearsal by instructing the conductor as to *tempi*, etc.—in public—had to come to an end. Too many cooks had been stirring the broth and for much too long a period.

But " Jack " persisted in jumping up, however heavily the lid of his box was sat upon; and to eradicate the nuisance strong measures and occasional exhibitions of temper—not always real—were required until the unwisdom of talking to the man at the wheel became sufficiently obvious.

Since the foundation of the Academy the rigidly carried out regulation that the boys should occupy one side of the room and the girls the other had existed. Except on musical business, no " Ensembles " or conversations were permitted. Universal opinion has long ago done away with such ridiculous restrictions; but that party-wall stood until 1888, and I am pleased to think that one of my first exercised privileges was to pull down a futile tradition. The students heartily appreciated the audacious action.

A severe blow was dealt me when, but a couple of weeks before taking office, the unexpected death of Walter Bache occurred. To the courage of that sincere artist and energetic pioneer—unselfish to the verge of eccentricity—music in

[1] His name is perpetuated by an Organ Scholarship founded by his wife, to whose generosity the dignified organ case now to be seen in the Duke's Hall is also due.

England is indebted more than has ever been understood. That he had accepted a professorship at the R.A.M. at a personal sacrifice solely with the purpose of stimulating an interest in modern musical thought, was evident when, after much pressure, he admitted that he was giving his time at the generous reward of half a crown per hour.

When, addressing the school for the first time, I endeavoured to express my sorrow at the removal of a doughty fighter and delightful companion, my feelings silenced speech and the written sentence had to be read by another. But I doubt whether there were many present who could realize how greatly such exceptional characters were needed at the time.[1]

Not many days after that, my old friend, Mr. Henry Littleton, who did so much for the spread of musical knowledge by bringing cheaper publications within reach of the multitude, also passed away.

I had brought with me from Italy a set of violin pieces, including a *Benedicite*—altered at Hallé's suggestion to *Benedictus*—which Lady Hallé did me the honour of playing at the " Pops " with a success not yet quite dimmed by forty years of fairly constant wear and tear. It was immediately transferred to the orchestra for Manns. One late night on the Lyceum stage a military-looking man, introducing himself as a Commissioner of Police, informed me that " my police band in Hong-Kong plays your *Benedictus* twice a week;" and, walking on a Yorkshire moor, I met a stranger who, evidently knowing me, said that he had enjoyed hearing something of mine at a hydro; and to a question regarding its title confidently replied, " *Nicodemus*." I understood, but did not contradict.

Notwithstanding new responsibilities, an Ode had to be written for the opening of the first Glasgow International Exhibition (Chorus and Military Band) to words by Robert Buchanan, and conducted by myself in May '88. The

---

[1] His name is now linked in perpetuity with that of his master in the " Liszt-Bache Scholarship."

gifted author enjoyed a reputation for combativeness, but I knew him only as a likeable and agreeable man. For what reason a portion of the Northern Press indulged in so furious an attack on his poetically-conceived Ode, *The New Covenant*, was best known to itself.[1]

Following so soon after my appointment, the visit to Scotland was made the occasion for public hospitality and many social attentions, some of which were shared by George Grove, and not a little amusing badinage passed between us on the subject of the " *tout* ensemble " in favour of our then rival establishments.

Shortly after my return, an operatic singer, well known at La Scala and at Covent Garden, called upon me at the Academy with the object of securing engagements, while making no secret of their urgent need. Requested to write to Glasgow in the hope that there might be some vacant dates in the programmes of the daily concerts at the Exhibition, I willingly agreed to do so, and asked her to return for the reply. But when she came again I could only express regret at the unfavourable nature of the answer and my inability to assist her. Two days later the newspapers announced that the unfortunate lady had been driven to the entrance of a fashionable hotel and immediately shot herself in the hansom cab. The incident impressed me deeply, and in many ways.

Not long after my appointment the need of help (in addition to that of an able assistant, Mr. T. B. Knott) became urgent, and I fortunately secured the services of a former student and one of the most eminent musicians of his day, to whose enlightened tuition many of our best-known composers owe their artistic prominence. The fatuous objection that the distinguished ex-Mendelssohn Scholar had left the Academy to study in Germany, met with my reply that the fact of a musician having been sent abroad to increase his store of knowledge seemed no very reasonable argument

[1] Besides contributing some part-songs for female voices, flutes and harps, to a not very successful play, *The Bride of Love*, I collaborated with him again.

against his engagement. But logic was never the opposition's strongest point, and Mr. Frederick Corder became and remained my trusted lieutenant until I relinquished the Principalship.

Cognisant as I am of the earnestness of their elders, it must be admitted that it was mainly owing to him and (in the instrumental departments) to the influence of Oscar Beringer, young Tobias Matthay, Emile Sauret, and the late Hans Wessely, that the Academy was so quickly enabled to modernize its courses of study. Their pupils have continued the good work, as the excellent results show.

Several cases come within my own ken in which Liszt Scholarship-holders have urgently requested to be recalled from the Continent and allowed to resume their studies at home.

The new appointment of a Curator, however, afforded further opportunities for attacks upon me; that of *The London Figaro* (July, 1890) took this form :

It has long been known that Dr. Alexander Mackenzie had discovered his duties at the R.A.M. were of a far more onerous character than he expected when he competed for the appointment. There has accordingly been a talk of resignation; and, indeed, there is certainly more than one musician in England who would do such simple though tedious duties equally well, and his resignation would have left Dr. Mackenzie to give proper time and energy to composing. Such an event would probably have been a gain instead of a loss to music. An arrangement has, I understand, been made by which Mr. Frederick Corder has been appointed, under the unmeaning title of Curator, to assist the Principal, who, therefore, for the present, will remain titular head of the Academy.

To these artful insinuations *The Musical Times* made reply:

Our contemporary has been strangely misinformed—and perhaps not wholly unwilling to believe. It is true enough, we should say, that Dr. Mackenzie " discovered his duties at the R.A.M. were of a far more onerous character than when he competed for the appointment," because no one then outside of the institution could have known the condition into which it had fallen.

There was a necessity to emulate at least one of the labours of Hercules. But it is emphatically not true that " talk of resignation " has been heard outside the circle within which the wish has been father to the thought.

Dr. Mackenzie has not and never had the smallest thought of resigning. He means remaining at his post and discharging his duties as heretofore. But this does not imply that he is to waste the time demanded by the higher interests of the Academy upon a crowd of smaller matters which, in such an institution, must be attended to by someone. Minor details will henceforth lie in the province of the " Curator," the Principal being left free for higher concerns.

This is the plain basis upon which our contemporary has built a fanciful structure, crowned with a " titular head " of pure imagination.

A similar statement had also to be made public by the Chairman. I regret to make any reference to these oft-repeated naggings, and the above specimen is only reproduced because it developed into systematic persecution and personal abuse from which I had ultimately to protect myself by more effective means.

Two formidable difficulties confronted those who had the Academy's rehabilitation at heart. The slipshod conduct of its " Local Examinations " (held in London and the great provincial centres) brought down a storm of remonstrances and complaints urging an immediate reform of their management. That these examinations, properly guided and controlled, must be of great value to musical education I never doubted; and that belief has been amply verified and confirmed. But that any proposition to interfere with the then existing methods would be met with hottest resistance was a foregone conclusion.

Further, consequent on the prolonged and fruitless negotiations, dating from before 1878, with the promoters of the National Training School for Music (under Sullivan's direction for a short time), the parent of the Royal College of Music, the breach between the younger institution had widened into something like unconcealed hostility. Friends were few and far to seek. The Academy, though " Royal and Chartered," was without a President, H.R.H. the Duke

Painted by René de l'Hôpital in 1923. Reproduced by permission of the
Royal Academy of Music

of Edinburgh having withdrawn from the anomalous position of sitting practically in opposition to the new institution honoured by the Presidency of H.R.H. the Prince of Wales.

For an untried new-comer like myself there seemed no chance of breaking down the fence which divided us, or of establishing the desirable conditions which I was determined to bring about. A happy thought gave courage to the resolve. Why not raise the standard of our examinations to one of greater usefulness and importance by asking the sister school to take an equal share in the responsibilities of their management? Confiding the proposal to Mr. Threlfall, we at once proceeded to pay our respects to my friend Grove at the College; and after some preliminary conversation—mainly concerning the weather—I diffidently offered the plan for his consideration.

" Mackenzie, I knew you had something up your sleeve! " cried the Director, slapping his knee vigorously. In a few days he led me to understand that, so far as he was concerned, a favourable opinion of the suggestion had been formed.

But we both found ourselves at odds with our respective authorities. My people, as expected, gasped at the proposal of " an unholy alliance," as one of them described it; and Grove met with strong opposition on the part of those who either imagined or preferred to think that the union might be unfavourably received by their Royal patrons. I am, alas, the only survivor of a company of ten at a private dinner given for the express purpose of finally assuring me of the unacceptability of the combination, and when I had the temerity—respectfully but firmly—to uphold my opinions, Grove and Parry were my only supporters against a powerful resistance. It was, however, not long before all was smoothed out, agreements drawn up and signed in the late Sir James Dewar's rooms at the Royal Institution (the event was duly toasted in his excellent champagne) in the presence of the late Lord Charles Bruce (the Associated Board's first Chairman), by Arthur Sullivan, John Stainer,

George Grove, Hubert Parry, Thomas Threlfall, and the
" onlie begetter " of the wicked scheme.

All this could not have come to pass without the consent
of the Royal President of the R.C.M. But the Prince of
Wales, too generously foresighted to disapprove so reasonable
an attempt at a peaceful solution of a tiresome problem, not
only commended it cordially, but graciously became President
of the newly-formed Board. H.R.H. the Duke of Edinburgh
also showed his goodwill by presiding at one of its first
public distributions of certificates, and personally assured me
of his pleasure at the union.

Encouraged by this, I felt that the time had come to
request the consideration of a return to his vacated seat
at the Academy. Armed with the authority of a recently-
formed Board of Directors I placed their desire before him,
and—again with the approval of the Prince of Wales—he
resumed and retained the Presidency until his lamented
death in 1900.

Thus a long disagreement came to an end within twelve
months after my appointment, and the ensuing results have
long since justified an action from which I have derived
lasting satisfaction and genuine pleasure. H.R.H. the
Princess of Wales did us the great honour to attend our
Distribution of Prizes in St. James's Hall in 1897, when the
Prince spoke with reference to these facts in the most encouraging manner.

CHAPTER XX

DREAM OF JUBAL: NATIONAL OPERA

HOW I contrived to complete two works during that very exacting year is not now easily accounted for; but an Overture to *Twelfth Night* (produced by Richter) and *Pibroch* [1] (which Sarasate made his own when he played it at the Leeds Festival in the following year) were written.

Former misunderstandings long since forgotten, Charles Hallé then kindly brought a commission for a cantata wherewith to celebrate the Jubilee of the Liverpool Philharmonic Society, at the suggestion of its President, Mr. Walter Clarke. Joseph Bennett supplied a poem—in my opinion the best cantata libretto ever handed to a composer. *The Dream of Jubal* fascinated me so much that its composition, though time pressed as usual, afforded me real enjoyment.

Although by no means a novelty, the union of recitation and music did not escape censure. " Mélodrame, in the French and here applicable sense, has never succeeded yet, and certainly will not now. In the *Dream* it is carried beyond the farthest point heretofore reached," said one writer. " The speaking voice cannot be made to blend with instruments," said another. [2] Nevertheless, the combination, with the effective assistance of Margaret Macintyre, Edward Lloyd, and the popular reciter Charles Fry, succeeded from the start and the work has had numerous performances at Festivals and elsewhere.

Notable in my recollection is one at the Albert Hall with

[1] Years ago a Highland piper at Blair Athol enlightened my ignorance by describing a pibroch as " Juist a sumphony, Surr." Not far wrong.

[2] The super-sensitive have also felt that the pianoforte labours under the same disability and is unsuitable in combination with strings, etc., etc.

Julia Neilson in the speaker's part, but Mr. Fry identified himself with the cantata on most occasions.

Turning again to Scottish music, *The Cottar's Saturday Night* then occupied me. The setting of Burns's poem was first performed by the Edinburgh Choral Union, and shortly afterwards at the Albert Hall, where the choir courageously grappled with a foreign tongue.

The music to Robert Buchanan's play *Marmion* was then written, and under odd circumstances. A pressing invitation from the manager of the Theatre Royal, Glasgow, had to be declined on the valid plea of lack of leisure, and, on my recommendation, a most talented young composer was asked to accept the offer in my stead. Much music, both vocal and instrumental, was required; time wore on, the production grew near, terms could not be arranged, and my friend—neglectful of a chance of gathering experience and some popularity—seemed reluctant to write for a necessarily limited theatre orchestra. The manager now made another and desperate appeal to me, and almost at the last moment I undertook to help him. Though involving work into the early mornings, the score was delivered in time—and practically gratis: a quixotic way of reading a lesson to a junior by severely punishing myself. The piece had a very successful run. But although my share in the production seems to have been worthy of special mention in the second edition of Grove's Dictionary, I never heard a note of that music—nor is any of it in my possession—as neither Buchanan nor I could be present at any of the performances.

When the Public Orator, in presenting me to the Vice-Chancellor at Cambridge (November 1888) as a fitting recipient of an honorary degree from the University, said, among other things:

Sed vatem egregium, cui non sit publica vena, qui nihil expositum soleat deducere, nec qui communi feriat carmen triviale moneta, . . . anxietate carens animus facit.

He was quoting the lines in Juvenal's *Seventh Satire* in

which a poet is mentioned as having nothing to do with the popular vein, and that I was not of those who coined the cheap song from the commonplaces of popular currency. May I have merited his approval?

As the little overseas University exists no longer, there can be no offence at this distance of time in telling the tale of a degree granted me *in absentia.* Notice of the accorded honour and a copy of the customary Latin oration were duly forwarded. The next mail brought an urgent request from the Speaker asking me to refrain from publishing his laudation. He confessed that, pressed for time, he had adopted Sir Hubert Parry's oration on the occasion of the presentation of August Manns to the Vice-Chancellor of Oxford—verbatim! Presumably on the assumption that our initials being identical the speech would fit either of us equally well. The worthy man need hardly have worried himself, as I had no intention of making any public use of the eulogy.

The honours of that day at Cambridge were enhanced by the fact that they were shared by Charles V. Stanford, then seated in the Cambridge Chair of Music in succession to Macfarren. We met for the first time on Drury Lane stage on the *première* of *Colomba*, when the young Irishman, five years my junior, offered his congratulations. Prolonged absences prevented further acquaintance either with himself or his works until personal convictions caused the *"Irish"* *Symphony* to make instant appeal to my sympathy. Nor was I slow to seize an opportunity for conducting it at one of the Novello Concerts.

By that time C. V. S. had several important works to his credit (*Elegiac Ode, Holy Children, The Revenge,* and a couple of operas), and had already risen to eminence. For exceptionally dexterous workmanship, unceasing industry, and a positively staggering rapidity in composition, I have never met his equal. That he could cast off his Irish brogues at will and adapt himself to any particular subject in hand added to my appreciation of an outstanding ability. In the long and varied catalogue of his works there are many really great things which justify the high place he now occupies in our musical history.

Thrice I took an active part in fruitless endeavours to establish National Opera. On the first occasion Rosa had architect's plans for a permanent home prepared, and, armed with these, we gained admission to the Mansion House without any result.

Again, the chairmanship of an exceptionally representative committee, backed by favourable public opinion, imposed many months' work upon me, as well as the privilege of presenting a petition to the London County Council and of being well heckled on that occasion. The necessity of an Opera House and the provision of a repertoire to obviate reliance on the success—or other—of a single opera formed the basis of our argument.

The so-called failure of *Ivanhoe* in 1891 invariably cropped up in opposition to our pleadings. "If Sullivan could not keep the Palace Theatre open, how can you expect to do so?" This was the burden of the song.

Now, that excellent opera enjoyed a nightly run of many months, was no fiasco, but a well-deserved success. But no management can hope to fill the house for long on the strength of one opera, were it even by the great Wagner himself. Whatever the circumstances may have been— certainly it was announced that several native composers had been commissioned to write for the theatre—Sullivan was followed by Messager, with whose work the venture ended. *Ivanhoe* should not have been blamed, but rather its prolonged exploitation with a double cast, and no alternative relief. In any case, Scott's hero served as a perpetual bogey to warn us all off the course.

The late Mr. D'Oyly Carte, asked by the London County Council for an opinion on our project, submitted a highly favourable one; and when I called to thank the already confirmed invalid for this unexpected support, he promptly said: "If I had had my way, you would not have been begging now." Though his own immediate interests were bound up in another theatre, he was a warm and unbiased sympathizer with our aspirations and struggles. Again I joined in a later attempt which met with the same perverse fate, when I made a futile vow—since then several times disregarded—to touch the nettle no more.

I took advantage of a much-needed leave of absence by a trip to Gibraltar, where an odd incident happened. A fellow-passenger and frequent visitor to the Rock—Mr. Ernest A. Sandeman—kindly offered to act as guide during a long walk on the day of arrival. Returning at dusk (just at gun-fire, after which no appeal gains admittance), I heard the distant tones of a violin, and in hopes of entertainment proposed to trace them to their source.

Soon we stood before a high house, much like those in Edinburgh, in the upper story of which a good performer was practising. "He is playing something of mine," said I to my doubting friend. "Surely I ought to know my own *Pibroch*?" To be listening to a quite recently published and exceptionally difficult work thus unexpectedly on a dark night in so unlikely a spot as "Gib" had a weird effect upon me. After mounting many stairs, I soon found myself giving a lesson to an astonished and very promising young "Scaup" (native of the Rock), the son of a regimental bandmaster whose name has now escaped me.

The short holiday was made the more agreeable by trips into Spanish territory and other amenities consequent upon introductions to officers of the garrison, which would not have been mine but for the strange occurrence.

CHAPTER XXI

HENRY IRVING

HENRY IRVING, at the outset of his stage career, had been my father's colleague at the Edinburgh Theatre for six months in '57, and I had known H. J. Loveday (his stage-manager) since childhood. The latter wrote to the effect that stalls for *Much Ado About Nothing* had been sent to me, but, to his chief's annoyance, the seats had remained empty on the dated evening. My explanation was immediately made during the next performance, *on* the stage behind the bushes which conceal Benedick while the hook is being baited for him in Act II. No apology was possible; I could honestly disclaim receipt of the tickets, for they had not reached me.

"There they were, like two front teeth out," said Irving, keeping an ear on his cue while accepting my statement.

It was not my good fortune to be connected with any of his successes at the Lyceum. The romantic drama *Ravenswood* was a congenial subject offering many opportunities to the musician, but pervaded with gloom, for it began with a funeral and ended with a double tragedy. The final tableau, as altered, helped greatly to relieve the depression. I played my music one morning to him in his room at the Lyceum, he sitting beside me at the little piano. When I had finished he asked the meaning of the music to the final curtain. This was the love-motive which ran through the play, given with all the strength of the orchestra, the idea being that Edgar and Lucy were joined in death, and an apotheosis of love the intention. After a moment he said that he had imagined a cold, desolate moonlight scene with the black plume lying on the sands. No more passed between us then, but on the

174

following morning I received this letter (evidently written soon after our meeting) which proves that the actor had not hesitated to adopt the musician's idea:

DEAR MACKENIZIE,—

You were right after all. Faust does, we hope, go to Heaven in the second part—and Edgar and Lucy I am sure go together. At all events your music will certainly send them there—and the moonlight—on the sea—I shall change to the breaking of the rising sun.

Sincerely yours,

4th July, 1890.   HENRY IRVING.

While not professing any knowledge of music, his unerring instinct for what was fitting or unfitting to a dramatic situation was remarkable. During our stage connexion he frequently deferred to my opinion with, "Well, you know best." I attributed his dislike to the clarinet—always alluded to as "Jem Baggs"—to the abominable sounds produced by his friend, Frederick Macabe, as a street-minstrel of that name in an entertainment, "Begone Dull Care," and more than likely the great little Robson had also helped to disparage the tone of that beautiful instrument.

But, in and out of season, his affection for the harp was evident. Until the dress-rehearsal of *Ravenswood* I had attended none, and was greatly pleased to find that the incidental music to exits and entrances had been so accurately timed as to need neither additions nor cuts. The only alteration was proposed by myself at the inevitable " call " after the first night. A disconcerting titter had gone round the house when the " Master " saved Lucy's life by courageously shooting a furious bull from the window, saying " There is no danger ! " the obviousness of the remark being indisputable. Might I not have helped the ludicrousness of the situation by certain trombone notes in the few bars of " hurry " accompanying the gallant deed, perhaps too realistically? Such at least was my impression, and confessing my supposed guilt, I struck out the bit of local colour which had helped the " moo-cow " (as Ellen Terry called it) to its end.

" Never mind, I got the best laugh in the piece," said

the imperturbable Henry, and thenceforth left the hall and fired " off."

He was endowed with nerves of steel, perfect control of himself, and the enviable faculty of, ostensibly at least, putting disagreeable matters behind him without further thought. Artistically fastidious in all connected with his productions, he not only maintained an excellent and complete orchestra, but sought the co-operation of the most distinguished composers: Benedict (*Romeo*), Sullivan (*Macbeth*, *King Arthur*), Edward German (*Henry VIII*), Stanford (*Becket*), and others.

I spent many days in his company at the end of the *Ravenswood* season, when he stayed for some weeks at Great Malvern with a party of guest-friends. For several summers we had occupied rooms in a small farmhouse at West Malvern. One morning he arrived with his friends to take us for a long drive. While he, the late Ernest Bendall (then dramatic critic of *The Observer*), and I were waiting to start, my landlord, the farmer, suddenly died in the kitchen, at the door of which we stood chatting at the moment. With his habitual kindness Irving instantly arranged for my little daughter to stay with his party as long as the sad circumstances necessitated.

And I have a lively recollection of spending an instructive evening with Miss Terry in a booth when a strolling company presented the classic drama of *Sweeny Todd*. My neighbour in the audience, an elderly, ruddy-faced lady upon whom I had made a favourable impression, embarrassed me by cordial invitations to share the contents of a large bottle of beer from which she partook freely during the entr'actes.

Byron's *Manfred*—as I have good reason to know—had a perpetual fascination for Irving, and, knowing that I had witnessed the run of Phelps's assumption of the part and could describe the production scene by scene, he frequently discussed the possibilities of an exceptionally brilliant revival with me. So it came to pass that I was asked to write the music and to arrange that the solo vocalists and chorus were to be supplied by the R.A.M. On two occasions the order

to start operations was withdrawn. He appeared unexpectedly at my house one Sunday afternoon to tell me that he had
definitely decided to put on the play at once and to know
how much of the music was finished. By this time I certainly
was prepared and produced my MSS. All was fairly ready
except the music to the scene in the " Hall of Arimanes,"
which he intended to surpass that of the Brocken in *Faust*,
and could not be written without a scenario before me.

But again he was overruled by the advice of his friends,
for two days afterwards I received the following:

MY DEAR MACKENZIE,
    I am afraid that I cannot come round to-day—having an appoint-
ment at Kensington which will keep me some time. I have only just
decided to begin my season with an original play—I have put off (for
the present) our talked-of *Manfred*. There are impediments in the
casting of *Manfred* (as my company now stands) which would make
the production impossible.
    I am going for a provincial tour after all, and shall re-open at the
Lyceum in December. You will have a real holiday, I hope. I need
one too. Every good wish,
Sincerely yours,

21 *July*, 1897.   HENRY IRVING.

Even then the thought was not dismissed, for he once
more alluded to it in a genial speech at the Annual Prize
Distribution of the R.A.M. three years afterwards in Queen's
Hall.[1]

The original play above mentioned was *The Medicine
Man*, who proved an inefficient and expensive practitioner.

Yet another scheme came to naught after I had been
called to Birmingham to discuss *Richard II*, of which a
printed stage-version with Irving's musical requirements,
marked by himself, I still have. For some reason or other
I had little faith in the fulfilment of the scheme, and only
a small portion of the music had been sketched before the
production was abandoned. His words to me at Birmingham,

---

[1] Three Preludes, *Astarte*, *Pastorale* and *The Flight of the Spirits* were first
heard at the late Robert Newman's London Festival in 1899. The popular
manager and enterprising friend of musicians is sorely missed.

"As if we were not all sent into the world to fight," were not without meaning.

While on a Christmas vacation spent in Florence a telegram arrived just as I was leaving for a long-projected visit to Naples. "Will you write Coriolanus. Book follows."

Most of the music was brought home with me.

I had never seen the "Chief" so keenly anxious about the staging of any play. Alas, *Coriolanus* was to be his last Shakespearean creation.

I spent a fortnight in the theatre, for we all worked loyally for the man of whose trials we were aware and whose energy in overcoming them we admired.

A few nights before the curtain rose I came home in the belief that my part of the work was done, but the morning brought a request for additional music for the Forum scene. Written on receipt of this, copied, and rehearsed on the following day, they complimented me on having supplied one of the most effective "bits." Indeed, on the actual night of the performance (April 15, 1901) I held a band rehearsal just before the doors were opened to the public. The Lyceum had passed into other hands and I had to deal with an orchestra inferior to that of former days. The unwelcome presence of deputies [1]—notably in the tell-tale brass—impeded progress at rehearsals, and though the "Chief" was aware of my difficulties he could no longer exercise his old control.

Occupying the O.P. box with his son H. B. and my friend Edward German on the first night, I was placed immediately above the trombones, of whose frequent slips I received the full benefit and had ample cause for many audible mutterings. At the subsequent gathering of friends on the stage, Coriolanus—in his most hospitable of humours—asked me, "Well, how did your horns behave?" Said I, "Not horns: trombones, and damnably!" Quoth the noble Roman with a twinkle in his eye: "Ah! that's why I put you in that box, old chap!"

The cynical utterance of a tired stage-hand at rehearsal

[1] Still thorns in the flesh of conductors and composers

to a pal, "Three knights!" (Irving, Alma Tadema, and myself), "that's about all I'll give it!" was not quite accurate, for the play ran for thirty-seven nights. The strains of the *Funeral March* to which Coriolanus had been carried as many times to his stage-grave were next heard when the great actor's coffin was lowered to its resting-place in Westminster Abbey on October 20, 1905.

CHAPTER XXII

AN ADVENTURE IN ITALY: THE PHILHARMONIC

AT the San Carlo (Naples) I witnessed the last of six performances of Mascagni's *Le Maschere*, which elicited no sign of approbation or disapproval from an audience firmly determined to show its displeasure by maintaining a frigid attitude from start to finish. A conspiracy of silence—rare operatic occurrence in Italy. As if to dismiss the work finally, the conductor, Mugnone, closed the score with a sharp slap and left his seat with an eloquent shrug of relief. The unusual plan of producing the opera on the same night in all the large cities had been adopted, thereby arousing the unanimous condemnation of Press and public. At Milan, I believe, the performance was not permitted to proceed.

In my opinion the opera was very far from deserving any such drastic treatment. The mistaken policy had rendered the composer unpopular at the moment, and Verdi's dictum, "*Torniamo all' Antico,*" which he endeavoured to follow, perhaps too literally, could not save him from the storm. Although the performance was a remarkably good one, I passed a cruelly depressing evening; the time-honoured audible method of showing dissatisfaction would almost have been welcome. Bizet's early *Pêcheurs des Perles* at another theatre did not much help to raise my spirits.

Accredited to some influential musicians our stay became an exceedingly pleasant one; an invitation to visit the Conservatorio was gratefully accepted, but the Christmas vacation prevented the formation of any opinion on work done, or of making comparisons with our own methods and results.

I avoided Ischia on account of the painful circumstances

recounted elsewhere; but lovely Capri and indescribable Pompeii enchanted us. A visit to Baiæ is not so briefly dismissed, as at the end of an interesting day our rascally guide persuaded, or forced, the *vetturino* to prolong the excursion, in the rapidly approaching dusk, as far as the abode of the Cumæan Sibyl.

In the evening of that day on which the news of Queen Victoria's death reached Naples, my wife and I were driven to Cumæ—one of the loneliest spots imaginable—to be escorted by a couple of lanky torch-bearing charcoal-burners through a long subterranean tunnel, carried across the coalblack stream which purports to be the real original river Styx, and set on a rock in its middle. No doubt an instructive experience if shared with other intelligent students of the classics, but not to be recommended when alone and at the mercy of ruffians bent on extortion. The Dantesque stage-setting of the scene in which the heated argument had to be conducted may have been exceptionally picturesque, but the situation was decidedly unpleasant. To an assumed indifference as to consequences and a slight, but sufficient, familiarity with Italian slang, an unmolested return to the upper air was due.

On returning to Baiæ, the guide, backed by a crowd of sympathizing friends—"pickpocket" writ large on every face—restarted the discussion on his own behalf; the same defiant tactics, aided by my wife's fearless attitude, enabled us to break through the ugly circle, which pressed closer and closer, and drive off at a surprising speed amid jeers and threats.

When, at a safe distance, I remonstrated with our honest little *vetturino* for taking us to Cumæ at that late hour, I was informed that noncompliance with the guide's orders would, on his next visit to these parts, probably be an uncomfortable one: " *Una bella bastonata, o forse qual' cosa di peggio* " (a nice beating, or perhaps something worse). He was forgiven. To have crossed the Styx was well worth all the excitement.

The directors of the Philharmonic Society honoured me by the offer of its conductorship, a position which I held, with varying emotions, for seven consecutive seasons.

At that time the conditions governing these concerts differed so much from those of the present day that they might well call for a more detailed record than can be given here. Be this one, therefore, restricted to some of my own experiences between 1893 and 1899.

One conductor being made responsible for the musical success of each season of seven, or even eight, concerts at a salary of one hundred pounds in all—his name figuring on the guarantors' list for a like sum—it may be guessed that the chosen individual enjoyed a sprightly enough time during the entire twelve months of office for a somewhat slender remuneration. Little is known and less is understood of the constant anxiety which fell—must always fall—to the lot of the Honorary Directors whose efforts were then often rewarded by more blame than encouragement—sometimes quite unjustly, I thought.

At a rehearsal in St. James's Hall, when a forceful odour of cooking from the restaurant below permeated the atmosphere, an eminent lady vocalist inquired, with many audible sniffs, as to its cause. Fully aware of the prevailing custom, I ventured to suggest that the Philharmonic Directors were being roasted as usual.

During my tenure of office the heat and burden of the day was borne by an Honorary Secretary (happily still living) of remarkable linguistic accomplishment, much musical experience and an immense capacity for work—Mr. Francesco Berger. Fortunately the conductor had no part in the selection of the artists, his duty being to submit programme schemes and such suggestions as might or might not be acceptable to the directorate. My connexion with that well-intentioned body remained from first to last a most agreeable one, and from the friendly relations formed with some of the most eminent artists of their day I derived both pleasure and profit. The onerous post, however, bristled with difficulties to be endured with as little impatience as possible. When the Italian Opera Season commenced many of the orchestral members employed at Covent Garden would become restless before the end of the already scanty enough rehearsals, giving indications that they were presently due at an operatic rehearsal. The like, and some other pleasantries, then evidently irremediable, could not now occur or be tolerated.

Just before stepping on to the platform one evening I became aware of the absence of one of the trombone players, and had to dispatch a note by cab to my friend Mancinelli at Covent Garden: " Please lend me a trombone at once." How the important instrument was dispensed with at the Opera I never knew, but the man arrived just in time to play his part—*a prima vista*.

Now and then difficult new works were a source of anxiety, not much relieved when writers of the analytical notes failed to return the only available score—often in MS. —in time to allow sufficient leisure for the adequate study it demanded.

The programmes are in themselves a history of the progress of our art in England since 1813.[1] That in its first year three symphonies by Beethoven were played, and that in the second the *Eroica* was tackled (with François Cramer as Leader and his more famous brother J. B. Cramer at the pianoforte) is sufficient evidence of the earnestness of the Society's earliest endeavours. When in 1858 George Macfarren suggested that " old and oft-repeated ouvertures should have a rest, and new and clever works, so far neglected, should be allowed an opportunity," he was doubtless hinting at the inclusion of home-products. Many years had to pass before British names are met with, and for long Sterndale Bennett's and his own appeared almost exclusively. But it is to be remembered that these two were about the only native composers fit to be drawn upon at the time. As other men

" The History of the Philharmonic Society of London." By Myles Birket Foster.

arrived, opportunities were offered more freely, though intermittently, Gadsby, Cusins, Barnett, Sullivan, Cowen, Corder and Stanford being the new-comers.

In 1883 I was the only favoured one during the entire season.

But it was not until Cowen's advent as conductor in 1888 that a settled policy seems to have been adopted, the doors opened wider and with greater regularity.[1] Sir Frederic has something like ninety British pieces to his credit during the thirteen seasons at the desk, while my own fifty-four programmes show the titles of at least fifty-three. The presence of these items—then considered a much more risky venture than now—evidently did not influence the sale of tickets detrimentally, for no call upon the guarantors was made in my time.[2] But orchestral fees, rents and all other expenses were on a much lower scale, and the demands made in most modern scores for so unnecessarily large a number of additional instruments was not so general. Unless the production of merely useless noise be the object, the game is not worth the candle. Few, if any, societies can now cope with the altered conditions—including a burdensome Entertainment Tax which precludes any hope of a surplus—and balance their accounts. Nor should composers complain about infrequent performances while creating obstacles to the success of their own works, and committing *felo de se* by scoring them thus extravagantly. Personally, I prefer to be played sometimes on two horns, rather than never on four.

A list of the virtuosi with whom I worked is of sufficient interest to be given in the order of their appearances:

(Pianoforte.) Joseph Slivinsky. Wassily Sapellnikoff. Clotilde Kleeberg. Otto Hegner. Camille Saint-Saëns. Ignaz Jan Paderewski. Leonard Borwick. Fanny Davies. Sophie Menter. Emil Sauer. Frederick Dawson. Ilona Eibenschütz. Bernard Staven-

[1] Sterndale Bennett conducted for eleven years; but Cusins easily beat all records by his tenure of office for seventeen seasons.

[2] It is interesting to note that during my Seasons at the Phil. the Guarantee Fund averaged £3,125, and that in 1897, my fourth Season, the figure was £3,300, the highest ever reached.

hagen. Cécile Chaminade. Eugène d'Albert. Mark Hambourg.
Alfred Reisenauer. Adèle Aus der Ohe. Frederick Lamond. Ossif
Gabrilowitch. Fanny Bloomfield-Zeisler. Moritz Mozkowski. Ella
Pancera.
   (Violin.) Gabrielle Wietrowitz. Willy Hess. Ladislas Gorski.
Emile Sauret. Frida Scotta. César Thomson. Willy Burmeister.
Franz Ondricek. Lady Hallé. John Dunn. Johannes Wolff. Louis
Pecskai. Tivadar Nachèz. Pablo de Sarasate. Charles Gregorowitch
Henry Such. Timothy Adamowsky. Leonora Jackson. Joseph
Joachim.
   (Violoncello.) Julius Klengel. Leo Stern. David Popper.
   (Vocalists.) Margaret Macintyre. Norman Salmond. Marie Brema.
Charles Santley. Liza Lehmann. Esther Palliser. Mde. de Vere
Sapio. Eugène Oudin. Camilla Landi. Ben Davies. Amy Sherwin.
Adelina Patti. David Bispham. Mrs. Henschel. Katherine Fisk.
Sophie and Gulia Ravogli. Blanche Marchesi. Emma Albani. Mar-
cella Pregi. Rosa Olitzka. Clara Butt. Mde. Alva. Ella Russell.
Plunket Greene. Ruth Lamb. Christianne Andray. Emma Nevada.
Evangeline Florence.

This catalogue of names, to which might be added those
of many eminent foreign composers, crowds my memory
with lively recollections. The sixth concert of the first
season introduced me to Tchaikowsky and Saint-Saëns.
The latter played his *G Minor Concerto* with brilliant effect,
ending the programme with *Le Rouet d'Omphale* under his
own direction. The impressions left were those of an unfailing perfection of pianoforte technique, combined with a
dryness of expression and an inflexibility of beat, which in
this case, however, fitted the rigid rhythm of the wheel.

I have never witnessed so automatic a manner of conducting. The clever Frenchman's compositions, invariably certain
of the effect aimed at, always attracted me, and my spoken
tribute in Queen's Hall, on June 2nd, 1913, on the occasion
of his farewell to England was a very sincere one. We were
frequently to meet again. A somewhat unbending stolidity
when playing or conducting, and a snappy manner of speech
by no means observable in his elegant music, may be best
described in his own tongue as " *sec.*" He was good enough
to express satisfaction with my efforts and wrote to me to
that effect.

When the famous Peter Ilitsch came to conduct his *Fourth Symphony* in '93 he seemed already a spent man, nor did he live very long after his visit; the weak voice, intense nervousness, and exhaustion after rehearsal, plainly indicated failing health. His unaffected modesty, kindly manner and real gratitude for any trifling service rendered, all contributed to the favourable impression made by a lovable man. Truth to tell, Tchaikowsky possessed no gifts as a conductor, and knew it; nevertheless, thanks to the assistance of an attentive and sympathetic orchestra, *No. IV* scored a complete success. I fear to have unwittingly provided an uncomfortable hour for him when, honouring the R.A.M. by a quite unexpected visit at a time when I happened to be exceptionally busy, I placed the baton in his hand and called upon a student to play his *B Flat Minor Concerto* at an orchestral practice.

The Philharmonic directors invited him to dinner at the St. Stephen's Club, after which he and I started on a long ramble through the streets until past one o'clock in the morning. I then learned that he was neither a perfect Wagnerite nor a devout worshipper at the shrine of Brahms, and gathered that his reception at Vienna had not been a pleasant one. Probably friend Hanslick had been at his courteous tricks again: "*Stinkende Musik*" was not a pretty expression to use in connexion with the popular Violin Concerto. He stated to me that the fight for recognition had been a hard one everywhere—but in England.

Without showing discontent or bitterness, the amiable Russian appeared melancholy and lonely; devoid of self-assertion and giving no sign of the passion and force revealed in his music. Eight months later I had the gratification of introducing the *Pathétique* (No. 6); its immediate success leading to a repetition by special desire at the next concert (February 28 and March 14, 1894). Whether the composer's intentions were faithfully reproduced or not, the effect was sufficiently striking to secure an exceptional success.

To be strictly accurate, I believe that the famous work had been previously run through by Manns at a rehearsal at the Crystal Palace; but the fact only came to my knowledge after the Philharmonic performance.

Under Sophie Menter's nimble fingers another Tchaikowsky *première* took place in that year, and the occasion serves to illustrate a conductor's trials.

Of the Russian composer's *Fantasie de Concert* only a pianoforte edition was published, and the by no means easy orchestral accompaniment had to be learned at rehearsal, as no full score was procurable.

In the same programme the pianist also played a *Fantasie*, *Zigeuner-Weisen* (orchestrated by Tchaikowsky), of her own, which I had to conduct from a MS. score which did not contain a note of the pianoforte solo part! To memorize at a day's notice and follow such tricky passage-work (à la Liszt) without visual aid was a much more dangerous undertaking. All went well, however; but my homily upon carelessness and laziness—for it was nothing else—had no effect upon the good-natured Sophie, whose oddities had often amused us when we met her in Italy.

We believed that when on tour no desire to acquaint herself with the objects of historic fame in the many cities visited was shown. She contented herself with driving from hotel to concert-room, or to the houses of hospitable friends. Probably she never saw the Duomo while in Florence. On the other hand, keenly interested in the cats with which she invariably travelled, her attentions were divided between them and the eternal keyboard. A child of Münich, with a strong spice of the merry Viennese, the thoroughly genial woman and accomplished pianist was a particular favourite with us all. Her full rich tone lingers in my ears.

Virtuosity and musicianship not being necessarily co-existent, a conductor's experiences are of a varied nature. While most of mine were delightful, some were terrifying while they lasted. *Rubato!* What crimes are committed in thy name! One young Russian, disregarding the orchestra as well as the composer's intentions, persisted in racing through Liszt's *First Concerto* at such a pace as to render the oft-recurring pizzicatos impossible of execution. My courteous explanation and remonstrance only resulted in a considerably accelerated *tempo* being adopted at the actual performance.

At one time a rage for " resonance " prompted certain virtuosi to insist upon the pianoforte-lids being open to their widest extent, notwithstanding the fact that an upright wooden obstruction prevented the conductor from seeing and controlling a considerable number of the orchestral members. This, however, concerned them not at all, as the baton-wielder would of course be blamed for any mishaps.

In one case, when conducting a Saturday concert in the absence of Manns at the Crystal Palace, it was necessary to erect a special structure to enable me to look over the obstruction; nor would the obstinate pianist realize that the dizzy height I occupied in fear and trembling would have to be removed in order to permit me to direct the remainder, and much more important part, of the programme from a less elevated position. Only to avoid a serious altercation did I consent to suffer the discomfort.

The fact that the fine *Symphony in B Minor*—which pleased greatly, but has not been often performed since—by the Russian Professor of Chemistry, Borodine, was given for the first time in England, reminds me that a young vocalist proposed to sing an item from one of his operas, and the score reached me at the last moment. To my horror the piece had been transposed by some genius, with the result that all the string parts descended a whole tone beyond the compass of the instruments. More than an hour of the following morning's only rehearsal was wasted on an attempt to make the performance possible. I had to call out every single note of the many alterations required, and these were patiently corrected by the members of the orchestra. Luckily the song was a short one and the accompaniment consisted chiefly of minims.

The vivacious young lady seemed to be unconscious either of the necessity of the proceeding, or of the valuable time and trouble expended on her behalf, and furthermore exhibited an irrepressible penchant for conducting while singing. After several fruitless remonstrances, her widely waving arms enabled me to pass my stick dexterously from my hand into hers; a transference which, causing some well-earned amusement, effectually cured her of the habit for the time being.

Adelina Patti sang but once to a Philharmonic audience, and on that occasion (April 3, 1895) received the Society's Gold Medal.

Though the selected songs were sufficiently familiar, I deemed it wise to suggest a private hearing in case of her absence from rehearsal. She amiably protested, but yielded to a request which proved well-timed. Cadenzas, being subject to the singer's individuality, ability or caprice, may become veritable mantraps to catch conductors unless they walk warily; and in "*Una voce poco fa,*" the Diva's version differed from those of others. At the end of a fatiguing rehearsal I coaxed a tired orchestra to run through the well-worn aria without the singer, when, without waiting for my beat, the band " came down " unanimously at the accustomed place and of course at the wrong moment. It was my turn to laugh.

Mdme. Patti, then just on the eve of a tour, might not have been so readily moved to say: " I would like to take you with me in my pocket," had a public exhibition of my incompetence not been avoided.

But these be tales out of school!

Meeting again at a friend's dinner-table after her retirement, I admired the popular singer's amazing vitality and keen sense of fun.

In 1905 (March 17) we celebrated the hundredth birthday of Manuel Garcia, " The Father of Laryngology," as Sir Felix Semon called him. That he was still a professor at the R.A.M. when considerably over eighty—at the time of my election—and continued to teach there for another ten years, proves the marvellous mental activity and physical energy of the famous singing master.

Another veteran, whose occasional visits gave me great pleasure during the early days of Principalship, was the popular pianist, George A. Osborne. The genial old Irishman's intimate acquaintance with Berlioz, Chopin, and all the great personages who figure so prominently in a most important period of musical history, made him ever a welcome guest. But his own cheery personality was sufficient to fascinate me.

CHAPTER XXIII

MORE PHILHARMONIC MEMORIES

IT was in 1889, when I filled Cowen's place at a concert
before he returned from Melbourne, that the quaint little
couple Edvard Grieg and his wife appeared. He had
played his *Concerto* and conducted in the previous year,
coming for the third and last time in '94. Although announced for another concert three years later, illness prevented
his arrival and his programme had to be entrusted to my care.

At our first meeting an extremely nervous disposition,
partly owing to delicate health, was apparent enough, and I
have reason to remember his final visit when his unconcealed
irritation at the absence of the percussionists from their
seats at the rehearsal of the last movement of his Suite, *Sigurd
Jorsalfor*, caused me to leave the hall and personally conduct
the delinquents from the street to their places, discipline
being yet in the making.

From Grieg I gathered that, at the outset of his career,
it was owing to Liszt's advice that he had developed his
talents in the direction of Norwegian folk-song and had
adhered consistently to the national idiom to which his
popularity is in a great measure due. Of Scottish extraction
himself, my *Burns Rhapsodie* (which concluded the concert)
led him to expatiate on the similarity of our countries' melodies
and their characteristics. I am not, however, yet convinced
of the existence of so striking a likeness as he seemed to dis-
cover.

Extremely particular regarding the smallest details when
rehearsing, none could fail to appreciate the Scandinavian
composer's artistic sensitiveness.

Would that space permitted a more adequate expression

of gratitude to Ignaz Jan Paderewski for his friendship and kindness, great artistic enjoyment, and many happy hours passed in his company. His *Concerto in A Minor* and the brilliant *Polish Fantasie* had entered early into the R.A.M. pianoforte repertoire, which had by this time been brought thoroughly up to date by the energetic work of my already mentioned pianoforte professors. The great Polish patriot, as posterity must ever think of him, honoured the school and its students by giving them a memorable display of his extraordinary powers. Of his large-hearted exhibition of gratitude to the British nation after the War no reminder should be needed here.

It was at the suggestion of a mutual friend, the late Mrs. Angelina Goetz—herself an accomplished musician—that a *Scottish Concerto* was written for and played by him for the first time at a Philharmonic concert in 1897; and to Paderewski I am indebted for many improving hints and a careful revision of the solo part.[1] The piece was ready for the previous season, but its production had to be postponed, as his tours left no leisure for preparation.

The debut was a successful one, and after repeated recalls he said: "If I play again I shall repeat the last movement." This he did, in spite of a stentorian demand from the gallery: "Without the orchestra!"

In recent years similar curtly-expressed requests and opinions have been known to issue from the same quarter. Whether my friend is the progenitor of the present loudspeaker I know not, but I imagine myself to be the first composer thus publicly honoured in Queen's Hall.

The publication of a work of the character of the *Scottish Concerto* is, no doubt, a somewhat costly undertaking, promising at best but a very limited sale. Failing to find a British firm willing to take the risk—even without a honorarium to myself—it was offered to a German house which,

[1] One of the most valuable gifts ever received by the R.A.M. is the " Angelina Goetz " Library, founded by the family in memory of their mother in 1903. It is open to the public and contains 350 modern scores, some of which cannot be seen elsewhere.

to my joy, immediately bought it for twenty-five pounds. The transaction is an example of many a better composer's difficulties, and the monetary reward of nearly a whole year's work in the available leisure hours.

Those works around which controversy was to rage so fiercely were yet unknown when, only at the threshold of an eventful career, Richard Strauss appeared at the invitation of the Society in 1899. The fine *Ton-Dichtung, Don Juan* and witty humoreske, *Till Eulenspiegel,* were already so familiar and cordially appreciated that a warm welcome awaited their daring composer; and on the occasion of its first performance here, *Death and Transfiguration* instantly made that deep impression which its earnest sincerity must always leave on the listener.

While my admiration of these masterpieces, and much else belonging to that earlier period of his remarkable activity, remains undiminished, I felt unable to keep further step with Strauss's intentions and methods in a like enthusiastic spirit. Whether my fault or misfortune, each succeeding work weakened an appreciation which was brought to a *Fermata lunga* by the ponderous futilities of the *Sinfonia Domestica :* but gladly renewed by the humour and silvery glitter of the *Rosenkavalier.*

Interesting, frequently amusing, were the differing temperamental peculiarities exhibited at the conductor's desk by our composer-guests. Contrasted, for instance, with Grieg's nervous anxiety over trifles, the German master's cool, almost indifferent demeanour, when rehearsing his infinitely more exacting and intricate music, was striking.

An evening in 1912, when a whole concert had again been entrusted to me, is gladly recalled, for I then met an artist whose personality occupies a separate niche in my memory. Busoni's playing—it seemed to me—bore so little resemblance to that of any of his contemporaries that comparisons need not be ventured on.

On the occasion referred to, a delay on the railway had caused a long stage-wait before his arrival, and extreme fatigue forbade exertion at the one brief rehearsal: even my careful preparation of Liszt's tricky *Totentanz* did not relieve an anxiety which was only dispelled by the confidence which his good-natured encouragement and modest self-possession inspired.

"Safe as a house," the performance was an exceptionally spirited one, the best I have yet heard of a work for which Busoni had an evident affection. On that night—in a transcribed Bach *Prelude* and *Fugue*—he revealed himself as an experimentalist in novel effects when producing an astounding whirlwind of sonority from the instrument. During an all too brief intimacy I learned also to esteem this earnest thinker for a rarely-unbiased interest in and liberal recognition of the merits of others, as well as for that absence of pose, fuss or ostentation which often marks the most highly gifted. The Italian maestro's early death deprived art of the services of a great musician and likeable man.

Joachim's historic connexion with the Society covered a period of fifty-five years: the boy of thirteen making his first bow (with Beethoven's *Concerto*, under Mendelssohn's direction) in 1844, and his last—appropriately with the same work—in 1899. What may have been his thoughts on the latter occasion? There had been a gap of six years between his last two appearances (of which there were forty in all), and even this final engagement was not in the original scheme of the programmes; but, as I explained, these matters lay outside of my province. Upon the intellectual conception of the masterpiece he loved time had made no mark, but that his wondrous tone had suffered he was aware when whispering to me, with a rather pitiful smile, "*Wenn's nur das verdammte Zittern nicht wäre*" (If only there were none of that damned shakiness).

I was particularly thanked for the accompaniment to the *Romance* from the *Hungarian Concerto*, a deceptively simple piece by no means easily followed. The concert concluded with Tchaikowsky's *No. IV*, to which he listened attentively at the wings. Whether the ageing purist entirely approved the realistic Finale, descriptive of the humours of Novgorod Fair, may be doubted. But it amused him as much as the chance of "letting it rip" diverted me.

None has excelled "Jo," as he was affectionately called here, in his interpretations of the "three B's" (Bach, Beethoven, Brahms); nor did he leave any successors, among his numerous pupils, capable of perpetuating so personal a style: it died with him. I cherish the proud memory of a long acquaintance with the great classicist.

Joachim only played once more with an orchestra in London (1904), when on the sixtieth anniversary of his first appearance in England he was presented with his portrait by Sargent. Three years afterwards he passed away at Berlin.

At Richter's suggestion I helped to persuade the Directors in 1896 to consider the adoption of the low pitch now in general use, and they courageously initiated a long-awaited reform. In spite of the willing assistance of our orchestral players, the welcome change was not effected without difficulty. As an immediate result, the intonation of the wood-wind could hardly be said to be *sans reproche* during the whole of that season. But what, for a short time, may have seemed a loss of brilliancy, has proved a lasting gain in practicability, and that we had been screaming a semitone above the rest of Europe for years is now a forgotten fact.

On my retirement from the desk, my friend Cowen returned to his old post. Resignation did not sever that long and happy association with the " Phil," upon which I might dwell longer if space permitted, for I conducted on a good many subsequent occasions, and my stock of interesting happenings is by no means exhausted.

CHAPTER XXIV

BRITANNIA: ROYAL CHORAL SOCIETY: *HIS MAJESTY*

TO our sorrow, Von Bülow died at Cairo (January 1894), where he sought alleviation of intense sufferings from which his doctors were unable to deliver him. I learned that he had been afflicted with three ailments, any single one of which would have made a much speedier end to a less resistant nature.

A few years previously the meagre attendance at his last recital in London had thoroughly disappointed him, and at a luncheon party given by the hospitable Henschel his annoyance was concealed with evident difficulty. This was my last meeting with a generous-hearted friend.

The reluctant withdrawal from a commission, mainly owing to the piecemeal delivery of the book, besides disappointing the Leeds Festival, also roused the displeasure of my collaborator. Neither author nor composer perceived that the day of lengthy oratorio was already drawing to a close, and had I guessed that the work was spinning itself out to such dimensions it would have been treated more concisely, although its two sections can be performed separately. *Bethlehem* was ultimately produced at the Albert Hall, when Barnby assisted me cordially in the choral preparations; but the usual single orchestral rehearsal could not be favourable to an adequate presentation of a new composition. Only British orchestras can be trusted to take these risks without courting defeat. *Magnifique, mais ce n'est pas la guerre!*

We celebrated the seventieth anniversary of the R.A.M.'s foundation in a worthy fashion at a concert of which the programme consisted entirely of works by past students: Bennett, the two Macfarrens, Sullivan, Barnby, Goring

Thomas, Maude V. White, Edward German and Corder. Not a few other names might have been included had time permitted.

All were now loyally working with me, and peace and plenty reigned. Our President, the Duke of Edinburgh, listened for the first time to *Britannia* (a nautical Overture), which, at the age of thirty-three years, still retains its popularity. Within a few days the second performance took place at a Richter concert. The great conductor, greatly tickled by its vivacity, averred that, when the second Dibdinesque subject appears on the tuba, the sonorous instrument represents a big whale trying to join in the sea-song; but I regret not to be able to claim the fantastic intention. The Overture also enjoyed the distinction of a political significance, quite unintentional, being attached to it.

Immediately after Hallé's death I was invited to conduct some of the remaining concerts of his season at Manchester, Leeds and Liverpool. In the latter city the Overture met with so exceptionally warm an ovation that it had to be played a second time with the same result. In compliance with a third demand only the final pages were repeated. These boisterous encores were, however, not entirely due to an excessive appreciation of the music, because on that very day the German Kaiser's ill-judged telegram to President Kruger had become known, and *Britannia* had been made the vehicle of a patriotic demonstration rarely witnessed in a British concert room. The occurrence had an amusing sequel when the piece had been selected, for a second time, to be played at Düsseldorf by the liberal-minded Buths, a few days later. A *Verbot* was issued and the offending work had the honour of being banned by the police. *Musica proibita!*

In connexion with a rehearsal of the Overture by the London Symphony Orchestra under Dr. F. Read at Reading, a remarkable incident happened. After the timpani had played the opening signal and the brass had given out the principal theme, the church clock chimed the identical four notes and in the same key. In the piece they are followed by an echo on the horns. On this occasion the clock deputized for them and entered just at the exact moment!

Charles Hallé and Joseph Barnby passed away suddenly within four months of each other. On the afternoon of the latter's death I agreed to an urgent request to take over his duties at the Albert Hall for the remainder of the season. As I had acted for him at several consecutive concerts during his enforced absence in 1891, in addition to those occasions on which I had conducted my own works, my acquaintance with the fine choral body was a fairly intimate one. But on becoming aware of the fact that the next concert was to take place two days following the popular conductor's demise, I resolved to urge its postponement until after the funeral, and for that purpose hurried to lay the proposal before a prominent member of the Council. To my surprise the suggestion was firmly, even brusquely rejected. The concert must be given on the advertised date. An exasperating and prolonged argument, during which I protested against the tastelessness of compelling the choir to sing *Judas Maccabeus*, or any other work, while its late chief was still unburied, producing no result, I rose to take my leave, and indignantly refused to accept the engagement.

The effect of that statement was even more surprising. "Why didn't you say so at once?" said the obstinate official. My demand being now granted, without further words I drove at once to the newspaper offices and arrived just in time to alter the next morning's announcements. *Redemption* —more appropriately the first one after Barnby's burial— was followed by *Faust* (Berlioz), *Judas*, *Messiah* and *Elijah*.[1]

On account of a recrudescence of the meddlesome interference to which I had been subjected, I took an early opportunity to disclaim any intention of accepting the vacant conductorship, as the Academy, Philharmonic and private

[1] In the Handelian Oratorios the marvellous flexibility and ease of Charles Santley's method astounded me. His carefully considered readings were perfect and he rightly deprecated the habit of making *ritardandos* before the final bars of the Arias.

work provided me with more than sufficient occupation. Some months passed before the election of Sir Frederick Bridge, who continued to fill the position with honour and credit to himself for many years.

Even at this distance of time the smart of persistent persecution pains the victim, but it shall be mentioned if only to congratulate my young colleagues on the *autres mœurs* which happily prevail in their day.

A student bearing a foreign name had been entered on the list of competitors for a scholarship at the Academy to be held by a British subject, and I had satisfied myself of the validity of the claim to be included. But to ensure against any possible doubt the case was submitted to the final decision of the donors of the prize, who unhesitatingly allowed the application to stand. So promising an opportunity to attack the Principal could hardly be ignored, and, encouraged by a preliminary shot fired by another righteously-incensed lover of justice, my old friend " the Barber" stropped his razor again:

The part that Sir Alexander Mackenzie played in this affair is scarcely an enviable one. It shows that he is unfit to direct the fortunes of such an important institution as the Royal Academy of Music, and the sooner he resigns or is superseded the better for all concerned. He may be a distinguished musician and this is disputed; but there can be no difference of opinion as to his incapacity as an administrator or principal of any institution, not only of the Royal Academy of Music, but of that hole-and-corner Society, the Philharmonic! " etc.

Then yet another censor of morals, pursuing the subject and the object, added this to other insults:

This infamous case is typical of all the transactions that go on in what I have repeatedly called the cesspool of academical life. . . . You may win scholarships in defiance of law, honour and common decency. I suggest that no further explanations are needed so long as our music schools, our concerts, our whole musical life are dominated by commercial men who, without shame, perpetuate feats of dishonesty from which the most hardened bogus company promoters might well shrink, etc., etc.

And much more to the like complimentary effect. What had I done to provoke such virulent attacks, suffered in silence

N   199

for eight years? The articles contained imputations which no man can bear with equanimity. The only possible steps —those leading to the Law Courts—were immediately taken. That decision becoming known, the following appeared in *The Times* and other journals on February 6, 1896:

The "London Figaro" *ats* Sir Alexander Mackenzie.
An Apology.

We regret that a paragraph appeared in *The London Figaro* on January 16th commenting on Sir Alexander Mackenzie in his public capacity as Principal of The Royal Academy of Music, in which un-founded statements were made reflecting on his character.

We desire to take this opportunity of withdrawing completely all reflections on *Sir Alexander Mackenzie* and hereby offer him our fullest and amplest *Apologies* for having caused him pain and annoyance by the paragraph in question, and we tender the apology both in his public and private capacity. Furthermore we trust that, in evidence of our regret for what has occurred, Sir Alexander Mackenzie will allow us to send in his name a cheque for 25 guineas to any musical charity which he may be pleased to nominate.

The London Figaro, 233 Strand, W.C.

This, and several more or less repentant announcements, did not, however, prevent the cases being tried before the Lord Chief Justice and a special jury on July 30, with a resultant verdict for the plaintiff and damages in both instances.

That the issue of this, the most disagreeable episode in my life, called forth many sharply-expressed, public reproofs and reprehensory comments on the behaviour of my detractors was only to be expected: but, though the obvious necessity of keeping on the windy side of the law had to be more strictly observed, the rancorous pursuit did not entirely cease, and what Jane Austen somewhere calls "the dignity of ill-usage" was not easily maintained.

Despite these unwelcome distractions, which affected my health so much that Stanford kindly undertook to conduct the last of the Hallé Concerts for me, that year cannot have been an unproductive one. The music to Barrie's *Little Minister* (November 6) was written for Messrs. Harrison and Maude, and a Comic Opera for the Savoy Theatre (February 20). In connexion with my share in the highly-succesful run of the former piece, be it said that, with the exception of "Duncan Gray," which old tune was incorporated in the Overture at the author's special request, the music is mine own. This because the reproduction of the Scottish idiom has deceived not a few.[1]

In 1890-91 Gilbert and Sullivan ceased to collaborate, and when the latter wrote *Haddon Hall* with Sydney Grundy, this excerpt from the librettist's public letter illustrates the attitude towards any new combination whatsoever.

As a humble but sympathetic student of dramatic and musical criticism, may I suggest that a short Bill be introduced into Parliament making it a penal offence to supply the Savoy Theatre with a libretto?

And two of the most knowing and accurate chroniclers of Savoy history[2] write freely of the prevailing " irreconcilable antagonism."

It was after the famous pair had worked together for the last time on *The Grand Duke* that I was asked to write an opera with F. C. Burnand and R. C. Lehmann, an offer which was gladly accepted. Alive to the risks, I was not surprised when Mr. Carte—like the war-horse sniffing danger from afar—confided to me, before I had been at work very long on the congenial task: "I see it beginning already: nothing but G. and S. allowed."

His Majesty had the advantage of an excellent company: Ilka von Palmay (a vivacious comédienne, good singer and conscientious artist), Florence Perry, Henry Lytton (who succeeded George Grossmith in the name-part), Kenningham, Billington and Walter Passmore. To the annoyance of the management the strictly enjoined rule of secrecy as to plot and title had been disregarded, and a statement that the book was a skit on "His Majesty" of Germany also appeared. Be that as it may, the Monarch of Vingolia's exceptional

---

[1] My daughter was the Jean of the original cast.

[2] "Gilbert, Sullivan and D'Oyly Carte," by François Cellier and Cunningham Bridgeman.

gifts, superior mentality and profound belief in himself were fair and amusing game enough, although in certain important directions not exactly favourable to success.

This is not set down in defence of an opera—which contained some charming and witty lyrics from Lehmann's pen —still less to bemoan its fate; but even before its production our work was, like others, evidently marked as unwanted. Sullivan himself had a similar experience with *The Beauty Stone*, which followed my opera, and had even a shorter run.

Arriving early at rehearsal one morning I found Charles Harris (brother of " Druriolanus " and stage-manager at the Savoy) seated at his table in a state of profound dejection. To an inquiry as to progress and prospects I received the depressing answer: "It is killing me! All is in a state of—— *kudos !* "

This being much too good to waste upon myself, I took Burnand aside to urge a repetition of the question. The same dispiriting assurance that the prevailing " kudos " would make an end of him was uttered, and I took upon myself to offer the encouragement that, should that be the case, a " tabloid " to his memory would be put up. A retort, courteous but forcible, to the effect that the suggested act of piety would be of no particular benefit to him ended the cheerful conversation.

Alas, the true word had been spoken in jest, for, to our sincere regret, the good fellow died within a few days. He was not permitted to witness a production on the preparation of which he had worked so willingly and well.

I paid occasional summer visits to New Brighton where my friend and ex-student, now Professor, Granville Bantock, was installed as Musical Director. Wending our way to a rehearsal of an orchestral concert through the beautiful grounds, Bantock halted on an eminence for the purpose of letting me hear his newly-formed military band which, at his signal, played a selection from a comic opera. After praising the performance I remarked, " Well, Sullivan does write some jolly good tunes." A roar of delight followed, and Bantock, recovering his breath, managed to splutter out something to the effect that I had just been listening to *His Majesty!* It had completely passed from my mind. But did not the lapse of memory perhaps indicate that, after all, I may not have strayed so very far from the Savoy path?[1]

[1] In this connexion I am reminded that, although the orchestral parts were duly returned to me after some performances in the Provinces, the MS. full score of *His Majesty* has not yet reached its rightful owner. The late Mrs. D'Oyly Carte's, and other endeavours to recover it were fruitless. I shall therefore be grateful for any information regarding the present whereabouts of my property.

CHAPTER XXV

GILBERT AND SULLIVAN: *THE CRICKET ON THE HEARTH*

REMINISCENCES are incomplete without a passing reference to Sir William Gilbert—with whom I had a slight but invariably pleasant acquaintance—and how I missed the honour of collaborating with him.

At a Benchers' dinner he asked me whether an opera without a male chorus would have any chance of success, my affirmative answer being based on the fact that I had just finished one on these very lines. I was, however, careful to point out that the possibility depended on a sufficiency of principal male characters to supply the missing links and preserve the balance of the vocal numbers, and gladly agreed to consider one of his early plays which, on subsequent consideration, I ventured to find unsuitable to the purpose. The unfavourable verdict was conveyed with greatest care in a letter which evoked a characteristically stimulating reply.

At our next meeting at the Garrick Club, W. S. G. had either forgotten or chose to ignore the circumstance, for he received me cordially and nothing more was said.

On December 9, 1909—a week before the production of *Fallen Fairies*—a lengthy interview was published in *The Daily Telegraph* in which the eminent author frankly stated that he had offered the libretto to seven musicians, six of whom had rejected it: Sullivan (who " would not hear of it "), Elgar ("who gave no reason for refusal "), Messager, Massenet, Liza Lehmann, Mackenzie and Edward German. I appear to have been the sixth refractory, and my dear friend Edward German—who supplied admirable music— the only tractable composer. Thus an opportunity was unfortunately lost of joining an author with whose name I would have been proud to be associated.

The publication of *King Olaf* brought Edward Elgar's name into sudden prominence by immediately stamping him as an exceedingly accomplished musician who quickly secured unanimous recognition. It was Stanford who enthusiastically drew my attention to the almost unknown new-comer's splendid gifts, upon which it would be an impertinence to dwell here and now.

Sullivan's ailing condition had caused serious anxiety for some time, but his death came as a shock to us all (November 22, 1900). We had been intimate for the past nine or ten years and the coolness existing between himself and the R.A.M. had long ceased. Macfarren had dubbed him " The English Offenbach "—a singularly inept comparison, for although the Parisian composer was assuredly not without a share of genius, not the faintest similarity exists between their methods, still less between the distinctive qualities of the libretti they set to music. But I am unwilling to believe that Macfarren intended to convey the disrespectful meaning so annoying to Sullivan and his friends. Anyway, the Englishman did achieve the longest-known uninterrupted survival of a series of comic operas which still defy time and fashion. I had to leave my desk during a rehearsal when he paid an unexpected visit to the Academy, to answer an anxious question as to the length of time I had taken to score *Colomba*, *i.e.* how many pages per diem! He was scoring *Ivanhoe*, and seemed very fidgety about completing it in time; but I had the impression that he was more in search of a hearty cheering-up than of the information I failed to offer him.

A lively recollection remains of a couple of days passed in his temporary home at Weybridge, and of being rowed by him to an island then occupied by the Carte family, little dreaming that the passenger would be asked to contribute to the Savoy repertoire shortly afterwards.

My warning not to leave any tunes lying about during

my visit elicited the smiling reply that he had "run dry" himself. He was then busy with *Utopia* and thoroughly pleased to be once more at work with W. S. G. "After all, there's nobody like him," said he.

We discussed metres, his preferences and the comparative difficulties their settings presented, our liking for Auber, "ships and sealing-wax;" but no musical politics crept into our conversation.

In three lectures given at the Royal Institution (May 1901), when I had the willing help of the Savoy company, I endeavoured to do justice to Sullivan's gifts, after an exhaustive study of his works, published and in MS.

Apart from personal inclination, it was not quite without an ulterior motive that my fancy turned to thoughts of a lighter genre of composition at this period. I was aware that a mawkishly-morbid, thoroughly un-British style, which I cordially detest, was rapidly influencing the minds of the talented young folks with whom I was in daily contact and for the public production of whose works I was responsible. While not foolish enough to imagine that tides can be stemmed, I was not afraid to wet my feet and thought that cheerful example might be better than precept or preachment.

Hence an application to Julian Sturgis, who suggested a version of *The Cricket on the Hearth* as a promising subject for a wholesome and lively English comic opera. The amiable author of *Nadeshda* and *Ivanhoe* could hardly have been induced to employ his pen so devotedly to the project by any expectation of financial gain.

We worked harmoniously together *con e per l'amore*. Completed in 1902, it was not until twelve years had passed that the *Cricket* chirped in public for a whole week at the R.A.M. A couple of performances took place during the Centenary celebrations in 1922, but the opera has not yet been heard in a London theatre.[1]

---

[1] The spoken dialogue is mainly Dickens's. Sturgis—who unfortunately did not live to see his opera staged—added charming and touching lyrics to the simple English story.

The Carl Rosa management made an offer for provincial purposes, but could not commit itself to a London production. I therefore, rightly or wrongly, withheld the opera. It so happened that Goldmark had also just written *Heimchen am Herde*, which was quickly secured by the Company; so, for the time being, there could hardly be room for a couple of crickets on the operatic hearth.

By chance I met Augustus Harris on the night of his return from Vienna, whither he had gone to hear Goldmark's setting. To my questions regarding its merits, the experienced impresario replied: " There isn't any cricket, and the hearth is a German stove! " A tersely-expressed verdict which seems to have been verified.

Absorbing scholastic duties preventing me from giving much, or any, attention to extraneous interests, their furtherance was neglected on this and other occasions. Of the late Mrs. Ada Lewis's kindness of heart, which prompted the gift of eighteen thousand pounds, in the foregoing year, to establish the fifteen scholarships bearing her name, another instance may be told. In the course of conversation over the tea-cups the lady inquired about my recent compositions, and when informed that this opera had just been finished her instant reply was: " Well, when you want a thousand pounds to help it on its way, you are welcome." What any other composer might have done under similar circumstances I know not; but let it be solemnly stated that the spirit moved me to decline the generous offer, with the cordial thanks I felt. To say, however, that the rash act has not been regretted would not be in strict accordance with the truth.

London Day by Day (a light orchestral suite) also came to be written for the Norwich Festival of that year. The whole point and climax of the first movement (*Under the Clock*), a series of snapshots over the persistently repeated four notes of the Westminster chimes, was missed at the first performance by the refusal of Big Ben to strike at the right moment. The gong-artist evidently found the single stroke expected from him too much to remember.

CHAPTER XXVI

A CANADIAN TOUR

AS interesting as adventurous was a tour through Canada, undertaken at the request of Dr. Charles Harriss in 1903 and accepted on condition that the contemplated Cycle of Festivals should assume a national character. Until then the Dominion had only seen German-American conductors and knew nothing of our music; therefore none other than British composers were to be represented on the programmes. Harriss, a Londoner (and a Tenbury boy of Sir Frederick Gore Ouseley's), had been working on patriotic lines for some years in the country of his adoption, and assented readily to the scheme.

The enterprise called for a greater amount of labour and financial risk and had farther-reaching effects than are realized after a passage of more than a couple of decades. Fourteen new choirs were raised and a number of existing societies were considerably augmented. Associate-conductors and executive committees in fifteen towns loyally co-operated towards the successful issue of a cycle, starting at Halifax (N.S.) and ending at Victoria (B.C.). Conducting three times daily (and a couple of rehearsals on Sundays) during five consecutive weeks, I take modest leave to doubt whether a better record of so strenuous an attempt can be shown. As many of the choirs were of tenderest age and not to be burdened with tasks beyond their untested powers, the works had to be chosen with an eye to " Safety first." Nevertheless, I was amazed at the results of their enthusiasm.

At a public banquet (honoured by the presence of Their Excellencies the Earl and Countess of Minto) given on the night of the State-opening of the Festivals in Ontario, I

took the opportunity of replying to a rather captious speech
—the solitary example of its kind—hinting at unnecessary
missions, by retorting that, while we were well aware of all
that had been done for music in the larger representative
cities, the rest of the Dominion was still a dry desert, and
that everyone needed reminding of the existence of such a
thing as British music. Of evidence that the yet uncultivated
land only needed ploughing there was abundance, for the
pioneers were everywhere received with open arms. Between three and four thousand voices were set a-singing.

There was no lack of ardour either on the part of the
singers or their hearers at St. John (New Brunswick), whence
we proceeded to Moncton where, although a small town,
I met an even larger choir again created for our purpose.
No choral work had ever been given there, and this was the
first occasion upon which an orchestra had performed; the
unique experience being mine of having every item on the
programme encored. The cantata (Elgar's *Banner of St.
George*), though a warm request was made, could not be
repeated. *The Little Minister* Overture had to be played
six times in three consecutive days.

At Halifax (Nova Scotia) we experienced deep snow and
an occasional blizzard. On the night of the first performance
I had to take a carefully calculated harlequin's leap from the
coach, which landed me into the stage-door, between the
violent gusts of wind. The steep streets became so dangerously slippery to the uninitiated that I accepted an invitation
to dinner only on the condition of being carried to and from
the hospitable club. The suggestion was willingly adopted,
and a quartet of stalwarts—one to each leg and arm—safely
deposited me at my destination.

Orchestral rehearsals were long and frequent. I was
compelled to hold one after the first evening concert which
began at eleven at night (we had been working since 10 a.m.),
and in spite of protestations that the lips of the wind
players could stand no more, dogged endurance enabled me
to get what I wanted.

Halifax had been musically active for some years, and could boast of a number of excellent resident musicians whose successful educational work was evident; the large choir was exceptionally well trained, and the defiant utterances of Sir Richard Greville would have delighted the composer of *The Revenge*.

The Montreal Symphony Orchestra did good service at this, the first group of concerts.

At "Bonnie Hamilton" (Ontario) the larger Chicago Symphony Orchestra of over fifty "pieces," did every justice to our compositions—of course hitherto unknown to it—and secured that cordial recognition invariably granted in crowded theatres, concert and drill halls, the latter holding from three to four thousand auditors.

Then to Brentford to face another newly-formed capital choir. The hardest day's labour was mapped out for us when starting, after an evening performance, we arrived at London (Ontario) at 2 a.m. The hour of 9.30 saw us rehearsing in the theatre, and at 12.30 we left by special train to give an afternoon concert in Woodstock, where I dispensed with the band—and food—contenting myself with a piano at the brief rehearsal held until the incoming tide of an eager public bade me stop. Noting that all the choristers wore badges of the Mackenzie tartan I had no fear of the result, knowing that they would follow their Chief when singing his *Cottar's Saturday Night*. When all had gone well, we sped back to London in time for *The Death of Minnehaha* and *The Dream of Jubal*. That perfect day ended with a reception and luxuriously appointed supper (frequently called luncheon in these parts) given by the Mayor. This brilliant function afforded further proof of the great interest taken by the municipal authorities; and another notable feature connected with the choirs was that representatives of all classes stood shoulder to shoulder in a common cause.

Sleeping-cars were not reached until 2 o'clock in the morning, and seven hours later I was quite ready for the

preparation of a concert to be given on the same evening in Toronto's magnificent Massey Hall. Mdme. Blauvelt, Ben Davies, Watkin Mills and Charles Fry joined our quartet of vocalists, and, with the Toronto Festival Chorus (350) and National Festival Choir (300), took prominent parts during the week.

Frequently when we played in theatres, the choir as well as part of the band occupied the stage, while I conducted in the centre of the house, from which conspicuous position all could see me. This happened again at Ottawa, when additional instruments and a military band (Elgar's *Coronation Ode*) occupied every available space, and the concert was again graced by the presence of the Governor-General and his amiable Countess.

The second section of the tour ended in Montreal, after a couple of concerts had been added; though only a single day's notice of the extension could be given to the local press, the large Windsor Hall was sold out on both occasions. Parry's *St. Cecilia's Day* was again performed and a repetition of *Jubal* had been requested, and as my forces were now thoroughly familiar with these cantatas, a more sympathetic rendering could not have been desired.

I now parted with the Chicago Orchestra which had loyally helped me through eighteen concerts and more than that number of rehearsals during fourteen days without hitch or trouble.[1]   On my entrance at the beginning of our last evening together I was received in old German fashion with a lusty *Tusch* (impromptu flourish on all instruments) from these hard-worked men, and the finish was a scene of gratifying enthusiasm.

A "Festival de Quebec," consisting of two concerts, was, for some occult reason, suddenly cancelled. My *Coronation March* and Harriss's *Coronation Mass* appeared on the programmes as *Marche du Sacre* and *Messe du Sacre*.

Hitherto all had passed off brilliantly, but trouble began

[1] The list of composers, on p. 218, whose works were studied, speaks for the band's zealous assistance and that of its conductor, Adolph Rosenbecker, whose place I occupied.

on our way to Manitoba, the long journey being held up for an entire night at a roadside station, the name of which was revealed, by the help of a dismal oil-lamp, as "Mackenzie."[1] The delay cancelled two preliminary rehearsals and a reception given by the Lieutenant-Governor, Sir Daniel McMillan, at Winnipeg. Hurried as our preparations had to be—I can see Impresario Harriss jumping into a passing fish-cart to rout out additional desks for the instrumentalists—the performances proved surprisingly good, as the large well-drilled choir was intensely eager for the fray.

On the first evening the only work by a foreign composer admitted to our programme was given by special request— *Elijah*. That Mendelssohn's masterpiece still awaited a *première* anywhere in 1903, and that I should be privileged to conduct it both amazed and gratified me. Upwards of 2,000 attended that concert, and among the audience at the succeeding matinée were 1,000 school children from whom our efforts seemed to meet with approbation. Some of them nudged each other whenever Miss Ethel Wood indulged in a flight into the upper register, and became positively apopletic with suppressed glee at the skirl of the bagpipes in *The Little Minister* music. Passing from gay to grave, *The Death of Minnehaha* was listened to by 4,000 adults on the same night. The cantata received every justice from the chorus and made a profound effect. Incoming trains brought many visitors; moreover, on my journey farther westward, I had occasion to note the keenness of the desire for music, and to hear of the well-intentioned efforts to raise more choirs. After the concert the Lieutenant-Governor gave his postponed reception and supper, at which we were made to forget that our train started for Brandon at 7 o'clock on the following morning.

"The Granary of the West" and "Baby" of the cycle had never seen an orchestra; but the recently-raised choir was much too keen about its work to fail. The associate conductor must have had much hard work, since a proportion

---

[1] Farther on we passed a station bearing my wife's maiden name, Burnside.

of the singers had to be taught the time-signatures and elements of music! This rag-time state of matters, though not applying to all its members, might well have discouraged the stoutest heart. The "Prairie Chorus," however, came out of the ordeal with credit to itself and Mr. Frank B. Fenwick, the resident musician. The manifest eagerness to establish a musical organization caused me to address the singers as the audience was reluctantly moving out, and those words of encouragement and thanks were as sincerely felt as they were spoken. All the seats had been disposed of two hours after the sale of tickets had been announced (three weeks previously). Owing to the foresight of residents in out-lying districts who had taken the precaution to send money-orders before the opening of the sale, many of the inhabitants were excluded from a concert in their own town. But it was impossible to meet the request to repeat the performance, as we had to leave for Vancouver on the same night. The attention of the audience was remarkable, and each piece might easily have been thrice repeated. Four hundred miles was not considered an unreasonable distance to travel for the pleasure of hearing music!

Here, alas, I bade adieu to my third orchestra (Danz's of Minneapolis), and with it went a considerable portion of my peace of mind.

Our eager desire to see the wonderful panorama of the Rockies was not gratified so soon as expected, for on waking up next morning we found ourselves but thirty miles from Brandon and likely to remain there, by reason of another wrecked freight-train in front. This became serious; the possibilities of making Vancouver in time to play on Monday evening (May 4) were fading rapidly. It took from Friday night to Monday evening to reach our destination, and that was only accomplished by putting on a fearsome speed during the latter part of the journey—by special permission—"consistent with safety." The return trip (under normal conditions) offered ample leisure to realize the nature of the track along-which we had been whisked—and be thankful. The surprising grandeur of the scenery made me forget all but the problem of keeping faith with the Vancouverians; and, after consultation, Harriss telegraphed to his agents to have the orchestra—an x quantity—ready for me in another hall at 6.30. There I rehearsed until the last moment; we then proceeded to the theatre in time to face the audience at 8.30. The chorus I had not met, but as the work in question happened to be my own *Cottar's Saturday Night*, I faced a chance which happily proved (chorally) to be no risk at all when I introduced myself on the public platform to a capital choir ready and able to save a most disconcerting situation. Doubtless my difficulty was Punch's secret, and sympathy played a large part in securing an unexpectedly good result—at least, in the estimation of a generously-disposed audience. Nevertheless, it was the most anxious evening I ever spent before the public. Lost time had to be recovered, and I dared not appear at the next forenoon's concert without a drastic drilling of so undisciplined and incompetent a band. A Chamber Concert was therefore hurriedly substituted in order to allow me to express my personal opinions to the musicians.

On the previous day my first words to the players conveyed a firm request to remove their pipes from their mouths during rehearsal. Unaccustomed familiarity and general demeanour necessitated the immediate assumption of mastery. To hesitate was to be lost. Ordinary courtesy went by the board and candid criticism worked wonders. I rehearsed assiduously the whole of that day, and at our appearance in the evening my friends were astounded at a vigorously-expressed demand for an encore. This had evidently never happened to them before; that none had ever wanted to hear them twice did not surprise me in the least. But the encouragement had the beneficial effect of rousing their mettle while raising me in their estimation. That I could give them " points " was now freely admitted, and a delegation waited upon me with a request to " come and have a drink after the concert." This invitation having been accepted, we now thoroughly understood one another. Thus after some, in several respects, rather uncomfortable days, we were enabled to perform even such works as *St. Cecilia's Day* very creditably.

The story ran as follows. Some weeks before I arrived the manager's advance agent approached the professional players in Vancouver offering them engagements. On seeing the music to be performed (their frankness one must admire) they honestly admitted that it was beyond their powers and experience, and that the offer could not be accepted. When, however, it was stated that other instrumentalists would of necessity have to be brought, an indignation meeting was forthwith held, at which the odd argument was advanced that, nevertheless, the members of the Union ought to be allowed to play the music as well as they could! Endeavours were then made to prevent others from appearing with me. I was told that on the day before my arrival on the scene a final attempt was made to dissuade the orchestra, gathered together from Seattle, Portland and Oregon, from performing; and even when I was rehearsing for the first time a meeting was being held outside.[1]

Fortunately the voices of these sweet charmers were ineffectual, and the strenuous opposition dwindled down to a curt refusal to let me have the services of a man (or even the instrument itself for a consideration) to play the side-drum.

Now here was an undertaking fraught with every good intention to music and musicians, one which could only result in benefiting the profession in the future, jeopardized by the action of its own members. In all probability I was better served by the absence of these men, for the least capable among them were loudest in clamouring for the " rights " of their precious Union.

[1] Nearer to America I never got than the purchase of a cabin-trunk to hold requisites for certain appearances at the great Chicago Exhibition of 1893. Saint Saëns, Joachim and others had, I believe, been likewise engaged to represent their countries, but the musical arrangements seem to have prospered ill, for, almost on the eve of departure, a short telegraphic message—doubtless also dispatched to the others—urged me to remain at home.

All this did not in the least upset my equilibrium or shorten my temper by an inch, for the counterbalancing pleasures were too numerous. But had the choral forces been feeble or less well prepared, the results might have been disastrous. I write in the hope that the then prevailing musical conditions no longer exist.

Between working hours our company availed itself of the Mayor's offer of a drive to Stanley Park, in which the huge trees, luxurious vegetation and magnificent views won admiration and astonishment. Nor did my countrymen of the St. Andrew's and Caledonian Society omit to complete the enjoyment of my visit to the " Garden City of the West " by calling a merry meeting of the representatives of the clans.

We entered the picturesque town of New Westminster on May 6 in the midst of a thunderstorm of tropical violence. Here Mayor Keary did the honours royally, his profuse hospitality being exhibited in divers ingenious ways, such as a sail and interesting visits to a log-sawing establishment and salmon cannery on the Fraser River, open-handed entertainments at his house, and, finally, by the illumination of the long and broad main street by electricity in the evening. The business of the hour was, however, not neglected before we sailed that night for the capital of British Columbia.

The German proverb, " *Alle guten Dinge sind drei,*" appealed forcibly to me when the steamer started several hours after the appointed time—probably because it was a " special." This third belatement since leaving Ontario was a less serious one, as I had all the afternoon before me for rehearsal, but it spoke volumes for the good-humour of the choirs which on each occasion waited patiently, and suffered altered arrangements without a murmur. This alert chorus distinguished itself by a remarkably fine quality of tone and quick responsiveness to the beat.

Many professional musicians of both sexes sang side by side with the amateurs, none shirking the long rehearsals. The aged Lieutenant-Governor, Sir Joly de Lotbinière, accompanied by many prominent citizens, officially attended the opening concert, entertaining us at luncheon on the following day. On that occasion he slyly thanked me for having brought so much "harmony" to the city. In my reply I modestly deprecated any such necessity, as so much "union" already prevailed. We both were delicately alluding to the fact that, at the moment, the number of simultaneously conducted industrial strikes did not exceed three!

The Mayor and Mrs. McCandlish also showed their good-will to the wandering minstrels by providing delightful drives through the surrounding country before their last concert. With which—an extra one, when Parry's and Taylor's cantatas were repeated—my duties ended; and after bidding farewell to many new-found friends, like Maeldune and his fellows, "Sadly we sailed away." There were moments when I experienced the sensation known as "a lump in the throat," and these occurred at Victoria, Vancouver and Montreal, when the choirs assembled at wharf and station to sing us out of sight—a tribute which invariably touched me deeply.

Though not privileged to perform in Quebec, the quaint beauty of the picturesque old city was shown me by an amiable cicerone, M. Lavigne (one of our associate-conductors), during a midnight drive to the famed Heights of Abraham, whence I enjoyed the gorgeous view over the St. Lawrence in brilliant moonlight before bidding farewell to Canada from the s.s. *Ionian*, which left at an early hour in the morning.

My reply to the oft-repeated question whether I had enjoyed any sport, was to the effect that I had killed four orchestras.

We had passed through the four seasons during these six or seven busy weeks—midwinter in Nova Scotia, spring in Ontario, summer in Manitoba, and midsummer in British Columbia. Each day brought new impressions and heightened interest. The indifference in the West to long journeys in search of an evening's music has already been mentioned. At stations on the vast prairie, where no vestige of a dwelling was visible, well-dressed people left the cars, stepped into their vehicles, and vanished seemingly into space. The picturesque costumes of mounted police, cowboys, Indians, Doukobours (Russians) coloured the constantly varying scene.

No information regarding the present state of matters musical in these regions is before me, but this traveller's tale of nearly a quarter of a century ago, of an artistic trip crammed full of pleasurable and anxious hours, humorous incidents, lavish hospitalities and speech-makings innumerable, truly depicts the then existing conditions.

In spite of difficulties and defects attendant upon an initial attempt to carry out so extensive an undertaking, the fact remains that many important vocal and instrumental works by W. S. Bennett, J. G. Bennett, Cliffe, Coleridge Taylor, Corder, Cowen, Elgar, German, Goring Thomas, Harriss, MacCunn, Parry, Sullivan, Stanford and William Wallace, had been introduced to an entire continent.[1] Blades of grass were made to grow where none grew before, inasmuch as fourteen choirs had been called into existence, orchestras were heard for the first time, and a general impetus given to music from one end of the Dominion to the other. This in no way detracted from the value of the efforts of those who had exerted their influence in the interests of the art in previous years in Nova Scotia and Ontario. They had done much and well. But it needed a far-reaching effort to cover the vast territory and to affect similarly so many fresh woods and pastures new. The egg was not made to stand on end without thought, risk, and, above all, enthusiasm.

The success of a scheme which undoubtedly left its mark was due to an English pioneer-musician who shouldered the entire responsibility, Dr. Charles A. E. Harriss of Ottawa,

---

[1] My principals were: (*Soprani*) Lilian Blauvelt, Millicent Brennan and Ethel Wood; (*Contralti*) Lilian Carter, Louise Clary, Jennie Rankin; (*Tenori*) Ben Davies, Wilfred Virgo; (*Bassi*) Reginald Davidson, Watkin Mills; (*Reciter*) Charles Fry; (*Accompanist*) Arthur Dovey.

who, since then, has directed several such artistic and patriotic enterprises throughout the Empire, with the able assistance of Dr. Henry Coward and others. Notably to his credit stands the formation of the huge " Imperial Choir " which, reaching the number of 10,000 voices at the British Empire Exhibition in 1924, earned richly-deserved popularity. Only the rare combination of an exceptional capacity for organization and highly-competent musicianship can achieve such —too soon forgotten—results.

The exploration of a wealthy mine of Canadian folk-song gave me interest and pleasure. Experts should have no difficulty in distinguishing between songs imported from France by the original settlers and those springing from the soil of their adopted country; in addition to which there is more than a flavour of the Indian, as well as of the older type of Scottish song, to be detected in them.

The outcome of my investigations was a *Canadian Rhapsodie*, played for the first time at a Philharmonic Concert in 1905.

CHAPTER XXVII

THE INTERNATIONALE MUSIK-GESELLSCHAFT CONGRESS IN VIENNA

IN February of 1905 an attempt was made to stimulate an interest in operetta on the music-hall stage. *The Knights of the Road* (by Henry A. Lytton)—an unpretentious piece of the tuneful English type once in vogue—had the advantage of a cast including Walter Hyde (now one of our most distinguished operatic tenors), Leslie Stiles, Cairns James, with the invaluable assistance of my friend Herman Finck and his admirably-trained orchestra, and ran for a month. If the venture did nothing else it induced King Edward and other members of the Royal Family successively to visit the Palace Theatre for the first time since " Variety " had replaced " Opera."

My election to the Presidentship of the *Internationale Musik-Gesellschaft* brought much additional work, in a hopeful cause, during the six years I filled that office. The Society then numbered many hundreds of the most notable musicians, professors and amateurs of all countries. Though the honour was by no means of my own seeking, many amusing glimpses into the idiosyncrasies of so large and mixed a membership, and the artistic enjoyment provided by the memorable celebration of Haydn's death during the Third Congress in May 1909, recompensed me for the time spent in its service.

Starting from Florence after a short rest, I travelled to Vienna via Venice. By chance, the journey from the Italian frontier (Villac) had to be made on the national holiday in celebration of Napoleon's defeat at Aspern. At every crowded station the picturesque costumes of the peasantry, patriotic Guilds and the military, offered a sight resembling a brilliant theatrical display. The interest was, however, tempered by the discomforts of heat, hunger and thirst suffered in closely-packed carriages, while the struggles to get within measurable distance of a buffet recalled the early days of Bayreuth, when a man in lawful possession of a sausage and a glass of lager was deemed a prime favourite of the gods.

Arriving many hours behind time, my first impression of the lively capital was that an insatiable craving for amusement effectually dissuaded its inhabitants from ever going to bed; and I looked forward with more pleasure to take a brief share in the merriment than in the endless series of lectures over which it would be my honourable privilege to preside within the walls of the University. May forgiveness be mine for the honest endeavour to skip as many of these as could discreetly be managed. An invitation to witness *Elektra* (under Weingartner) at the Imperial Opera awaited me, and occupying a front seat in the stalls—my neighbour the eminent Frenchman, Vincent D'Indy—we had the full benefit of the splendid orchestra delivered at closest quarters. The opera was given magnificently and, dramatically, unbowdlerized; for instance, the wretched king, preceded by the stampede of wild cattle, was savagely throttled on the ledge of a window, *corum populo*—an æsthetic episode omitted, I think, at Covent Garden. Mdlle. Marcella, equally fine an actress as a singer, surely the most realistic *protagonista* imaginable. The intermittent appearances of many beauty-spots we did not fail to admire.

At the end, however, the hitherto silent D'Indy crystallized his opinion into these words: " Three drunk women." I differed from him only in degree; the mother seemed to be a confirmed dipsomaniac, the sister a hopeless neurotic, and Elektra an incurable epileptic. Methought to have been living in St. Bart's with an occasional visit to Bedlam. Some of the German members suggested that their Herr President had probably heard that opera for the first time, to which he replied that he had just heard it for the last time: the small jest was duly circulated, and by no means to his detriment.

On returning to London my impressions were recorded in an "Epic," of which this excerpt should serve as a sufficient excuse for withholding the remainder.

> When shriek joined shriek, then came the tug of war.
> I thought so when you quarrelled with your Ma,
> Whose added yells made matters really serious;
> The orchestra, as well, became delirious.
> It squeaked, banged, roared, with emphasis percussive,
> The hideous din could hardly have been worse if
> Lucifer's own private band had made it,
> Himself had written, scored and played it.

Delegates from every Government, representatives of all nations, made up a concourse of music-lovers probably larger than had ever been gathered together. To an appropriately-named guide, Dr. Guido Adler (friend Hanslick's successor in the Chair of Musical History), I was indebted for safe conduct through the manifold duties of an exacting week.

After—as representative of the British Government—I had declared the Congress open, his Excellency Graf Stürkh (Minister of Education) followed with an eloquent address of welcome. I was to see more of this courteous man who, when in occupation of a more dangerous post in the Ministry, met his death, during the War, by assassination in a restaurant.

Viennese *bonhomie* found its natural expression when the famous Burgomeister Karl Luegger invited us all to a banquet at the Rathhaus. His popularity was unbounded; so was his outspokenness. When I presented myself that evening at the Rathhaus, he pleaded the excuse of approaching total blindness for inability to distinguish faces, adding, however, that he could recognize me.

"Ah, because of my lighthouse!" said I, pointing to a shiny scalp.

"*Kommens! Wir verstehen uns!*" (Come! We understand

each other!), he chuckled, dragging me to my seat beside him.

More than seven hundred guests were present in the spacious hall, in which a lavish feast was spread: food, wine and tobacco of exclusively Austrian produce. Picturing, in my speech on the previous morning, an imaginary meeting with Haydn, Mozart, Beethoven, Schubert and Brahms in the streets of Vienna, I had not forgotten the names of the popular dance composers Lanner, Gung'l and Strauss; and the Burgomeister had, in consequence, as he informed me, instructed the orchestra to enliven us with specimens of their genius.

When the Chief Magistrate addressed us, my table-neighbour whispered that the genial speaker was a doomed man; indeed, he only lived another year.

A humorous speech, delivered in homely dialect, did not end without some caustic references to his predecessors in office for having permitted the remains of the composer of their beautiful National Hymn to be removed from the city in which he died to Eisenstadt, at the insistent request of the Croatians. These, and other acidulated remarks, revealed that the several nationalitites under Austrian rule were not a quite happy family.

Having had no leisure to prepare a reply, I secured the Burgomeister's willingly-given permission to take some mild liberties concerning himself before I mounted the platform. Expressing regret at finding him to be merely a Doctor of Laws, I suggested that the first duty of our Congress was to confer upon him a degree really worth having—a Doctorate of Music. Recklessly bantering the pundits and professors by assuring the assembly that none of us was half so learned as we looked, I managed to shock some serious-minded and important delegates to the Congress, for observance of etiquette was strictly preserved among a class which seemed to be unduly concerned about its dignity. The audience was amused and a most agreeable sojourn prepared for myself. Nevertheless, the many onerous obligations were, I trust, dutifully fulfilled. Among them was a lecture on Mendelssohn—a subject chosen with special reference to the centenary of his birth in 1809—at the University.

I was prevented from joining a pilgrimage to Eisenstadt, where a Mass and other works were sung in the Bergpfarrkirche (Haydn's burial-place), and a reception held by Fürst Nikolaus Esterházy von Galanthia. Some enthusiastic London friends had provided themselves with a gigantic wreath, intending to lay it reverently on the composer's grave. A suitably large vehicle hired, the floral tribute placed thereon, they solemnly proceeded to the church—but unfortunately to the wrong one. They had driven to Haydn's first resting-place on the outskirts of the city. No one being about, after much knocking of doors they unearthed the sexton, who, in roughest Viennese, informed them, *"Der Haydn liegt überhaupt holt gor nit hier!"* (Haydn doesn't lie here at all), and gruffly bade them depart. Much fatigued, and with a now completely dilapidated garland, they drove back to the Bristol to be received with unseemly mirth.

We were honoured by an invitation to a reception at the Hofburg, at which I looked forward to a glimpse of the aged Kaiser Franz Josef, who, however, was represented by the Archduke Leopold Salvator on the occasion. Anything less like a similar function at our Court of St. James's can hardly be imagined. In addition to the male members of our society, a large number of generals, officers, and officials attended, their brilliant gala uniforms, plentifully adorned with much-coveted decorations, making a brave show. Entering the large reception hall by a mean and narrow back-staircase, I noted among the gorgeously arrayed company an elderly woman (of the charlady type) in rusty black, standing before an unmistakable pantry door busily wiping tumblers and glasses. The dame eyed us with an amused curiosity.

We stood three-deep in a queue which encircled the entire room (I, as President, at the head) awaiting the tardy arrival of the Erzherzog. Kept thus for a considerable time, the hum of conversation naturally rose high at intervals, but whenever the buzz exceeded the bounds of decorum an ancient, long-bearded and be-robed Chamberlain, who occupied the centre, called us to order by rapping loudly on the floor with his long white wand of office. The company certainly kept old Polonius knocking busily like a human woodpecker.

Learning that I had not travelled direct from London, conversation with the Archduke confined itself to "*das liebe Florenz*," as he called it—probably not without a remembrance of the House of Habsburg's lengthy but unwelcome stay in Italy—but of music no word passed. After he had made a round of the extended circle and departed, many footmen entered carrying trays laden with bonbons, every variety of pastry, sweet Sekt and wine-cup for the refection of the guests. Quantities of confectionery found their way into pockets. It should, however, be stated in fairness that those receptacles were not attached to the coats of members of our society. The strange custom seemed to be purely an indigenous, but nevertheless, a very odd one.

On leaving, I noticed the lady in faded black still grinning at the pantry door while assiduously wiping her dirty tumblers. That typical old Wienerin knew and must have seen much in her distinguished official capacity; yet I firmly believe her to have been the only native person present who wore no Orders.

The Congress was extremely well-planned and managed. Its artistic side was irreproachable, and the courtly hospitality dispensed on a lavish scale. From an historical point of view, among the most interesting performances were the revivals of Haydn's operas (again under Weingartner's direction), *L'Isola Disabitata* and the comic *Lo Speziale*, with their grotesque dresses, childlike humour and quaint music.

At the close, my final remark, "*Auf Wiedersehen* in London," was received with enthusiastic cheers. Although the bow was drawn at a venture, the idea materialized two years afterwards; but not before I had returned to Vienna on another pleasant errand.

CHAPTER XXVIII

THE SUN GOD'S RETURN: FOURTH CONGRESS OF THE
INTERNATIONALE MUSIK-GESELLSCHAFT IN LONDON

EVERY available opportunity seized to enlarge the so-called " rabbit-warren " in Tenterden Street only helped to make its maze of tortuous passages more bewildering; no additions could transform the old building into the semblance of a decent housing for its useful purposes. The ominous fact that, at the rapidly approaching termination of the lease, a national institution in vigorous health would be without a shelter had stared the authorities in the face for long, and every economical device had been practised in order to meet the ugly situation. These efforts were aided by a generous appreciation of impending danger on the part of our professors, whose claim to a more solid recognition of their services (though from the first I had made it my business to ameliorate the conditions to some extent) merited a much more liberal scale of acknowledgment than could be afforded.

Unduly irritating negotiations, protracted by prohibitive demands, proving utterly hopeless, the sudden relief, at the eleventh hour, from doom by the unexpected discovery and quick acquisition of a new site can readily be imagined. The load of care was lifted on June 10, 1910, when the foundation-stone of the new building was duly laid, in the absence of our Royal President, by Lord Strathcona.[1]

That our object had been patiently achieved by careful financial management and our own endeavour without public

---

[1] The Band of the Royal Engineers (conducted by an ex-student, Neville Flux) performed a programme of music by Edward German, Sullivan and Corder, to which was added a specially-written eight-part for voices by myself, " My Soul would drink those Echoes" from Byron's *Manfred*.

help or, notwithstanding assertions to the contrary, private donations in the brief space of twenty-two years, justified the pride shared with my colleagues on that day.

A cantata on which I had worked for a long time before discarding it on account of its length and other reasons, was then produced at Cardiff. The book, rewritten by J. Bennett, appealed much more to me in its new form. Our pleasant days of collaboration had been of long duration, though we sharply disagreed on many musical matters, and this was the last time we were to work together. After his retirement he withdrew to a remote place in his native Gloucestershire, and soon succumbed, as I believe, to the depressing effects of inactivity and ennui. I am his debtor for many acts of private and public kindness.

The Sun God's Return, with the effective aid of Miss Percival Allen, Walter Hyde, and a capitally-trained chorus, had a warm reception from a large audience. The verdict of the critics—delivered in some cases with Nasmythian vigour—was, however, so unfavourable that the work had only one other performance in England. To Dr. (now Sir) Henry Coward I owe that second opportunity, in Sheffield, for which he earned my lasting appreciation of his courage.

An excellent German translation offered the chance of testing the effect of the *Sun God* in a country never conspicuous for clemency of judgment upon our music. This wish was speedily gratified by an arrangement generously made by my friend Eisner von Eisenhof with the committee of the famous *Wiener Singakademie*. One could gather from the Press that the choral portions made unusual demands upon the singers, but our meetings were of the pleasantest and they (trained by Richard Wickenhauser) served me most willingly and well. Compared with the responsive alertness to which similar bodies at home have accustomed us, the Austrian choir moved more heavily and necessitated a corresponding amount of increased exertion on the part of the conductor. A short choral work by a German composer preceded mine.

Taking my experiences in connexion with Cardiff and

Sheffield into account, I was more than astonished at the unstinted praise accorded to the Cantata by the entire Viennese musical Press. Out of the many samples these three quotations will suffice:

We were more attuned by the other cantata, which sings in refined tones of the "Sonnen Gott's Heimkehr," the composer conducting his well-devised, ripely-thoughtful and carefully-written work: a youthful work of age. Mackenzie's music moves more in inner than in outward effects; and as he shows himself everywhere an experienced master and sterling musician we follow him unhesitatingly from darkness to light.—(Max Kalbeck in *Neues Wiener Tageblatt,* January 20, 1911.)

The work throughout contains good, even excellent music. In several moments beautiful and refined melody is revealed. To the honour of the Tone-poet be it said that the dangerous proximity to Niffelheim has not once led him to don Wotan's blue mantle. There was strong applause: on the whole an interesting evening.—(*Wiener Allegemeine Zeitung,* January 20.)

The choral writing combines technical skill and sonority, even in the plastic lines of a number of lyrical solo passages, and more fully in the reticence of the whole work, with its aristocratic absence of any violence of characterization. Always distinguished and well-schooled the music gains also in inspiration in the third part. The composer who conducted, received every honour.—(*Neue Freie Presse,* January 17.)

Thus Baldur passed the examination to which he had been submitted. H.I.H. Zita, Duchess of Parma, now the unfortunate ex-Empress of Austria, honoured the concert, and amiably congratulated me at its close. A merry supper, with speeches galore, followed the performance. When the company rose (about 3 o'clock) I imagined that the genial evening had ended. Not so! We left the restaurant to proceed to a café to consume the popular *Knickebein*—composed of raw eggs floating in some alcoholic decoction—until a much earlier hour.

Our proposal to hold the Fourth Music Congress in London was not made without due consideration of the responsibilities it involved. The project could only assume the shape of a voluntary effort to be backed by generously inclined lovers of music, and in a short time the Guarantee

Fund amounted to over £10,000. King George graciously granted his patronage, and Mr. A. J. Balfour willingly acceded to our request to act as President.[1] The Lord Mayor (Sir Thomas Vesey Strong) and certain City Companies offered ready help, and the complicated arrangements for sectional meetings, lectures, etc., were solved by the kind manner in which we were met by the University of London.

Some of us succeeded in winning our colleagues over to the opinion that this great gathering promised a rare chance of making our visitors from afar acquainted with the works of living British composers and of informing them definitely as to our progress in the art. We had had none but German music at the previous Congress, and that the strangers should be given a liberal dose of ours—*nolens volens*, while they were at our mercy—was, be it confessed, my fervent wish.

Thus twenty-eight composers, thirty British singers and players, and the following societies took part in a long chain of chamber, orchestral and choral concerts:

The Magpie Madrigal Society (Lionel Benson).
The Huddersfield Choral Society (W. G. McNaught).
The Choir of the Westminster Catholic Cathedral (R. R. Terry).
The Choir of St. Paul's Cathedral (G. Martin).
The Westminster Orchestral Society (Lennox Clayton).
The London Symphony Orchestra: Strings (Arthur W. Payne).
The Queen's Hall Orchestra (Assistant-Conductor, Dan Godfrey).
The String Band of the Royal Regiment of Artillery (E. C. Stretton).
The full Band of His Majesty's Coldstream Guards (J. Mackenzie Rogan).

Certain details find a place here in connexion with a unique event in our musical history. The head-quarters of the society were in Leipzig, and the delicate problem concerning the London habitat of a Congress office, Information Bureau, the sale of tickets, and other important matters, was solved by Messrs. Novello's compliance with our suggestion

[1] In the preface to the " Report of the Fourth Congress of the International Musical Society " (Novello & Co.)—to which readers are referred—it is stated: " No financial aid has been received from any Governmental or Municipal Authority, and the funds have been raised exclusively through the munificence of numerous private individuals and a few musical societies."

to act as business managers. Our success not only owed much to their energy, but the whole scheme could not have been carried out without the facilities so freely offered by the firm.

On the first day it was my privilege to welcome and introduce the delegates representing the Governments of fifteen nations to the President, after which Mr. Balfour, in one of those thoughtful and eloquent speeches in which he excels, addressed the visitors.

Hubert Parry then, in happy terms, referred to the " wonderful hardihood of the foreign members coming here in the spirit of generous enterprise to inquire if it is really true that, at last, there is some music in this country! " Good, seasonable banter!

The great Elizabethan, Restoration, and later periods were amply represented, and I believe that the event which gave the greatest satisfaction and earned unstinted praise then, and afterwards in the German press, was the special Service in St. Paul's under the care of the late Sir George Martin. His highly-trained choir offered such strikingly fine renderings of Gibbons, Purcell and Byrd that the eulogies were richly deserved.

The band and pipers of the Coldstream Guards (Director J. Mackenzie Rogan) also met with unqualified approval. As for the rest, I fancy that few of us 'scaped a whipping, more or less mild.

The many antiquaries, whose chief interest was centred in the historical concerts, may doubtless have preferred an enforcement of the rule which governed the programmes of our " Antient Concerts " and prohibited the inclusion of any work not, at least, twenty years old. The omission of *The Beggar's Opera*—seemingly the only British one worthy consideration—appeared to be a serious defect in the scheme. But there were no Playfairs or Austins to enable us to satisfy their curiosity. The late William Farren, when director of our dramatic class, suggested it as suitable for production at the R.A.M., and I, rather hastily, agreed to the proposal.

But on paying a visit to one of the early rehearsals I noted that the uncombed plot and dialogue retained so much of the æsthetic simplicity of its period that my error was realized in time. I therefore confessed to the dear old actor that we had overlooked the fact that the R.A.M. was an educational institution, and our modest curtain never rose upon a classic which might not have appealed to parents and guardians.

I keenly wished the differing English, Welsh, Irish and Scottish musical characteristics clearly displayed to the foreigners, but an appeal to my friend, Charles Stanford— *par excellence* the representative of his country's music—was unsuccessful, for he preferred to conduct the fine prelude to his *Stabat Mater*. To emphasize my own nationality a bagpipe chanter was mercilessly added to the wood-wind in the score of *Tam o' Shanter*, a specially-written *Scottish Rhapsody* (*No. III*).

The few composers who did not conduct had the benefit of the experienced Dan Godfrey's services. The list of items presented is too long for detailed mention, but the efforts of our then living composers—Vaughan Williams, Stanford, Parry, Walford Davies, Carse, Holbrooke, Bell, Cowen, Corder, Elgar, Ethel Smyth, Edward German, William Wallace, Balfour Gardiner, Norman O'Neill, Charles Wood, and Coleridge Taylor—did honour to an exceptionally gratifying display of native genius.

It was hardly surprising that towards the end of the conference many of our guests showed signs of fatigue. Had not eighty-five papers of an erudite nature been read, ten concerts been listened to, and six receptions of a generously hospitable kind been attended within six days? Messrs. Novello provided an admirable opportunity for an informal gathering on the first evening. The Lord Mayor's invitation to the Mansion House satisfied more interests than those merely musical. The Worshipful Company of Grocers entertained in the lavish manner for which the City of London is famous. A flood of champagne arose, sufficient to float the Ark, and more than once rapidly dried up. Ararats of plovers' eggs—in an r-less month the oyster's substitute—disappeared as quickly. If appreciative curiosity meant anything, then that dainty was undoubtedly the success of the Congress. I had to answer innumerable inquiries regarding the ornithological species to which it belonged, and sincerely hope that none was misled by the assurance of the repeated reply, "*Kiebitz Eier.*" For all I know, it may have been the cause of much subsequent scientific speculation on the bird's relation to, and influence on, British Art.

By the courtesy of Viscount Burnham, a genial reception took place at the offices of *The Daily Telegraph*, whence, after witnessing the printing of a great newspaper, the delegates passed into "the Street of Ink" refreshed, and with the morning issue in their pockets. The Government also bestowed its blessing by inviting the male foreign members to a luncheon, after which the presiding genius, Earl Beauchamp, kindly escorted the company through both Houses of Parliament to Westminster Hall. Keenly appreciated as the gratifying recognition was by us, we did not consider it necessary to inform our friends that this was the first time that a body of musicians had been entertained by the British Government.

A jovial banquet celebrated the conclusion of an exciting week, when the Lord Mayor made a humorously appropriate and sympathetic speech, which, followed by some remarks by myself, was responded to by Dr. Herman Kretschmar (Joachim's successor at the Hochschule in Berlin), Dr. Guido Adler (Vienna), and Dr. Echorchéville (Paris). The bandmaster contrived to play a goodly number of National Anthems, but the many countries represented could not all receive that customary honour; the missing tributes were, however, enthusiastically supplied by unprepared vocal efforts—with odd results. Alas, several of these melodies shed their popularity within the succeeding three years.

My words were limited to congratulations on the powers of endurance displayed while listening to so much of our music, which seemed to have had no more serious effect than that of producing mild attacks of home-sickness in a few of the less robust of our guests. Far from apologizing, I pointed out that it would have been easy to have done justice to other worthy names had time permitted. I also anticipated some remarks subsequently made by the frank-spoken Parisian delegate concerning the differentiations noticeable in our works.

Kretschmar (Berlin) confined himself to expressions of admiration of English life, the enormous street-traffic, the wonderful trees in our public parks, and the kindness of the poor to animals. "Nobody can leave this marvellous country without a strong desire to return and stay here for ever!"

The Frenchman spoke so much more to the point that this excerpt may usefully be quoted:

In the first place there is that mixture of races that gives to the Islanders the poise of their character. Have we not seen represenetd in one and the same programme the Scotchman (Mackenzie), the Irishman (Stanford), the Welshman (Parry), and the man from the Midlands, the Anglo-Saxon Elgar? Moreover—and this is a very English characteristic—your music is wholesome. It avoids that perpetual sense of irritation with which continental music is afflicted, that aggressiveness which in France gives the impression that our music is always, so to speak, levelled vindictively at someone! Your Art is that of a people of sporting habits, which pays more attention to its muscles than its nerves. . . . This zeal for the mingling and concentration of the most widely different elements is so much a part of your temperament that our labours at the Congress have been given a quite unforeseen instance of it, which has earned our admiration in all its aspects.

Delivered with evident sincerity, these opinions indicated that our wholesome and muscular music had made a favourable impression on the speaker.

So ended an enterprise—difficult of repetition and hardly estimated at its full value at the time—which made strenuous calls upon the energies of many who lent willing aid to ensure its success. M. Echorchéville presided over a final Congress in Paris in 1913, which I could not attend; and, to our sorrow, the gallant musician met his death fighting in the Great War.

Then the North German section, from Leipzig, took upon itself to declare the society dissolved; an attitude beyond the right of any unit to assume. Suspended, moribund though the I.M.S. was, its British section, resenting the proclamation, declined to accept dismissal and continued legally to exist until its committee, with the consent of every section, brought it to an end. At least, it met an honourable death at its own bidding, and not at the command of another's.

Unfortunately, I could not invite the strangers to the R.A.M. The new building was not yet at a stage of advancement to be shown, and the old home was in a transition state preparatory to our approaching migration. When we were fully equipped and ready to receive our students, a famous architect, then entrusted with the plans for the construction of the new Conservatorium in Vienna, visited me in order to glean any useful information. Similar erections in that capital being on so gigantic and imposing a scale, no more than a few complimentary remarks were expected, but he and several attendant experts expressed high approval of the handsome exterior and spacious interior of the school. That which compelled their frank wonder was the lavish manner in which the class-rooms were furnished. Such comfort! Such carpets! The latter greatly impressed them. I recollected my own impressions when shown over the old Vienna School of Music with its bare-floored rooms containing cheap tables and a few skinny chairs. Even No. 4 Tenterden Street has no cause to be ashamed, I thought. But when my visitors exclaimed, " Your English Government must treat the art of music with an astonishing liberality quite unknown to ours," it became necessary to ask them to bestow their admiration upon someone else, as the Government had not contributed one farthing towards either the building or its equipment; and I explained that all they saw had been done by our own unaided efforts. Famos! Kolossal!

CHAPTER XXIX

WOMEN COMPOSERS: EISTEDDFOD HUMOUR: HANS RICHTER:
PAOLO TOSTI: AND SOME OTHERS

IT was not so easy to be off with the old love as some of
us imagined. When the students played Haydn's *Farewell
Symphony*, blew their candles out, and left me alone at
the conductor's desk, my few valedictory words were uttered
with difficulty—certainly with mixed feelings of sadness and
gladness—for here I had already spent the best half of my
life, and I almost felt that my appointed services were at an
end.

The official opening of the rejuvenated school, though
work had been in full blast for three months, had to be postponed until the completion of the Duke's Hall provided the
fitting moment. In the unavoidable absence of our President,
H.R.H. the Duke of Connaught and Strathearn—whose
undiminished interest and sympathetic encouragement the
Academy has enjoyed for a period of over twenty-five years
—his son H.R.H. Prince Arthur graciously consented to
preside at the ceremony, when an orchestra of ninety students
and a female choir of a hundred voices took part in a short
concert in which the most notable item consisted of a motet,
Sing unto God, in fifty parts, for ten separate five-part choirs,
with organ, harps, trumpets, and drums. This unique and
complex piece of music, by Frederick Corder, proved an
extraordinary feat of ingenuity such as could only have been
attempted by a master of his craft.

To the best of my belief, during my student-days neither
female professors nor girl-violinists were seen in the Academy.
It was not until Mde. Norman Neruda—who, a child of

235

nine, made her first appearance at a Philharmonic concert—
blew her tempter's pipe in the early 'seventies, that

> Little hands clapping, and little tongues chattering,
> Like fowls in a barn-yard—when barley is scattering
> Out came the children running.

Violin worship soon spread itself to that of the 'cello.
Now, there is hardly an orchestral instrument, from double-
bass to piccolo, that is not in the hands or on the lips of
capable lady performers.

The best-trained female teachers had a long tussle for
recognition. My own conviction of their worth and desire
to help met with constant opposition from an unexpected
quarter: the rooted objection of young women to be instructed by members of their own sex! Strange logic! Were
not the pupil's future interests identical with those whose
capabilities they refused to acknowledge? These obstacles
were overridden *poco a poco*, and the present list of female
teachers contains the names of thirty-seven full professors
and thirty-five "subs" in active service.

Like Sheridan's Spanish Fleet, the female composer was
not yet in sight. Augusta Holmès—an Irish girl born in
Paris (1847), and a pupil of César Franck—is the first one
of lofty ideals and serious achievement within my early ken.
Possessed of great personal charm and firm resolution, the
pioneer-composer gave a stimulating impetus to a new
development of female talent which no amount of maiden's
prayers had been able to call forth. Why so little of her
virile music was ever heard here is due either to unbelief on
our part at the time, or to the lady's own indifference in her
later years. But Henry J. Wood, in his early conducting-
days, did give us a hearing of her symphonic poem *Irlande*.

Special opportunities for watching the progressive results
of half a century have been mine, and I may venture on the
supposition that there are more *Compositrice*—some exceptionally gifted—now working in this country than elsewhere.
The movement culminates successfully in the person of an
Englishwoman whose artistic endowments and gladiatorial

vigour fall no whit below those of her predecessor. My friend Dame Ethel Smyth's championship of the cause has effectually silenced the once familiar, now forgotten, remark, "Good—for a woman!" and deserves in fullest measure, the recognition which her music—irrespective of sex—has won for her.

Friends, when twitting the recipient of many University degrees and other honours, forget that the catalogue is incomplete without the mention of " Pencerrd Alban," a Bardic title bestowed on him, to the accompaniment of a brass band, on the famous rocking-stone at Pontypridd one fine morning at eight o'clock. Always in cordial sympathy with the aims of these national festivals, their time-honoured rites and quaint ceremonies adding a peculiar interest, I agreed to serve on two occasions as principal adjudicator at the Eisteddfodau held there and at Newport (Mon.).

Great changes, both in music and manners, have doubtless taken place in recent times, but my experiences in 1903-4 must be included in my list of adventures, for, despite the venerable Arch-Druid's repeated opening formula, " Is it Peace?" I then saw but little tranquillity.

At the conclusion of the Eisteddfod at Pontypridd— where I learned much regarding the inner workings of these meetings—the constable who had attended to me all that day cheerily informed me that it was " Quite safe, sir," when I rose to leave. The utterance might have been made with less confidence at Newport in the following year, when a splendid body of well-groomed stalwarts were received with prolonged howls of disapproval on appearing on the platform to compete with another male choir. An ugly interference with the wooden benches began, a cordon of police was drawn round the hall, and sufficient order restored to allow us to listen to an admirable rendering of an unaccompanied Psalm by Mendelssohn. To add to the turmoil, a violent thunderstorm broke out just at the right moment. I was given to understand that the cause of the disturbance was the unfair advantage taken by the offending choir in having secured the services of a London trainer in order to improve its methods of singing! Small wonder that the intonation became slightly uncertain during the last few bars, considering that the singers, immovable as rocks, had faced the ravings of the crowd for nearly thirty minutes! The second, and inferior, choir, having had no such exciting trial to undergo, kept in tune and gained the prize which I rather reluctantly awarded to them. Only hard facts count on these occasions.

Hungry and tired, I left the box in which we had been cooped all day, and mounted the platform to bid the committee good-bye. They detained me with offers of cigars and refreshment, but the repeated invitations to remain excited my suspicions, and to a final query the answer came, " They are waiting for you." What manner of greeting, friendly or other, awaited me, or who " they " were, did not affect my determination to go at once. That decision being made definitely known, the late "Mabon" (the miners' popular M.P.) ordered a cab to come to another entrance, and, insisting upon accompanying me, we drove through back streets to my hotel, in which, following a hint, I remained for the rest of the evening. Music hath charms!

One may readily believe that, after a lapse of twenty-six years, the more serious appreciation of a higher-class musical education has worked wonders; indeed I have reason to know that this is the case. But at the time of which I speak, it grieved me deeply to witness the possession of rare natural gifts and exceptionally beautiful voices spoiled by uncontrolled excitement and a deplorable disinclination to profit by well-meant advice.[1]

Though Hans Richter and I had met occasionally in earlier years, it was not until the Birmingham Festival of 1885 that the intimacy was formed which lasted until the great conductor left England; during that long period I received nothing but kindness and encouragement at his hands.

At his request, my *Violin Concerto* was played immediately

---

[1] Sir Hubert Herkomer, R.A., who had spent much time and trouble in an attempt to foster a greater interest in his own art, told me, during our homeward journey, that he had reluctantly arrived at a similar conclusion.

by Rosé, at Vienna, and he always found a place for a work of mine in his London programmes—indeed, often rallied me on my supposed laziness.   This generous readiness was shown when the second performance of *Britannia* was given by him, within a few days, without any communication having passed between us on the subject.

The burly Hans, who certainly behaved liberally towards one or two of us in whom he took an interest, once excused himself to me for not introducing more of our compositions to the Austrian public on the grounds that he had to avoid the spiteful suggestion that he was repaying us for the popularity he enjoyed in England; nor was I disinclined to believe in the sincerity of his diplomacy.

Our early orchestral upbringing, many musical sympathies and opinions shared in common, and, above all, the joy of exchanging them in his own vernacular in the days when his English was a source of delight to all, made it easy for us to become more than mere acquaintances.   Outside his own intimate circle of German friends it was thus my chance privilege to learn more of his character than any of my colleagues.   Identified as he was with those splendidly sane interpretations of the classics and the works of his adored master, Richter's innate likings extended over a far wider range of music than his admiring public was permitted to guess.   Any poking about with the baton into the leaves of Beethoven's scores in search of effects undreamed of by the composer roused his ire, and there was cause enough at times. His cordial detestation of ultra-modernism in art and posturings of every kind was unconcealed.   Richter's scrupulous care over seeming trifles came within my ken when we both had announced a performance of a little-known symphony by Mozart, and discovered the " clash " too late for either of us to withdraw the work.   An obvious misprint of one note in the viola part had puzzled me; and in answer to a request for his opinion he suggested an alteration with which, however, I could not agree.   I then substituted another note, and immediately received a message to the effect that he had adopted my view. All this with reference to a single quaver. Always helpful, when the "Ninth" was performed at the Philharmonic (with the assistance of the Leeds Choir) in 1899, he came to the R.A.M. in order to write into my score Wagner's strengthening alterations in the wind parts of the Scherzo.

Seated opposite to him at supper after the concert at which Elgar's *Enigma Variations* were so successfully introduced to the public, I heard the enthusiastic terms of admiration, shared by us all, which the conductor addressed to the composer.

Some time before his departure from Manchester, Richter's precarious state of health caused great anxiety to his friends. It must have been at the time of his last appearance at Covent Garden (not many months before the "Declaration") that he asked me to dine alone with him at Oddenino's, when I found him much more like the hearty, frolicsome Hans of old than I expected. That night, at least, he seemed determined to have a good time, for we sat late, talked incessantly, and after good red wine (*quant. suff.*) he insisted upon finishing with champagne. After a long evening's interchange of vigorously delivered judgments upon all and sundry, he declared, with genial satisfaction, "*Wir hob'n uns weidlich ausg'schimpt!*" (We've thoroughly abused everybody), and that he felt relieved. Parting at the door of his temporary abode in Bedford Square Mansions, I saw him no more.

"When I retire, I shall occupy myself with Bach, only Bach." Coming from one whose artistic life had been chiefly devoted to Wagner, the statement conveyed much and was seriously meant.

Soft, long drawn-out wails, as from a distant siren, "*Hu . . . uh!*" alternating with nudgings and mutterings; "*Ma, che genere di musica!*" "*Hu . . . uh! Io mi ne vado!*" "*Hu . . . uh!*" "*Mamma Mia!*" "*Che Porcheria!*" "*Dio bono!*" The admonition, "*Stai zitto, non puoi scapare,*" was whispered by my daughter into the ear of a sensitive Italian musician during a certain German Opera at Covent Garden. My tastes, formed in the schools of several countries, permitted a sympathetic understanding of Paolo Tosti's internal sufferings when music spake uncomfortably and in an unfamiliar tongue to him.

Our friendship dated from an invitation to meet his artistic compatriots at a well-known restaurant (then consisting of one small room) which reached me *via* that eccentric master-caricaturist, Carlo Pellegrini—" Ape," but better known as " Pelican." Exceptional popularity did not spoil Tosti, who, aware of his limitations, invariably spoke as modestly of his own talents as he liberally acknowledged the merits of his colleagues, and whose house and helping hand were ever generously open to his own countrymen as well as to native-born musicians. To my knowledge, he was a better friend to the latter than he got credit for.

My family became firmly attached to the kind-natured, amusingly satirical, at times irrepressible, man of the world, who rarely failed to appear at my house on Sunday mornings to exchange greetings and merry sallies.

But there were two Tostis. Among other later publications, the *Quattro Canzoni di Amaranta* go far to prove that he deserved a much higher reputation than that of the mere drawing-room melodist by which he was chiefly known, for he was a skilled and serious musician, with a rare knowledge of his beloved Italian art generally, and Opera—past and present—particularly.

Long-deceased violinists both, we discovered, one evening at a friend's house, that De Bériot's *Scène de Ballet* had been one of our favourite *chevaux de bataille*, and forthwith essayed to perform it from memory. Beginning as accompanist, I presently seized the violin and continued the solo part, while Tosti rushed to occupy my place at the piano. Thus, turn about, we managed to finish the piece to the amusement of the company, whose duty it became to award the palm to the worst player. I fancy that the verdict was given in my favour.[1]

[1] Under the stage name of Mdlle. Baldi, the charming and witty Lady Tosti appeared in *Colomba* as Lydia. Our friend survived her lamented husband who died at Rome in 1916.

Nature did not endow me with that somewhat overrated gift, the sense of so-called " absolute pitch," although—as a violinist—I easily acquired it. But my " ear " has always been exceptionally keen; indeed, I have often thought that too delicate a sense of hearing may be the reverse of a blessing. It was my lot to experience one of the most distressing afflictions that can befall a musician, when, from overstrain, his ear not only deceives him, but when every musical sound causes acute suffering.

Hubert Parry's diary records that, as the result of a cold, he heard some notes a tone and a half higher than their normal pitch. And Manns complained bitterly to me that for a considerable time certain wind-instruments sounded a third higher than others, although, as a conductor, he had to conceal the fact.

I had to conduct a full orchestra on one occasion at St. Paul's, and at the rehearsal the brass sounded like nothing earthly; while the horns, in particular, provided a series of agonizing aural stabs. At the following day's performance I could only get through the piece by automatically following the first violins and totally ignoring the blatant chaos produced by the orchestra. Nor was my anxiety relieved when during a choral rehearsal at the R.A.M. the male voices treated me to similar, though somewhat less painful, effects. The phenomenon lasted for several weeks; in time, however, my hearing was gradually restored to its normal condition.

CHAPTER XXX

SOME " MIGHT-HAVE-BEENS " : THE WAR AND AFTER

LABOUR conquers everything. If that ancient adage always proved as accurate as stimulating, the sum of many a composer's opus numbers would be considerably augmented; but ruins of reluctantly discarded projects and reams of damaged music paper, representing so much fruitless occupation, raise doubts regarding its reliability. "These are our failures," said the Beau, pointing to a heap of spoiled neckties. My collection of " might-have-beens " is a fairly large one, and is mentioned merely in evidence of much love's labour lost.

There was a Grand Opera in four Acts, dealing with Duke Alva and the Netherlands on a Meyerbeerian scale, of which a large portion was sketched before the hopelessness of a production deterred further progress.

Also, a Comic Opera in three Acts (by B. C. Stephenson) completed and—shelved. Then, partly-written, the attractive *Luthier de Crémone* (translated and adapted at my request by Sutherland Edwards), the libretto of which was lost without hope of recovery. When almost fully sketched, the same unkind fate pursued a one-act opera on a Cornish subject by F. Corder. The book passed into Augustus Harris's hands at his own bidding, not many weeks before his death; but, after that event, search and inquiry failed to restore it to its owner.

The chief expenditure of time and thought was the composition of an Oratorio in three parts on the subject of "Paradise Regained." I had made a selection from Milton's wondrous lines with the view to a short sacred work, and shown it to Alfred Lyttelton, who, to my astonishment, not only urged the adoption of the entire poem, but assisted me enthusiastically in reducing it to reasonable dimensions. Engaged on this engrossing task, we met frequently and corresponded constantly, with the result that I devoted the leisure of several years to the completion of *The Temptation*. My friend's death in 1914 discouraged, and the War prevented, me from giving further attention to its future.

There are retrospective moments when I incline to corroborate Bülow's assertion that composition was the most expensive amusement he knew.

Premonitory signs of the ghastly calamity about to befall Europe were not wanting, though their significance passed unperceived at the time. I recall several visits from foreigners during the immediately preceding months, who expressed a keen interest in the Academy. One of them, a Swede(?) of polished manners and a perfect command of our language, while disavowing any intention of making use of his voice except as an amateur, asked me to hear him sing; and a professional interest in architecture also prompted the request to be allowed to inspect the interior of the building, over which I personally conducted him. On returning a few days later, the musical enthusiast frankly admitted that he had visited the Royal College to have his voice tested again, with the result that he proposed to take a course of lessons in Milan. Could I recommend a reliable teacher there? This led to a conversation in Italian, but on being addressed in German he professed to have but the scantiest knowledge of a language so closely allied to his own. The statement seemed an extremely odd one.

We parted amicably and the incident was forgotten until, during the early months of the War, a courteous letter of thanks—without a clue to the sender's address—for my patient attentions recalled it. An admirable sample of polite cynicism.

Another case was of a much less agreeable kind. One evening when I had left the school to attend a meeting of the Associated Board, a stranger, speaking no English, insisted upon seeing me instanter on the plea that an appointment had been made with him (untrue). Unable either to converse with or get rid of the importunate, the R.A.M. officials called me to the telephone, over which a harsh, insolent voice informed me that its owner (an Austrian) brought recommendations from Viennese friends (untrue) and must see me at once. Was I returning to the Academy that evening? No, I don't sleep there! Eventually I agreed to meet him on the following day. Behold, no Viennese, but an unmistakable Berliner of rough speech and irritating manners. Herr Müller, a tenor who had sung in the Albert Hall (untrue), wanted to see the Academy as he was leaving London that evening. Why? To numerous strange questions my answers became more and more curt.

" Your professors, of course, are chiefly Germans? "

" Certainly not. Do you think that we can't do without them? "

" Where can I see Sir Parrree? "

" Go to the Royal College."

" And Sir Henree Voot? "

" Go to Rome; he is there just now."

" How can I get quickly to Charring Crrross? "

My door then opened suddenly and the parting guest was speeded with the advice to " ask the hall porter." Totally unfit to conduct diplomatic inquiries, the pseudo tenor—whose wish had nevertheless been foolishly gratified—left me mystified, though happy in the knowledge that I had been uncommonly rude to him. Evidently, however, London's spacious buildings had become of sudden interest to someone or other.

Nor were these the only booby-traps within my recollection. This is not a detective story, but there were occasions when I felt inclined to consult Sherlock Holmes in his rooms, close by, anent the possible object of these visits and a long series of anonymous communications, in prose and verse, which reached me, from various bogus addresses in London, during these anxious years.

Not long before the " Declaration " my *Cricket*, ætat

twelve, sang for a week in a series of excellent performances (with a double cast) on the Academy hearth. Many of the young actors and actresses whose lively support gave me so much pleasure are now well known on the English operatic stage. To mark its appreciation of the event, the student-company presented me with a silver kettle, which " began it" by sending forth clouds of steam—produced by liquid oxygen —at a merry tea-party, none guessing that our stage would henceforth be occupied solely by female students who, when put to the test, thought it great sport to continue the operatic and dramatic classes without interruption during the grim time before us.

Of these four years memory retains but a confused jumble of nightmarish happenings now impossible to co-ordinate sequentially.

The male students, younger professors, the then lately appointed secretary, Mr. J. A. Creighton[1] and his clerical assistants, disappeared, leaving only a few youngsters in what had become a girls' school. The young women contrived to combine many varied patriotic duties and a consistently regular attendance at their classes with never-failing cheerfulness and amazing self-possession; indeed, my admiration of their endurance and calm behaviour, from the exemplary Lady-Superintendent (Mrs. Florence Russell) to the youngest pupil, is as warm as ever. After a raid, when—as it chanced on several occasions—some of their own or their neighbours' dwellings had been mauled, I invariably found them in their seats at rehearsal as if nothing particularly disturbing had occurred to upset their equilibrium. Far, indeed, from any public performance having to be omitted, or signs of slackness either of discipline or zeal observable, a determination to uphold the normal standard of excellence and the honour of the institution was exceptionally keen.[2]

[1] Able successor to the regretted Mr. F. W. Renaut, who died, after a prolonged illness, a few months previously.
[2] To my hard-worked staff of highly competent female substitutes (with the kind-hearted deputy-secretary, Mr. P. Quarry, in command) more than a passing word of gratitude for its eager and faithful service is due.

One would rather forget than remember the trials of those days, but who can refrain from acknowledging the support and confidence which that splendidly-resolute spirit —prevailing among all and in every corner of our land— inspired in those in authority? To me it was a source of daily wonder and pride. When on leave from France, our lads seemed at once to be irresistibly attracted to their Alma Mater, where an affectionate welcome from young and old awaited them. How often have I noted the sudden transition from boy to man. Some, alas! paid us their last visit.

Early in 1919 it became my sad duty—on behalf of the Incorporated Society of Musicians—to read from the pulpit of Southwark Cathedral the long list of all the ascertainable names of our professional colleagues who had fallen for their country.

Even more touching, because personally nearer to us, was the solemn Service in memory of the lost students of the two united schools, when the choirs of the Royal College of Music and the Temple (under Hugh P. Allen and Walford Davies) sang an impressive Motet by Parry, and other works, and the violinists of the Royal Academy played Corder's *Elegy* and my Postlude *In Memoriam* in the ancient church, with an indescribable effect upon a large assembly of mourners.

Shortly after the Armistice, so large a number of students flocked to the Academy from all quarters of the globe, as if to recover lost and precious time, that the wishes of many intending entrants had perforce to be disappointed. Then arose the trying question of the admittance of those ex-Service men who had to be tested individually before their claims to Government aid could be granted or withheld. That responsibility was of the gravest, since the decisions affected not only their own vital interests, but, in no small measure, those of the musical profession. Placed between sympathy and duty, these often distressing and occasionally lively interviews brought me into contact with all sorts and conditions of " human various." Even in very favourable cases, the pitiful fact remained that the most valuable period for study had been irretrievably lost.

A prevailing belief that proficiency in our art is attainable within a limited space of time, and that the possession of a voice (more or less) suffices without further musical (or other) knowledge, was frequently confirmed. Not a few seized the chance of getting off uncomfortable office stools or quitting uncongenial occupations in hopes of a fancied soft job.

One weedy little man, well over forty, treated me to a self-confident display of childish fooling on the keyboard, and in answer to a question stated that he was a tailor by trade.

" And what is the matter with tailoring? You'll just have to go back to it," said I.

Then came the reply, " Oh, it is such nervous work! "

As my inability to concede that my own profession was a less nervy one did not improve his politeness or diminish his persistency, I fear that we parted on unfriendly terms.

Alternating between tragedy and comedy, these critical sittings occupied my daily attention for many months and were conducted in the keenest spirit of fairness. During the ensuing three or four years the R.A.M. became the busiest hive of tractable working-bees imaginable, for very few of those—there were hundreds—deemed worthy the liberal Governmental help disappointed us in the results of the educational opportunities placed within their reach; indeed I was able to congratulate a goodly number publicly on their assiduity and well-merited success.

The grievous personal loss caused by the passing of Hubert Parry affected me deeply. An attempt to do justice to his worth, in a lecture given at the Royal Institution not long after his death in 1919, necessitated a careful reperusal of his compositions. Though familiar with them all, I was unsuccessful in my search for information as to whether a revised and expanded edition of his last cantata, *The Vision of Life*, had remained in manuscript or had been printed. In what would presumably be called a psychic dream by the illuminati, Parry entered my room and said gently, " You are quite right, Mac; the new edition is printed and ready for Norwich." My eyes were streaming with tears when I awoke, and so vivid was the impression that I could hardly persuade myself that I had not been visited by my old friend. The statement regarding the cantata proved to be correct. My " vision " might, however, be readily explained on less far-fetched grounds.

The privilege of an intimate association with three successive Directors and of having been on friendliest footing with all connected with the sister-school at South Kensington, affords me unmixed satisfaction. That its present chief, Sir Hugh P. Allen, extends the same amity to me adds to the pleasures of memory.

The prized " Fellowship " granted me (the first offered to anyone not belonging to the corporate body) sums up the tale of a long period of combined endeavour conducted in unbroken goodfellowship.

On the occasion when, my approaching retirement becoming known, my colleagues of the R.C.M. honoured me with an invitation to an informal dinner at their institution, I heard the voice of that other friend, the versatile, impulsive, kind-hearted Irish genius Charles V. Stanford for the last time.

Jack was in danger of becoming a dull dog during wartime had he not sought and found recreation and distraction in the composition of an opera in one Act by Eleanor Farjeon —an authoress of inherited literary gifts and musical talent— entitled *The Eve of St. John*. Whether the merry little piece pleased its hearers, five years after completion, as much as it cheered me while in its making, matters not. It was mainly owing to the generosity of the Committee of the Carnegie Trust—always helpful to the aspirations of young (!) composers—that, by relieving me of the expense of supplying the copied material (full score, orchestral parts, etc.) I was able to offer it to the British National Opera Company in hopes of a production, which eventually took place at Liverpool in April, 1924. Thanks to the goodwill of a talented cast (Doris Lemon, Muriel Brunskill, Walter Hyde and William Michael) under Julius Harrison's skilful conductorship, I have never been present at any *première* of mine which gave me less anxiety or more enjoyment than on that occasion, when I had the cordial co-operation of all concerned.

Not all the names of the many men, eminent in every department of Art and Science, within whose orbits chance and good fortune have carried me, can appear in these pages; to not a few of them I owe not only valuable instruction and the pleasure of congenial intercourse, but a wider interest in much that lay beyond the scope of my vocation. Among these the very greatest were invariably the most unassuming and frankly out-spoken.

None drew me so near, by sheer force of personality, as that heroic figure in science, the late Sir James Dewar, whose friendship I prized for nearly half a life-time. Though permitted on more than one occasion to watch the supple fingers at work on some wonder in the making, of these triumphs it behoves an ignoramus to be silent; but of his love and knowledge of art and literature I may safely speak.[1]

No mere dilettante, this man of rare imagination, in whose heart—after the fascination of scientific research—music undoubtedly held the first place, but an arts-man of genius and a critic of generous sympathies and sharp judgment. While close intimacy failed to penetrate the modest reserve which guarded any reference to his own brilliant achievements, Dewar's encouraging interest in genuine endeavour and honesty of purpose was unsparing in its liberality. Shallowness, ostentation or commercialism—for which he had a keen scent—met with fiercely-expressed contempt. While many shared the hospitality so lavishly dispensed by

---

As a bed-ridden boy of ten (the result of an accident) he had chosen to occupy a couple of years' enforced leisure with violin-making, and always asserted that this delicate manual training had served him well in his future career.

Lady Dewar, only a chosen few gained much knowledge of the complex character of a host whose keen sense of humour and exceptional kindness of heart it was my peculiar advantage to enjoy unceasingly. Shortly after my appointment to the R.A.M. he joined its Board of Directors, aiding me with advice and support until his death in April, 1923. The man of eighty retained his mental and physical alertness to the end.

This Wizard of the North was devoted to his beloved Royal Institution of Great Britain, and in it I have been privileged to give forty-five lectures on diverse musical subjects. A precious memento of a series of three on Verdi's *Falstaff*, in which I dealt expansively with the merits of the libretto and the music,[1] is a kindly recognition from the aged composer himself. The lectures found their way to him through Boito by means of an excellent translation into Italian (published by Ricordi), and brought me a fine photograph inscribed:

[handwritten inscription] Genova 20 nov. 1894 / A D. A. C. Mackenzie con grande piacere e profonda riconoscenza G. Verdi

On exceptional occasions, when we both became fearsomely " Doric " while arguing, I have known Sir James talk freely about some problem which absorbed his attention at the moment. But Henry Savage Landor's silence regarding either his proposed or completed explorations was even more rarely broken. Anything more unlike the typical traveller fit to face hardship or danger could hardly be imagined. The slim, apparently frail little man, of gentlest feminine manners, would suddenly disappear from our ken

---

[1] Alberto Randegger assisted me enthusiastically by selecting and preparing the many musical illustrations.

and as unexpectedly return, placid as ever, as if from Brighton instead of Tibet. Perhaps Dewar gained more information than I did, for the acutely observant chemist had every faith in Landor's statements. The fragile-looking dare-devil was certainly no poseur, and I believe his books to be accurately truthful.

That I never knew a dull moment is due to the fact that so many friends, following as many dissimilar vocations, have with unfailing kindness and forbearance provided those happy hours which they allowed me to share with them.[1]

[1] The A.C.M. Club, restricted to four members (including myself as President) was founded some years ago to celebrate the birthdays of Col. J. Mackenzie Rogan, Edward German and Herman Finck; but our natal days occur too frequently to be reliable as to the accuracy of their dates.

CHAPTER XXXI

WHEN the R.A.M. commemorated the hundredth year of its existence—that celebration being the last public event in which I took a conspicuous part—I had just completed thirty-four years of office. All our energies were devoted to an exceptional effort to make the festival worthy the proud occasion, and the immediate response on the part of past students to the call upon their services gave proof of the centenarian's vitality and their affection. An idea of this activity may be gathered from the statement that twelve chamber and three orchestral concerts, six operatic and two dramatic performances took place during the fortnight's rejoicings, which began with one of the most impressive Thanksgiving Services ever heard in St. Paul's, and ended with a brilliant Pageant and Masque written for the occasion by the popular dramatist Louis N. Parker, a former student.

The music was "All-British:" some of it written expressly by composers educated in the Academy, and performed by its alumni. Reference must be confined to these latter peices and the artistes who took part in the concerts given in Queen's Hall, as the familiar names of the young performers (not including those of the orchestra) who appeared on the platforms in some capacity or other, nearly reach the number of seventy.

"A Song of Greeting" (W. H. Bell); "Song of Rosamund" (Montague Phillips); "Eventide" (York Bowen); "Judas Iscariot's Paradise" (Adam Carse); "The Willow Song" (Edward German); Overture "Youth, Sport and Loyalty" (Mackenzie).

Soloists : Misses Myra Hess, Isobel Gray, Lena Ashwell, Marjorie Hayward, Caroline Hatchard and Clara Butterworth; Messrs. Ben Davies, Robert Radford and Lionel Tertis.

Of three operas—*The Yeoman of the Guard, The Cricket on the Hearth,* and *Nadeshda*—a couple of performances were conducted by Mr. Henry Beauchamp; the work of the dramatic class being shown in Shakespeare's *Twelfth Night, A Winter's Tale,* and in scenes from *Romeo and Juliet,* and *A Midsummer Night's Dream,* under the direction of Mr. Acton Bond.

Their Majesties the King and Queen, H.R.H. the Princess Christian and Princess Helena Victoria, with our President H.R.H. the Duke of Connaught, K.G., honoured the first orchestral concert by their presence and graciously expressed their warm appreciation. It was a joy to see Sir Henry J. Wood at the desk, for to that eminent conductor's care and energy the success was largely indebted.

The profound impression made upon a crowded congregation in St. Paul's Cathedral has already been mentioned. An eloquent sermon by the Bishop of London (Honorary Chaplain to the Academy) was admirably suited to the occasion and a largely-augmented choir did fullest justice to the well-chosen music, the selection and direction of which had been entrusted to Dr. Charles Macpherson. The effect of his solemn *Te Deum* is unforgettable.[1] Our girls in white and scarlet—wearing specially-designed, chic black velvet caps, naval and military uniforms and academic robes—made a brave show of colour, and the unexpected burst of music by the band of the Welsh Guards after the " Amen," as the procession moved slowly down the nave, provided a dignified close to a devotional function unique of its kind.

The poet-musician's Masque, " A Wreath of a Hundred Roses," with its humorous lines in honour of the makers of the Academy's history, crowned our efforts in an exceptionally effective manner, the years 1822 and 1922 being splen-

---

[1] Alas, this gifted musician—and lovable man—known to me since his boyhood—died suddenly on the 28th of May, 1927.

didly impersonated by the distinguished mother and daughter
(both former pupils), Julia Neilson and Phyllis Neilson-
Terry.

> *Academia, dulcis Mater,*
> *Nos alumni, te cantamus,*
> *Te cantamus, te clamamus,*
> *Te, o Mater adoramus!*

Thus the burden of the final chorus, preceded by a long
procession of students of which each group bore its national
banner. Few nationalities were unrepresented in this splendid spectacle, for had not the wave in favour of education which immediately followed the " Peace " filled our
school with students from nearly every country? Besides
those of native birth, our Overseas and European students,
there were Chinese, Japanese, Cingalese, Indians and Negroes
keeping step together! I was able to assure inquirers that
none but present pupils was taking part in Parker's Pageant;
fortunately at the time our contingent of male students had
been very considerably increased by the holders of the
before-mentioned Government grants, which ceased a few
months later. The witty music, comprising apposite quotations from popular works by dead and living ex-students,
was selected and conducted by F. Corder, the whole production being in the experienced hands of Cairns James.

So prolonged and varied a festival entailed a great deal
of planning on the part of the authorities, professors and
willing workers—such as Messrs. J. B. McEwen, Dr. H. W.
Richards, F. Corder, Welton Hickin, and William Wallace,
aided by the Secretary, J. A. Creighton, and his staff, who
contrived to carry out the intricate details without a hitch.
A costly scheme withal, but well worth the expenditure.
Surely no other School of Music, here or elsewhere, has yet
commemorated on so elaborate a scale.

At the concluding banquet, Viscount Burnham, in whose
family the furtherance of native art is traditional, said, in
an eloquent speech from the Chair, that the century the
R.A.M. had covered was " the whole history of musical

education in this country—in the Empire." He was followed by many men of mark in the Arts and Sciences: Sir James Dewar, Sir Aston Webb, Sir Owen Seaman, Lord Blanesburgh, Mr. Louis N. Parker, and the keenly-interested Chairman of the Associated Board, Mr. Ernest Matthews (who, in recognition of his services, received the honour of Commander of the Victorian Order from His Majesty), at probably the largest gathering of the most prominent members of the British musical profession at one dinner-table.

Marking the event, the King most graciously honoured the Academy and the musical profession by conferring the K.C.V.O. upon me. I deplore the sad fact that neither of my Chairman friends and helpers, Thomas Threlfall and Edward E. Cooper (Lord Mayor in 1920) had lived to witness the results of the projects to which they dedicated so much of their time and energy. The former did not see the R.A.M. enter into possession of its own house, and the latter died a few months before the Centenary celebrations.

Our equally-enthusiastic Mr. Philip L. Agnew (long a member of the Committee of Management) succeeded Sir Edward E. Cooper and immediately proved himself to be a liberal-minded occupant of a by no means easily-filled official seat.

Shortly afterwards a long connexion with the Royal Philharmonic Society (dating from 1883) received exceptional recognition from its Directors by their kind inclusion of my name in the list of the honoured recipients of the Society's Gold Medal.

L'ENVOI

TWENTY years have passed since I delivered myself of certain opinions in two lectures entitled, "The Latest Phases of Music," at the Royal Institution, knowing well enough that they would draw some spinous comments upon the writer. But I have lived to read daily endorsements of these freely-expressed beliefs. I enlisted the services of a distinguished team of youngsters, who have since risen to fame in our world of music, as illustrators of the numerous excerpts needed to support my arguments.

Occasionally I acted in that capacity myself, as when I played eight bars by Max Reger and faithfully repeated them backwards with an equally intelligible result. I also essayed, with little Miss Myra Hess, the child's part in extracts from an "Album for Children," which could only have been printed for no other purpose than to train and sensitize the ears of the youngest pupils to the æsthetic value of ugliness, and to which some of the foremost Frenchmen of the day had lent authority by contributing to it.

All this, and more of its like, had its funny side, but I, for one, could only take my pleasures sadly.

Whither have these experiments in the new art, which in their earlier stages we were advised to regard merely as passing phases and momentary expressions of the age, led us? By this time results ought to have answered the question definitely. They have; and in the expected manner. Promising expectations have degenerated into monotonous conventionalities more tiresome and less grateful to mind and ear than those which they were intended to displace. Tolerated, then encouraged, a succession of enterprising revolutionaries and irresponsible humorists continue to export pretentious extravagances which can be accepted seriously only by those who are heartily welcome to any artistic enjoyment they may derive from tomfoolery *in excelsis*. Better for us, however, had the infectious goods never been permitted to pass our custom-house.

There is no need to repeat Dogberry's indignant call, for there will be no lack of those eager enough to "write me down," etc., now as then. I remain impenitent.

Musical education [1]—most earnestly conducted in this country—which very rightly concerns itself with such important subjects as aural training, musical appreciation and æsthetics, has long been confronted with certain troublesome anomalies. May not the good done in one class-room be neutralized by the adoption of so much meaningless, ear-corrupting stuff in another? Some of us have long deplored the fact that so many composers, performers and, notably, teachers—mainly actuated by an irrepressible desire to be "in the movement"—unthinkingly aid the mischief done to native art and the younger generation. The necessary pianoforte is not so harmless. Of all the media through which taste and judgment may be formed or spoiled, the domestic instrument is obviously the most influential. Some of those ultra-modern keyboard concoctions now in vogue ought to be censored stringently. And what sort of muddled brains are being prepared for future musicians and teachers when young pupils are cruelly made to memorize page after page of shapeless incoherency, conveying nothing to them or to anyone else?

> Really anyone would take us
> (Anyone who did not know us)
> For the most unpleasant people!
> Hiawatha seemed to think so,
> Seemed to think it not unlikely!

Thus Lewis Carroll somewhere.

---

[1] Now able to add the greatly increased facilities afforded by disks and rolls which record the most eminent conductors' readings of the classics and interpretations of the master-works of musical literature by famous performers —mechanical aids to instruction, in every branch of our art, of an undeniable importance, so long as the easy provision of ready-made music is not permitted to interfere with or discourage personal effort—a growing danger of to-day.

Let not those placed in the privileged position to reach and teach the great listening multitude—military and other bandmasters, B.B.C. Directors, etc.—underrate its musical intelligence. The populace accepts what is offered, but does not always get what its immensely-improved taste and growing critical discrimination deserve. The most ardent progressionist arrives at a border-line over which conscience forbids him to step. Mine, though brought up on fairly strong pap, began to call me early.

Merely to say that there are indications of a repudiation of aggressive extremists on the part of a large section of the musical public is to understate the truth.

Revolt, not an hour too soon, is not only in progress, but in direct action. To what else can the revived interest in chamber music, folk-song, the early periods of our music, lecture-concerts for children, wholesome community singing, the ever-growing popularity of Bach and Mozart (those great vacuum-cleaners), as well as other reassuring signs, be attributed but to the craving for relief from the infliction of incomprehensible and unlovely noises?

My own lasting belief in British talent is being more than justified, and many gleams of satisfaction brighten my twilight. A surprising number of musicians of high merit are rapidly wiping out any vestige of the once proverbial sneer, "*Englische Musik, keine Musik*" (English music, no music). Most of the imported works by contemporary foreign writers convince me that ours are their equals in all essential respects. Our pianists and singers meet, in three countries at least, with cordial acceptance; and the foreign distrust of British scores is being removed, thanks to the untiring assistance of conductors such as Henry J. Wood, Dan Godfrey, and others. All honour, then, to the men and women whose achievements cause this welcome change to come to pass.

To put it plainly, very few composers, dead or alive, who have effectually helped to redeem the reputation of British music, but have been compelled to seek a livelihood in some other more or less congenial branch of their profession. In lifting this corner of the veil behind which they assuredly have not been working in hopes of much, if any, monetary reward, I might suggest a more sympathetic attitude towards their exceptionally unselfish endeavours; and this, while by no means presented as a plea for leniency, might be granted without damage to the value of critical judgment.

All those gratifying improvements above mentioned have not yet removed certain moss-grown prejudices. In one respect, at least, *plus ça change, plus c'est la même chose.*

Perversely inconsistent with the universal acclamation of music as an ennobling power in the life of a people is the demand for a perfection attainable only in those countries where Opera is heavily subsidized and carefully nursed, but in which, nevertheless, it is not tolerated except in their own vernacular. Always presupposing a faint interest in that ever-burning question, the excessively fastidious might well wait before insisting on ideals evidently unwanted in every European land but our own. French *Fausts* in Berlin, or German *Tannhäusers* in Paris or Milan, are unthinkable.

The annual return of that limited period during which we may enjoy those perfect performances given by the world's greatest operatic artists is gratefully hailed by all. The delight and instruction we derive by their all-too-short visits are admittedly inestimable. Nevertheless, the tender spot remains untouched, unalleviated, and may the fervent hope be realized that future endeavours to remove the slur will be successful.

There is no lack of admirable artistes or thoroughly satisfactory material in each and every department needful to the establishment of National Opera, for its own sake, and in our own tongue. Yet praise and support are somewhat parsimoniously spread over those courageous attempts to relieve it from the deplorable struggles of a hand-to-mouth existence. To the inexhaustible number of arguments in favour of permanent Opera in English—and at moderate prices—none need be added here, but this final growl from an old dog may not, however, be omitted.

The strangling effect of the impost yclept "Entertainments Tax" upon the educational efforts of our operatic companies, choral and orchestral societies, surely requires no explanation.

*   *   *   *   *   *   *

The inevitable step into the shade of retirement, after an unprecedentedly long continuation in office,[1] was not taken until eighteen months after our Centenary celebrations, when the election of my successor (Dr. J. B. McEwen) was announced at the same moment.

On the numerous manifestations of kindly feelings which moved me so deeply—a generous recognition by the University of Oxford the culmination—I may not dwell. Referring to a portrait (painted by René de l'Hôpital and presented by the thoughtful Chairman, Mr. Agnew) which is honoured by a permanent place on the Academy walls, my final words to all were spoken in Queen's Hall:

It is an assurance that a past-Principal may still be on view, I hope, for many generations to come. It also helps the realization of my inability—even if I wished it, which I don't—to adopt a minor key or to strike any dismal chord in this official swan-song, because I have been made so happily aware by the directors, committee, colleagues and students, that I quit a position with evidences of an amount of goodwill and esteem which should satisfy and gratify the most ambitious musician ever born to be overloaded with credit and honours.

No, this is the occasion for a cheery " Good-day " rather than the " Good-bye " which is more likely to be among my very last utterances.

Such work as I have been privileged to do in the public service has had the helpful accompaniment of countless pleasurable friendships, fulfilled hopes and aspirations. One thing I am bound to miss— that is, the constant daily contact with the infectious spirit of youth; but I console myself with the fact—at least, it pleases me to think so— that sufficient of its essence has been absorbed to last me, to keep me still going for some time.

Well, I tried to do my best. A somewhat drooping plant, now a flourishing tree, is left in the care of a younger gardener, under whose eye it will continue to spread its branches wider and wider as it grows older and older. I may say that some personal leisure will not be

---

[1] Dating from studentship, my connexion with the school covered a period of sixty-two years up to 1924.

unwelcome to me, for as a famous, very serious Judge said on with-drawing from his beloved Court, "I don't feel dead yet." And so, my young friends, I take a sincerely affectionate leave, wishing un-bounded success to the old School, its new Principal, and its past, present and future students.

These sentences shall also conclude the narrative of a lifetime spent, boy and man, in the service of British music. Whether the story be worth the telling must be left for others to decide. In view, however, of the perhaps excep-tionally varied nature of the incidents and experiences re-counted, it may not be without interest to the friends of music; and this scrap of personal history might even be a profitable reminder of the strivings of many yesterdays, when the younger members of my profession discuss the conditions, hopes and aspirations of their own day.

INDEX

T

TAIN, 71
Tannhäuser, 35, 36
Tausch, Julius, 94
Tausig, Carl, 125
Taylor, Franklin, 47, 138
Taylor, Mrs., 102
Terry, Ellen, 17, 149, 176
Thackeray, W. M., 56
Thomas, Ambroise, 67
Thomas, Goring, 110, 113, 118
Thorndike, Herbert, 123
Threlfall, Mr. Thomas, 162, 167, 256
Tietjens, 35
Tonnelier, Mme., 50
Toole, J. L., 7
Tosti, Paolo, 240
Tours, Berthold, 38, 40
Trebelli, 35
Tristan, 36, 40
Tschaikowsky, 99, 185, 186
Tussaud, Mme., 17

U

UHLRICH CONZERTMEISTER, 28

V

VALLERIA, MME., 111
Verdi, 67, 108, 180, 251
Vienna, 145, 220 *et seq.*

Vieuxtemps, 48
Volkmann, R., 116

W

WAGNER, RICHARD, 36, 55, 101, 108, 118, 124, 128
Wales, H.R.H. Edward, Prince of, 45, 151, 167
Wallace, William, 255
Wallace, W. Vincent, 42
War, the, 244 *et seq.*
Webb, H., 6
Webster, Ben, 7, 53
Weiss, Mr. and Mrs., 8
Wessely, Hans, 165
Wigan, Alfred, 6
Wilhelmji, 72
Williams, Rosa, 101, 128
Wilson, Hilda, 132
Wilson, John (tenor), 11
Wilson, Professor ("Christopher North"), 4
Wilton, Marie, 6
Wittgenstein, Carolyne Sayn-, 127, 152
Wood, Sir Henry, 49, 236
Wyndham, R. H., 64
Wynne, Edith, 53, 63

Z

ZELGER, 8
Zimmermann, Agnes, 45

Made and Printed in Great Britain by
The Greycaine Book Manufacturing Company, Limited, Watford.
F.25.827